T0309946

MURRAY TALKS MUSIC

MURRAY TALKS MUSIC

Albert Murray on Jazz and Blues

Albert Murray

Edited by Paul Devlin
Foreword by Gary Giddins
Afterword by Greg Thomas

UNIVERSITY OF MINNESOTA PRESS
MINNEAPOLIS | LONDON

The publication of this book was assisted by a bequest from Josiah H. Chase to honor his parents, Ellen Rankin Chase and Josiah Hook Chase, Minnesota territorial pioneers.

Published by the University of Minnesota Press
111 Third Avenue South, Suite 290
Minneapolis, MN 55401-2520
http://www.upress.umn.edu

ISBN 978-0-8166-9955-1 (hc)
ISBN 978-0-8166-9842-4 (pb)
A Cataloging-in-Publication record for this title is available from the Library of Congress.

Printed in the United States of America on acid-free paper

The University of Minnesota is an equal-opportunity educator and employer.

22 21 20 19 18 17 16   10 9 8 7 6 5 4 3 2 1

"We shall hear music, wit, and oracle."

—Shakespeare, *Troilus and Cressida,* and epigraph
to the *The Thomas Mann Reader* (1950)

CONTENTS

Foreword: St. George and the Blues   ix
GARY GIDDINS

Introduction. Albert Murray: Making Words Swing,
on and off the Page   xvii
PAUL DEVLIN

MURRAY TALKS MUSIC

"Art is about elegant form"
Interview with Wynton Marsalis, 1994   3

"Finding ourselves in the role of elder statesmen"
Interview with Dizzy Gillespie, 1985–86   32

"How did Basie come by the name Count?"
Interview with Dan Minor, 1981   71

"Human consciousness lives in the mythosphere"
Interview with Greg Thomas, 1996   84

"Hear that train whistle harmonica!"
Talk at St. John's University with Paul Devlin, 2003   96

"A real conservative? I'm not one. I'm an avant-garde person."
Interview with Russell Neff, 1989   105

"The blues always come back"
Liner Notes to *Revelations/Blues Suite*, Alvin Ailey
Dance Theater, 1978   114

Second Lining, Third Liners—and the Fourth Line
Notes on a Jazz Tradition, 2003–2004   119

"Basie's a special guy"
Interview with Billy Eckstine, 1983   122

"It's not bad being Huck"
Interview with Janis Herbert and Foreword to *The World Don't Owe Me Nothing: The Life and Times of Delta Bluesman "Honeyboy" Edwards*, by David "Honeyboy" Edwards, 1997   130

Three Omni-American Artists
Foreword to *Mitchell & Ruff: An American Profile in Jazz*, by William Zinsser, 2000   134

"I know the world that these sounds come out of!"
Interview with Paul Devlin, 2006   138

"Flexibility, the art of adapting, and the necessity of continuous creation"
A Talk on Jazz, Delivered in Morocco, 1956 or 1958   150

"We really integrated Fifty-second Street"
Interview with John Hammond, 1982   153

"No better example of the ungaudy"
Biographical Sketch of Count Basie, 2004   161

"It's a mistake to think of any art form in terms of progress"
Interview with Susan Page, 1997   166

"There was no gap: educational gap, cultural gap, between music education and what Negroes were doing in music"
Interview with Robert G. O'Meally, 1994   174

The Achievement of Duke Ellington
A Discussion with Loren Schoenberg and Stanley Crouch, 1989   186

Murray's Final Published Nonfiction Statement
Jazz: Notes toward a Definition, 2004   219

Afterword: The Blues and Jazz as Aesthetic Statement   227
GREG THOMAS

Acknowledgments   239

Appendix A. Albert Murray's Canon of Jazz
Arrangements, 2001–2002   243

Appendix B. American Patterns and Variations on Rhythm and
Tune: An Ellington–Strayhorn List, 1990s   255

Index   259

FOREWORD
St. George and the Blues

GARY GIDDINS

"This is one of my guys" or "These are my guys" was often how Albert Lee Murray would introduce to friends and colleagues the disciples he attracted in the 1970s, and we were all proud to bear the inclusionary tag. We were, in fact, his guys, which meant not so much reading his books, though of course we did, as absorbing his conversation and reading from his book list. Indeed, his guys (a modest, diverse group: men and women, black and white, young and not so young) recognized each other not by a secret handshake or a coded phrase but by our libraries. You might attend, say, a party thrown by a friend of a friend, and notice on the shelves volumes such as John A. Kouwenhoven's *Made in America,* Susanne Langer's *Problems of Art,* Constance Rourke's *American Humor,* Lord Raglan's *The Hero,* Roger Caillois's *Man, Play, and Games,* or André Malraux's *The Voices of Silence* mixed with the more usual suspects (Douglass, Mann, Melville, Hemingway, Faulkner, Al's friends Ralph Ellison and Robert Penn Warren), a book or three on jazz, and Murray's own work. You'd ask if the host happened to know Al Murray, and invariably his or her eyes would light up. Like Kilroy, Murray had been there.

A dazzling savant and a thoroughly original prose stylist, Murray was also a dedicated mentor, a responsibility that gave him much pleasure, bringing the world to enlightenment one person at a time. A master discourser (this book is proof) and an intellectually munificent friend, he could, at his best, radiate extraordinary charm and wit. He disdained the old Freddie Keppard myth of the trumpet player who puts a cloth over his right hand so no one can steal his stuff. Al loved the fact that the great jazz musicians, however unlevel the playing field, gave away everything they knew to anyone smart enough or capable enough to imbibe it. Art is not a secret. Ideas are not secrets. Other than the few days when I studied with him in an actual classroom, I do not recall ever taking notes when we visited, yet I always parted from him with a head full of notions and paradoxes ("you can tell how serious a writer is by what he reads," "read for the good parts, don't worry about the rest") and titles of records, books, and gallery exhibits to catch up on.

And he followed through. I had read *American Humor* before I met Murray, but I didn't know Rourke's posthumously collected essays or her other books, which provided an occasion to meet up at the Strand, the largest secondhand bookstore in New York, to pick up battered copies of *Troupers of the Gold Coast, Trumpets of Jubilee,* and others. In every bookstore we visited, incidentally, he was instantly recognized and welcomed, and I was introduced as one of his guys. For several years, he encouraged me to read Mann's late masterpiece *Doctor Faustus.* Dutifully did I crawl inch by inch through Serenus Zeitblom's unfathomably knotty and discursive narrative, until life intervened and I gave it up. Then one autumn the moment clicked for me and, with Zeitblom no longer unfathomable but still discursive, I downed it, reveling in its transformative power, like a time-release drug. After turning the last page, I called Al, who excitedly asked if I had *The Story of a Novel,* Mann's account of its genesis. I did not. "I'll be right there," he said.

Now, being right there was no little matter, as I lived on East 15th Street and he lived on West 132d Street. On the other hand, how many people do you know who can talk about *Doctor Faustus?* He arrived an hour later to lend me the out-of-print volume, discuss (actually discourse on) Adrian Leverkühn's pact with a Schoenbergian devil, and listen to some Ellington. Al had a velvety, raspy-soft voice and he talked a mile a minute, but his musical commentary consisted of apothegms and japes (of Johnny Hodges: "You wouldn't think a guy who looks like Sir Cedric Hardwicke could play like that"), which made me laugh and shake my head in wonder and hear things in a different way. He came over a few times when he was interviewing Count Basie for his as-told-to autobiography *Good Morning Blues.* Basie stayed at a hotel not far from me, and after a particularly illuminating session with him, Al would want to share some of it. One time he phoned from Basie's suite with a note of urgency: did I have the Chatterbox album with Claude "Fiddler" Williams? This was a scarce "bootleg" LP of a 1937 Basie radio air check, broadcast in Pittsburgh and treasured by jazz lovers as the only surviving instance of Williams—who usually played guitar with Basie—soloing on violin. Al dashed back to Basie, LP in hand, and returned that evening to tell me the story.

Murray had pressed Basie on why he fired Williams in favor of guitarist Freddie Green, and the great man shrugged off the matter, insisting that Williams didn't fit. Al mentioned how good he was at the Chatterbox. Basie insisted that no recordings existed of Williams soloing with his band. So Murray, armed with the evidence, played "Lady Be Good" for him. After a suitably pregnant pause, Basie looked up and said, "Sounds pretty good." They laughed, and he allowed that John Hammond forced the change. But that could not go in the book. Nor could Basie's hilarious tale of a recording session at which John suggested that Lester Young take over Herschel Evans's solo on "Blue and Sentimental." Basie said that if Hammond wanted Herschel to give up his signature solo on a tune he wrote, he would have to ask him himself. John made an end run, suggesting the idea to Lester, who drawled it to Herschel, who produced a large knife to pare his nails, as John made a quick retreat. Count Basie loved and owed Hammond, and nothing that reflected poorly on him could go in the book. Still, not to deny "Fiddler" his historic footnote, Murray inserted this line into Basie's narrative: "I don't remember exactly when he cut out, but I did know that he was still in the band when we went to Pittsburgh, because he's on the air checks of those broadcasts . . ."

Al's bright and dustless apartment, neatly arrayed with books and records, with his conspicuously uncluttered desk at a window, a swing-arm lamp clamped to its rear (first time I saw it, I bought one for my desk, though I never figured out how to keep things so neat), was presided over by his wonderfully welcoming and classically beautiful wife Mozelle, and home to their daughter Michele, a former dancer, who became the arm he leaned on in later years. My visits followed something of a routine: we'd talk for a while, then we would listen—he could always produce a few amazing Ellington tracks he knew I had not heard. Then we'd toast the day with a scotch or cognac; sometimes we would take a walk to the radically politicized Liberation Books down the street or to a surviving, shuttered monument from the old days, like the Savoy, waiting to be reborn. Ever stylish, he had a cool loping way of walking, unexpected in a man who spent twenty years with the Air Force, and he would speak of Harlem as if it were the New Jerusalem. He radiated energy, optimism, and the spring of youth, and it is jolting to realize that he was pushing sixty when we met, and that his literary career was really just getting under way.

He was absolutely in clover back in 1974. Martin Williams, another mentor and the most influential jazz critic of his generation, had left journalism to direct a highly innovative jazz and American culture program at the Smithsonian Institution. That year, he devised a concise but intense invitation-only clinic for young jazz critics to study with a faculty made up of himself and Dan Morgenstern (the critics), Jaki Byard and David Baker (the musicians), and Albert Murray (the theorist). Murray was unknown to me, but Williams urged me to read *The Omni-Americans* (1970), and after that I didn't need anyone to tell me to push onward into the sublime *South to a Very Old Place* (1971) and the 1972 University of Missouri lectures collected as *The Hero and the Blues* (1973).

Murray embodied a man with a plan that depended on patience, confidence, and longevity, all of which he possessed in abundance. Though hardly anyone knew it then, he had worked on his fiction as early as the late 1940s, but published very little (no more than one story, in 1953), and he did not began to freelance until the 1960s. Born in Alabama in 1916, schooled at Tuskegee Institute (Ellison was an upper classman) and New York University, he signed up with the Air Force in 1943, and in 1962 retired as a major, with the pension that allowed him to devote his life exclusively to his writing. Having bided and ripened all those years, his work gushed forth. In its counterintuitive way, *The Omni-Americans* was as redemptive a polemic as any Black Power tract, excoriating angry black and condescending white writers whose emphasis on social-science clichés produced a new stereotype: the ghettoized culturally deprived "Afro-Zionist," who seeks cultural salvation in Africa while neglecting the American legacy. For Murray, that legacy (and this is the heart of his argument) reflects so comprehensively the black influence as to prove that in the high-and-low matrix of cultural stability, the "fittest elements survive regardless of the social status of those who evolved them." He would no more answer to a patronizing victimhood than to any other instance of second-class status. He was a partisan of American Negro culture and all its triumphs. At the Smithsonian he remarked of the Italian sixteen-volume *Duke Ellington on Records,* then in progress, "This is the kind of project they should be funding in those black-study courses."

Murray offered a bitter pill to the 1960s civil-rights generation, many of whose most eloquent spokesmen he dismissed, sometimes with the kind of suck-it-up chiding one might expect from a major. Confronted, however, with dragons of arrogance and fakery, he set forth like St. George and with the same results. For example, he left William Styron's *The Confessions of Nat Turner* a-moldering in the grave, concluding almost nonchalantly, "It is hard to believe that either the author of Uncle Remus or William Faulkner could ever have written, 'The life of a little nigger child is dull beyond comparison,' to say nothing of presenting it as the conception of a Negro, certainly not one who has reached page 138 of a highly poetic 428 page confession." He infuriated his own detractors with his obstinate preference for the quaintly anthropological *Negro* to the roots-driven *African-American,* which seriously bugged him (having asked me the geographic origin of my family, he said, "Do you consider yourself a Russian-American?"), or the vernacular *black,* which he mocked for its imprecision (what about the browns and beiges?) but used all the time: for example, "A Short History of Black Self-Consciousness," in *The Omni-Americans.*

For a young jazz critic, Murray provided more than liberation. He provided a sword: the language and aesthetics to cut through the brambled triteness of borrowed prestige and establish a new domain in which blues music, as he writes in *The Hero and the Blues,* defines "the rugged endurance of the black American," and by extension everyone everywhere who understands that "blues-idiom dance music challenges and affirms his personal equilibrium, sustains his humanity, and enables him to maintain his highest aspirations in spite of the fact that human existence is so often mostly a low-down dirty shame." In 1976, he delivered the fullest measure of his aesthetics in *Stomping the Blues,* a novella-length essay, Aristotelian in its authority and expanded by dozens of illustrations into a paradigmatic purview of how blues music's values embody ritual responses to life; he explored the music's origination and the individual geniuses who stylized it into art of universal import, and he did it with a prose that makes you tap your feet. *Stomping the Blues* remains the foundation on which much contemporary music writing is built.

The copiousness of Murray's vision was such that, like the Constitution, it could accommodate other visions—even those that he tended to underestimate at the time he wrote it. *Stomping* offers a bold photograph of and a few telling phrases about Charlie Parker, but in those years he was tenaciously ambivalent, at least in conversation, about Parker and schools of jazz that he believed abandoned dance, swing, and blues. Obviously, Parker exemplified those virtues and Murray knew that, but his enthusiasm was tempered by a partly generational resistance that he shared with Ellison. Significantly, Al moved on in a way Ellison did not, or perhaps he simply returned to an earlier enthusiasm (see this volume's astonishing interview with Dizzy Gillespie), which he suppressed in the 1960s and 1970s, in reaction to a commonplace inclination on the part of younger observers to honor bop at the expense of its predecessors. In any case, one of the several eureka moments in his delightful 2001 poetry collection, *Conjugations and Reiterations,* is the transition from a lyrical invocation of Basie to Parker "shouting the blues / that many intervals higher / and thus / with an even more captivating / velocity of celebration." He was eighty-six when he published that book. Four years later, the final volume in his quartet of autobiographical novels appeared. *The Magic Keys,* a largely tranquil meditation in which his alter ego Scooter enters the jazz life in New York, spurred me to reevaluate the novels. I had initially discounted *Train Whistle Guitar* as a left-hand indulgence, deeming its so-and-so and so-and-so verbal rush as little more than an addendum to the way such locutions powered his essays. Now the image of Scooter settled in his tree, searching the horizon, strikes me as an indispensable metaphor; and his determination to leave Gasoline Point yet take the best of it with him as an act more of courage than nostalgia; and the beat of the prose not an echo but a prognosticator of the chuffing locomotive that promises him the world. The jury may be out on the novels, but I'm as optimistic about the verdict (Paul Devlin's comprehensive and forthcoming study of Al's fiction will help to sway it) as I am that posterity will honor Al Murray's entire oeuvre with rapt attention. In the end, the fiction, criticism, essays, memoirs, poetry, letters, and transcribed conversations are of a piece. The first time Al and I talked about Ellison's *Invisible Man,* he raised his right hand over his head, as if reaching for the top shelf, a physical expression of its stature. I'm pleased to find my own arm levitating, at least figuratively, as I think of Albert Murray and his life's work: top shelf.

New York, 2015

ALBERT MURRAY

Making Words Swing, on and off the Page

PAUL DEVLIN

> **WYNTON MARSALIS:** *You know many will say it doesn't really make sense to talk about music one way or the other. To speak about music in general is a waste of time—*
>
> **ALBERT MURRAY:** *I wouldn't agree with that. It's possible to make it accessible to people who otherwise would not appreciate it. I mean, that's what education is about. They're against education if they're against that.*

After my friend and mentor Albert Murray passed away in August 2013 at age ninety-seven, Lewis P. Jones III, the Murray family's executor and attorney-in-fact, asked me to go through Murray's papers and effects with a scholarly eye, a privileged task. It soon became clear that there was a significant amount of unpublished or uncollected commentary on music. Much of this commentary offered important glosses or new perspectives on Murray's previously published statements—not just on music, but on art in general (and his distinct theorizations of it). Most of that material has made it into this book. Murray was happy to talk, at least once, to almost anyone who asked him for his time, if and when he happened to have the time. He also spent a lot of time explaining, clarifying, researching, and promoting jazz—and so it is fitting that those conversations of which there is a record have resulted in another book largely about music.

This book is not a miscellany of his unpublished or collected works—there are numerous works that remain uncollected on subjects other than music (such as visual art). The works collected here add up to a coherent book about music—a resounding coda, or rather, as Murray might have called it, a swinging out chorus to his oeuvre on music, which includes his landmark treatise on jazz aesthetics, *Stomping the Blues, Good Morning Blues* (the thoroughly researched autobiography of Count Basie, as told to Murray), his essays in *The Blue Devils of Nada* and *From the Briarpatch File,* and his representations of music and musicians in his fiction, including freight-train-hopping blues guitarists, fearless barrelhouse piano players, wise blues divas, and the diverse personnel of a jazz orchestra at the height of the swing era. This book serves simultaneously as a coda to that body of work and as an introduction to his canonical texts.

For Murray, art is neither created nor appreciated in a vacuum. These interviews are prisms through which to view his approaches to aesthetics, creativity, history, and ultimately, a life well lived. As Murray notes in one of these pieces, art has a particular existential function:

> You wake up in the morning and realize that if you really look hard at what some of your possibilities are, life is a low-down dirty shame that shouldn't happen to a dog. You could either cut your throat right then and get it over with, or you could try to pull yourself together to be ready to stomp at the Savoy by 9:30. What is likely to help you to do that? Not money, power, all those things. Getting your head straight will help you to do that. And that's what the function of all art is. And of course, blues is an art form, and that's what it can do for you. It keeps you from giving in to the melancholy, or the sense of defeat, or the sense of uselessness that you have. You get it together so that you really want to do something elegant *yourself.* You're *inspired* to dance, to get with it, to get it on, to be yourself, to be with somebody else. . . .
>
> Well, you know, one of the basic fallacies with so much twentieth-century art journalism is that they confuse art with rebellion and revolution. Art is really about security. The enemy is entropy, the enemy is formlessness. Art is about form. Art is about *elegant form.* If you're going to be just for tearing down something, that is as ridiculous as trying to embrace

entropy, then you're gonna embrace chaos. If you want to try that, go down to the waterfront and try to embrace some waves coming in. You'll do much better trying to surf on the waves. You've gotta be elegant to surf. You go out there and hug those breakers coming in, that would be exactly the same thing as hugging a monster from the depths of the earth. They are always defeated by what Thomas Mann calls "life's delicate child." And man prevails through his style, through his elegance, through his control of forces. Not through his power, but through his control.

It is up to the critic, scholar, or expert otherwise to assess the relative levels of style, elegance, and control at work. Some of this moral-aesthetic riffing will sound familiar in outline to Murray's longtime readers. Murray riffs on these ideas throughout the book (among many other things). I wanted to include these quotes up front to let new readers know what angle this is all coming from. There is not a technical discussion of music here (not by Murray anyway—there is just a dash of it from some of his fellow discussants, such as Dizzy Gillespie). Murray's approach to music comes from the perspective of belles lettres; it is philosophical, poetic, historical, anthropological, and metaphorical.

This book is primarily a collection of Murray's unpublished interviews on music—all of them but one heretofore unpublished (while one published in a truncated version appears here in its full length)—and secondarily a collection of prose pieces on music, all of them but one published piecemeal. A previous collection of interviews, *Conversations with Albert Murray,* was published by the University Press of Mississippi in 1997 and edited by Roberta S. Maguire of the University of Wisconsin. The interviews in that essential book span from 1971 to 1996. Most were done in relation to book publicity. The interviews in *Conversations with Albert Murray* contain some of Murray's finest riffs, explanations, and extrapolations. Two of his most wide-ranging late interviews, both published in 1997 (originally in the *Georgia Review* and *Callaloo,* respectively), just missed being included in *Conversations.* He included them in his 2001 essay collection *From the Briarpatch File.* There are several others of note, in print in either books or periodicals, or on the Internet and not included here. Each piece in this book was transcribed or retyped by me, from either cassette tape or existing text.

In my selection process I asked if a work offered a substantive commentary on music and if that work was not primarily about something or someone else (such as Ralph Ellison or Romare Bearden). Music was the subject of most of Murray's unpublished or uncollected material. Jazz in particular is the major topic. Murray had a lot of wisdom to share about jazz, above and beyond what he published while alive, and which he usually leavens with generous wit, while never losing sight of the value of jazz as a metaphor with applicability to other fields.

Jazz is perhaps in perennial need of clarification and explanation. It has been the subject of endless, exhausting, often interesting, and occasionally preposterous debate for decades. But over the past decade such debates seem to have become more frequent and intense, undoubtedly owing to the rise of the Internet and social media. More people have more to say and the business models of most Web sites are based on fishing for clicks.

Recent years, say 2010–15, were tough on jazz—rhetorically, at least. There were attacks on the word *jazz* itself along with so many poorly conceived jazz think pieces, published on the Internet. And then, of course, there was Adam Gopnik's completely wrongheaded and error-filled attack on Duke Ellington in the *New Yorker* in 2013 (made possibly by Terry Teachout's hostile 2013 biography of Ellington, which gave a green light to a variety of negative attacks). It was disappointing to see a magazine that did right by Ellington in 1944 (in one of the finest profiles in the history of the magazine) and again in 2010 (in a review of perhaps the best book on Ellington—Harvey Cohen's *Duke Ellington's America*) let a critic with no expertise declare Ellington to be a second-rate pianist and then wildly misrepresent the nature of his recorded oeuvre. Would the *New Yorker* allow a writer to be so cavalier in assessing a ballet or opera legend, or a revered European composer? Anyone with even a cursory knowledge of Ellington had to be horrified. A few months later, the *New Yorker* ran an antijazz piece titled "Sonny Rollins: In His Own Words," a satirical work by a young white writer, yet accompanied by a prominent photograph of Rollins and not originally labeled as satire. Because the *New Yorker* is not the *Onion* (at least it didn't used to be), people did not immediately read it as satire.

In a 1983 interview included in this book, Billy Eckstine presciently tells Murray *"whitey is gonna run our legends down."* Murray replies without hesitation, "I know that." This is one reason why jazz repertory that sought to immortalize black composers and performers, a project in which whites participated in many heroic ways, was so urgently needed in the 1980s. A small army of whites assisted in helping to secure the historical status of black legends from the time of Eckstine's statement through today. But the lapses in standards at even the best publications make the need for continued vigilance apparent.

In "The Achievement of Duke Ellington," Murray's 1989 discussion with Loren Schoenberg and Stanley Crouch, the trio of experts riffs on Ellington's monumental oeuvre and comments on some rarely discussed recordings. Their conversation provides powerful counterinformation to the anti-Ellington bandwagon. (Teachout's book is in many ways like an updating of James Lincoln Collier's disgraceful 1987 biography of Ellington that Murray and Crouch discuss in the piece.) The old canards that Murray worked so hard to put to rest keep reappearing, yet because he loved to talk he ended up talking often enough on the record to leave a book of new mallets for the never-ending game of whack-a-mole (or whack-a-troll).

This is an era in which greatness is suspect. African American greatness in particular is especially suspect (that holds true in any era, of course). When American cultural insecurity and racial weirdness combine, figures such as Duke Ellington and Louis Armstrong can become targets for writers with contracts to fulfill and editors with click quotas. As Crouch says in "The Achievement of Duke Ellington," "when somebody is as great as Duke Ellington: *that's often hard to believe!* Some people have a very difficult time addressing something as big as this." Writing about the arts is often a bureaucratic upper-middle-class endeavor and thus tends to reflect that socioeconomic formation's general desire for leveling, for toppling those who have struck out and achieved magnificent results, and for demanding that the world conform to its narrow vision. The other side

of the coin of leveling is the promotion of mediocrity, especially if
there are points to be scored.

In any case, jazz is a cultural prism, and thus it will continue to
be a subject of contention. And because Albert Murray had much
more to say, and said it on the record, it seemed like a good idea to
collect it and publish it now. Murray provides correctives to many
misconceptions circulating out there, as well as a guide to clear thinking about the art form (and so much else).

Yet Murray's interviews here are not only on music. Murray
always brings in the topics he was most concerned with and wrote
about extensively: literature, visual art, social issues. Any conversation with Murray organically branched out despite attempts to contain it, and eventually covered an array of topics. In his 1994 interview
with Wynton Marsalis, for instance, Murray establishes and defends
the theoretical foundation of Jazz at Lincoln Center, but ventures far
beyond music to questions about the viability of the human species
and the human proposition. That interview is in some ways one of
the legs of a tripod supporting the rest of the book, along with the
Dizzy Gillespie interview and the Schoenberg and Crouch interview.
But each piece is different from the next and in each, new ideas are
expressed and paths explored, despite some occasional and unavoid-
able repetition.

In each interview, Murray makes some sort of significant comment about music—historical, theoretical, or illustrative. This book
presents Murray the sage and philosopher, Murray the polemicist,
Murray the mentor and educator, Murray the raconteur, and Murray
the historian and journalist. In the interviews with Dan Minor and
Dizzy Gillespie, Murray (as interviewer, as journalist) is concerned
with the historicity of the music they made. In his lecture at St. John's
University, he explains Ellington's achievement in further detail and
with illustrative musical examples and comparisons not offered elsewhere. For instance, here he juxtaposes Ellington's "Daybreak Express" with Forest City Joe's swinging harmonica blues "Train Time"
as examples of different iterations of locomotive onomatopoeia— with
Ellington's being a fully orchestrated statement, while Forest City
Joe was working on the folk level, yet both created thrilling works
of art. In his interview with Robert G. O'Meally, Murray provides

enlightening clarification of his positions on music vis-à-vis African American literature—positions that he and Ralph Ellison shared, but were never explained as clearly as Murray does here. In his interview with Greg Thomas, music appears in the context of American studies. In his 2006 interview with me he offers valuable insight on Jo Jones— and a dozen other topics, including his interest in the work of Charles Mingus in the late 1950s. His 1997 radio discussion with Susan Page is another strong defense of Jazz at Lincoln Center, along with one instance of providing an opinion on hip-hop (which he almost never discussed, in print or in person).

Murray had intentions for some of this material before he fell ill in the summer of 2005. His final novel, *The Magic Keys,* was published in May 2005 and after that he was going to turn his attention to some of his earlier material, including his taped interviews with Jo Jones, which I edited into the book *Rifftide: The Life and Opinions of Papa Jo Jones,* published by the University of Minnesota Press in 2011. For instance, Murray had intended to publish his remarkable interview with Dizzy Gillespie in its entirety (as it appears here). A sliver of it had been published in Andy Warhol's *Interview* magazine (which commissioned it) in 1986. This had apparently gone thoroughly unnoticed—it took me years to track down a copy of the issue on the Internet, and that took some guessing (based on the month it was submitted) and mistake purchases. There was no citation for it *anywhere*; it was as if nobody had ever seen it. In fact, none of Murray's friends or acquaintances I asked ever remembered seeing it or hearing about it. Murray hadn't saved a copy of the published version, perhaps because he did not like the way the piece was edited. In 2004–5, Murray was thinking about ways to publish the interview—which is of comparable quality to some of best *Paris Review* interviews, in which one accomplished writer or scholar interviews another.

There are other pieces for which his intentions are unknown. His interviews with Dan Minor, Billy Eckstine, and John Hammond, conducted as part of his extensive research program for *Good Morning Blues: The Autobiography of Count Basie,* are such pieces. He never mentioned them to me. For a variety of reasons, it seems like a good idea to publish them and there are no compelling reasons not to. Other works here were either done in public (broadcast on the radio, in the case of the Schoenberg and Page interviews) or with the understanding that they were on the record and would or could someday become public.

Murray and Speech and Writing: When a Great Writer Is Also a Great Talker

Albert Murray was a major twentieth-century writer. He was an original and innovative prose stylist, especially in his four novels and in his experimental memoir, *South to a Very Old Place* (1971). Singular and unprecedented, his writing has left its mark on the English language. It is a style with many partial antecedents yet no clear source. To call it a synthesis of down-home idiomatic speech, the rhythms of jazz and blues, and traces of the influences of Hemingway, Faulkner, T. S. Eliot, Twain, and H. T. Lowe-Porter's translations of Thomas Mann would not be inaccurate, but it does not fully describe its bouncing buoyancy, to quote the title of an early Ellington composition. Indeed, Murray has described jazz, and Ellington's compositions in particular, as providing him with models for structuring his essays and novels. As lively as his prose is, it can be challenging, knotty, and is best not approached casually. Murray might be said to be a writer's writer. He was showered with awards. He was profiled in the most prestigious magazines. His books received almost universally wonderful reviews, and even the occasional early (as in early 1970s) bad review that took another ideological position couldn't help, at the same time, praising his prose style and admitting a certain admiration. His books have had long lives in print. Each of the five books he published prior to 1980 was in print circa 2000.

And yet, Murray was also a talker's talker. What I shall attempt to do here is describe his engagement with orality in order to better understand his evolution as a writer and thinker. He started out as an actor, first in high-school productions at Mobile County Training School from 1931 to 1935, and then at Tuskegee Institute (where he earned a B.S. in education) from 1935 to 1939. Originally, he hoped to become a playwright. He directed the college theater at Tuskegee for several years. A program exists from a 1938 performance at Tuskegee of a one-act play he wrote. He loved the sound of words. He had a shelf of poetry memorized and he would often recite it with gusto and dramatic flair. I remember being at Murray's one afternoon when the writer Julia Blackburn stopped by to talk to him for a book she was working on about Billie Holiday. Murray was delighted to learn that her father was the poet Thomas Blackburn, a contemporary of W. H. Auden and Dylan Thomas. Murray then launched into a recitation of poetry from that era. He relished such opportunities.

Murray could and would speak in a variety of registers. These days such toggling between idioms is called "code switching" (a stark, too-technical-sounding phrase, if you ask me)—speaking in different accents and idioms to different audiences, often done by those who have moved from blue-collar and/or strongly ethnic backgrounds into bourgeois or predominantly "white" situations. But Murray would change up his speech all the time. He could sound like the fellas in a pool hall one minute and roll his r's like a professor from the nineteenth century in the next. He was equally comfortable at parties of elite writers and artists at the American Academy of Arts and Letters as he was in his Lenox Avenue barbershop on an ordinary day. He loved to laugh and tell jokes and amusing anecdotes. I saw him carry on with famous writers and musicians in the exact same way he'd carry on with doormen, store clerks, the bartender at his club, the butcher at Esposito's pork store near the Lincoln Tunnel, and so on. Butcher/baker/candlestick maker, doctor/lawyer/Indian chief, Kenneth Burke, Maya Deren, Nat King Cole—it didn't matter.

Murray was an absolute stickler for proper grammar in nonfiction writing. In fact, in his 2003 talk at St. John's University he explains Porter G. Perrin's concept of "levels of usage" and credits Perrin's *Writer's Guide and Index to English* (1942) as his inspiration for formulating his oft-discussed conceptions of folk art, pop art, and fine art. (Perrin changed "levels of usage" to "varieties of usage" in the 1959 edition.) And yet, Murray could be nongrammatical in his speech when and if he felt like it: he'd occasionally say "ain't," for instance, and he'd occasionally use a double negative (formerly proper grammar, in Chaucer's time). Murray was possessed of what the eminent theorist of rhetoric, composition, and pedagogy, Peter Elbow, in his book *Vernacular Eloquence: What Speech Can Bring to Writing* (2012), has called "vernacular literacy." Murray knew how to "mispronounce the words correctly" (a Yogi Berra-esque phrase he was fond of) and did so—and relished doing so—when he felt it was appropriate. He revered the African American vernacular idiom. He told an interviewer once that one benefit of living in Harlem, even though he could have afforded to live elsewhere, was being close to the idiom as it was spoken every day. He inscribed my treasured copy of *South to a Very Old Place,* "For Paul, who is way down into the idiom." At times someone will glance at Murray's work and accuse him of elitism or snobbery, but he actually had no trace of either. His conception of culture did divide art into three broad categories, but these categories were always informing and enriching one another. In a similar process, speech is always informing writing.

Murray's friend Dan Morgenstern, prolific jazz critic and historian and Director Emeritus of the Institute of Jazz Studies at Rutgers, wrote in his introduction to the 2002 edition of *Good Morning Blues: The Autobiography of Count Basie* as told to Albert Murray (1985) that at first he was surprised by the Murray–Basie pairing: "Basie was laid back, laconic, taciturn, the incarnation of the man-of-few-words, while Murray was intense, animated, a brilliant and enthusiastic talker, a veritable verbalist. What I should have known is what this wonderful book made obvious: that Albert Murray is also a brilliant listener, and that these two remarkable men shared a gift for editing—Basie of music, Murray of speech." Murray knew how speech should sound on the page. His thoughts on collaborative autobiography in this book (extensions of and elaborations on other pieces in his essay collections) reflect his ongoing concern with and theorization of this difficult topic.

Murray's adoptive father, Hugh Murray, was illiterate. He asserted this on the U.S. Census in 1920, 1930, and 1940. Certainly, he too could have had *vernacular* literacy, as did the many characters in Murray's fiction. Hugh and his wife Mattie Murray raised Albert from a baby through high school. Hugh Murray was a laborer who also managed semipro baseball teams in Mobile, Alabama (teams that at one point included young Satchel Paige). Al would sit in the dugout with the rule book at the—as per Hugh Murray—ready to provide angles for argumentation with an umpire. Before he ever stepped onto a stage or discovered Sheldon Cheney's *The Theatre: Three Thousand Years of Drama, Acting, and Stagecraft* (1929), Murray was concerned with links between text, speech, and sound. How did the words in the rule book, mediated through ten-year-old Albert,

shape Hugh Murray's performance in his arguments with the um-
pires? Undoubtedly, young Al thought about this stuff.

I realize there is something a little questionable in valorizing
the casual speech of a major writer. I will attempt to explain and
offer some insights into the issues of speech and writing pertaining
to Murray's career, and his achievements in and enjoyment of both.
Murray was raised in an African American community on the Gulf
Coast, not far removed from slavery in terms of orality, lore, and resilience. He knew numerous former slaves, including Cudjo Lewis,
one of the last persons to be imported from Africa (in 1859) on the
Clotilde, the hulk of which still sat in a nearby river during the 1920s.
In his fiction Murray immortalized the "tell-me-tale-time" of his elders, the front-porch and fireside discourses of his youth. As he proceeded through college and graduate school, becoming deeply read in
Western literature, his affinity for down-home speech—its inflections,
themes, and ritual occasions—never left him. Some of his greatest
accomplishments as a writer—in *Train Whistle Guitar* and *South to a
Very Old Place*—include literary renderings of the African American
Gulf Coast vernacular transmuted through the modernist technique
he so carefully studied and practiced.

For Murray, the transitions between vernacular and written
modes were seamless. One of Murray's accomplishments is to have
created a similarly balanced protagonist in his fiction, equally at
home with his down-home heritage and with the world of higher education. As literary scholar Bernard W. Bell has noticed, Murray's
protagonist, Scooter, "seeks to reconcile his Southern African American vernacular tradition with his literacy as a college graduate to attain wholeness as a cosmopolitan contemporary jazz musician." Bell
claims that "the main theme of the protagonist's quest [is to] affirm
both the vernacular and literary traditions." But he doesn't just affirm them—he brings them to bear upon one another. Murray's friend
Ralph Ellison said this somewhat differently. In Ellison's second
novel there is a character named Reverend Murray—undoubtedly
based on Albert Murray—who makes a cameo appearance. At one
point Ellison's central character Reverend Hickman says: "Reverend
Murray's education didn't get him separated from the folks."

The conflict between speech and writing goes back at least to

Plato's *Phaedrus* in which the character Socrates condemns writing in favor of speech. Jacques Derrida, in his reading of the *Phaedrus,* claims (as I understand it) that since the invention of writing, speech always already contains traces of writing's procedures, making the distinction Socrates insists upon quite artificial. In his landmark work *The Signifying Monkey: A Theory of African American Literary Criticism* (1988), Henry Louis Gates Jr. explores the tension between speech and writing in African-diasporic rhetorical traditions, noting that myths of Esu focus on writing while tales of the signifying monkey focus on the vernacular. Gates writes: "As figures of the duality of voice within the tradition, Esu and his friend the Monkey manifest themselves in the search for a voice that is depicted in so very many black texts." (In Murray's *Train Whistle Guitar,* the barrelhouse pianist Stagolee Dupas entertains young Scooter and his friend Little Buddy with tales of the signifying monkey.) Murray aspired to render the particular into the universal. His works shuttle between "the local nitty-gritty" and its universal implications—or rather, shuttle the local nitty-gritty into universal implication. But before doing that, he determined to strike a balance between the traditions of orality and literacy in the African American idiomatic dimension of American culture.

Between 2001 and 2005, I had the good fortune to spend a lot of time driving Albert Murray around, assisting him with shopping and working as a sort of literary assistant and typist, all the while learning as much as I could from him. I've written about this elsewhere and won't rehash it, except to relay an anecdote that may prove illustrative. One day, circa 2004, during our shopping routine on the Upper West Side of Manhattan, we were chatting about his legacy. On that day in the car, Murray mentioned recently rereading some of his books and finding that, in his opinion, they stood up. There was nothing he wished to change, nothing he wished he had not written. And then I recall, as he was buckling his seatbelt as we were about to pull away from the Duane Reade on Amsterdam Avenue—and a more mundane moment couldn't be imagined—he said with a laugh, "Hell, I might be Socrates, man!" Not quite knowing what to say at the time, I just laughed. I thought for years about whether I ought to repeat that, as it risks making Murray sound immodest. But he sometimes said immodest things with a laugh—part of an American tradition.

"Why is Albert Murray not better known?" has been a familiar refrain over the last twenty-five to thirty years. Beginning with Stanley Crouch's important 1980 essay "Chitlins at the Waldorf" in the *Village Voice,* various writers have pondered why Murray was not better known and have tried to create audiences for his work. A 1995 piece in *Kirkus Reviews* mentions an "Albert Murray revival" then under way. On C-Span in 1996 Brian Lamb asked Murray, "Is this the most attention you've ever received?" Murray says no, he had received more in the 1970s. Plenty of pieces over the next few years began with the assumption that he was not well known and asked why. An excellent article by Ayana Mathis in the *New York Times Book Review* in 2015 asked the question once again. There are numerous possible explanations.

Ultimately, like so many thinkers who were ahead of their time, Murray was simply too at odds with the order of things. It sometimes seems that Murray's work is about to gain some kind of traction—and then it doesn't. Murray often said that he wrote his books for the most sophisticated reader he could imagine. That is part of the problem—not a problem with the books, but a problem with finding a wider audience than he's already found. There is also a political dimension. A certain type of bourgeois white liberal recoils from Murray's work because reading it can feel like reading forbidden thoughts—thoughts that reject "the folklore of white supremacy and the fakelore of black pathology." Some white liberals are attracted to this, but others are made nervous by it. There is a young white historian in Britain today who is bent out of shape because Murray's vision of African American history and community is more positive than his own bleak and narrow conception of African American life. In 1974, a European critic speculated that young African Americans would dislike Murray's fiction. He did not have enough knowledge of African American life and culture to imagine that at that very moment young writers and students such as Toni Cade Bambara, Larry Neal, Stanley Crouch, Henry Louis Gates Jr., James Alan McPherson, Ernest J. Gaines, and Robert O'Meally were gravitating toward Murray's work or already appreciated it. Conservatives have never been too fond of Murray's work either—not when they have actually read it, at least. *Newsweek* had an inkling of all this, back in 1970, when it titled its review of *The Omni-Americans* "a different radical." Murray liked that a lot.

Murray was unlike Socrates in most respects—he didn't use the Socratic method or believe in gratuitous skepticism or ask deliberately dense questions. He didn't loll around or waste time. Far from condemning dance, as Socrates did, he was a historian of dance and a skilled dancer. The most important difference between Murray and Socrates is that Murray did not condemn writing. He strongly identified as a *writer* above all else and, as mentioned earlier, was a stickler for grammar and mechanics. Again unlike Socrates (or at least the image of him that has come down from Plato), Murray was organized (incredibly so, as one would imagine an Air Force major would be), busy, intense—a type A+ kind of personality, but with a wink, and a worldview informed by Hemingway's "winner take nothing."

At the time of his statement in the car, I figured that what Murray meant with the comparison was that he would not be properly or fully appreciated or understood in his lifetime. That was certainly true. But now I look at it a little differently. Now I think "I might be Socrates" might mean *some of my best material was never written down!* Murray would riff at a mile a minute. There are a hundred afternoons I wish I had on tape. And, of course, I was late on the scene. Murray had been holding court for decades before I was born.

Thank goodness a nice cross section of his speech was recorded and a good amount of what was recorded is presented in this book. That in itself is amazing because Murray was reluctant to be recorded. Sometimes even when he agreed to it initially, he'd quickly say "Turn that thing off!" when he wanted to feel like he could speak more freely. And the thing wouldn't have got turned back on. So, the fact that so much recorded material exists—and that each piece here is substantially different from the next—is something of a miracle.

There is another angle to "I might be Socrates." He was like Socrates in the sense that he was an educator. Murray was, in a manner of speaking, at the center of a giant, informal university. The Germans of the eighteenth century certainly knew how to organize a university (the model on which most universities in the United States are structured), but theirs is not the only way. Murray was at the center of something perhaps resembling an ancient Greek university, and its curriculum often circulated through talk. Among the ranks of alumni are numerous writers, musicians, and academics of renown. Plato had a university and Socrates taught Plato, so perhaps it could

be said that Plato's university really began with Socrates. Aristotle's
school could perhaps be called a university as well. A school, it seems
to me, can cover one endeavor—such as cabinet making or painting or poetry. A university deals with the universe—as Murray did
every day by trying to come to terms with "The Cosmos Murray"—
the vast swirl of his interests and influences, enough subjects to create
the departments needed to fill a university. Another skeptic might
say, "You're just describing Murray's active social circle." Murray's
enormous social circle, comprised of many writers, artists, musicians,
Air Force officers, and others close to his own age, is a separate thing
entirely.

Albert Murray University was a real (if informal) educational
institution centered on Albert Murray in New York, just as there was
an "Albert Murray Jazz Club" centered on him in Morocco. Henry
Louis Gates Jr., in a tribute to Murray he delivered at the American
Academy of Arts and Letters in November 2013, noted that "[Mur-
ray's] literary inclinations ran strongly toward the paternal. He took
deep satisfaction in that role, and there are many who can attest to his
capacity for nurturance besides me." Gates goes on to list numerous
notables. Murray felt a duty to teach. It was a multidecade peripatet-
ic operation. Lewis P. Jones, Murray's literary executor and the sole
trustee of the Murray estate, recalls that he would often see Murray
riding a bicycle, with a basketball under one arm, en route to shoot
around in Harlem's parks. (Murray kept this up through his seven-
ties.) Jones would run into Murray from time to time in this fashion and they'd talk about books and ideas for hours on the streets of
Harlem. Although Jones grew up around the corner from Murray in
Harlem, they first met, in only-in-America style, in Cambridge, Massachusetts, in 1973 when Jones was an undergraduate at Harvard
and was coediting a special issue of *Harvard Advocate* and organizing
the Alain L. Locke Symposium. Jones wrote to Murray, inviting him
to contribute a piece, thus beginning a forty-year friendship. Novelist Leon Forrest wrote to Murray in an unpublished 1974 letter:
"For whether you meet Al Murray (or the Merry Mister Murray, or
Brer-Uncle Murray—or more precisely Mr. Albert Murray, Sir) in the
flesh, or in the living flesh of his prose-intelligence, 'The University of Major Murray' (why not?) is something 'your nephew' hasn't
stopped talking about."

It might be said that a university is a factory for the production of knowledge whereas a school is a facility for the sharing of knowledge. Albert Murray University did not require term papers but it did require progress. As the writer Sidney Offit noted on several occasions about his good friend: "with Murray you knew you made the cut, but you were always being tested." Murray never required anyone to simply read what he'd read. He always wanted to hear of new things and new developments. He was always looking for new riffs—extensions, elaborations, and/or refinements. And the movement of knowledge was fluid. Murray wasn't always lecturing from on high. There was always a conversation going. I don't mean to say that Murray learned from his acolytes, but he had no problem learning along with them. For instance: once I had to give a presentation on Mark Twain's *Pudd'nhead Wilson* for a graduate seminar. I told Murray about it. He hadn't read it, but he owned a copy, and he read it in what must have been one sitting so that we could talk about it. I remember telling him about it on the phone around 10 a.m. on the day I was to give the presentation in the evening, and him calling me around 4 p.m. to discuss the book in detail. (If this sounds familiar, it is because Gary Giddins relays a similar story about Murray and Thomas Mann's *Doctor Faustus* in his Foreword.) Because he seemed to have read almost everything, he was quick to admit he hadn't read something. "Can't read everything, man!"

Murray was astoundingly curious and his zest for acquiring information and perspectives was matchless. He was always buying new books, reading old books, watching documentaries—informing himself about the world, even as late as age eighty-nine. When Murray was looking into buying a cell phone (which he referred to as a "pocket phone" when he'd ask to borrow mine), he asked me how they worked. I didn't really know—they communicated with a tower, or whatever? No, no "or whatevers" in Albert Murray University. He instructed me find and bring him information about how they worked, but he wanted me to read it first and learn as well. Then, he bought one on 125th Street, circa 2004. Toward the end he stopped reading, much as William Shakespeare and Wallace Stevens did toward the end of their lives. Among the last new books he read, around 2007, were *Romare Bearden: The Caribbean Dimension* by Sally and Richard Price and Jenny Davidson's novel *Heredity*. (While I was inventorying his books and papers in the fall of 2015, I was surprised by how much he kept up with newspapers and periodicals after 2005, as I found more later clippings than I had expected.)

Murray was, to borrow a phrase from his favorite poet, one of those "great masters who have shown mankind / an order it has yet to find." And as such, like many great sages of the world, he spoke the truth and let others deal with its capture. As important and essential as Murray's books are, they do not reflect the interests of the whole man or the depths of his knowledge. They represent the tip of the iceberg.

As his career progressed, he became much more restricted as a writer in terms of topics he chose to comment on and opinions he offered. His first book, *The Omni-Americans: New Perspectives on Black Experience and American Culture* (published when he was fifty-four, in 1970), was freewheeling, opinionated, and pulled no punches. It is still fresh, incisive, and urgently relevant to understanding the history and contemporary culture of the United States. Albert Murray of 2000 would not have written exactly the same book. He became exceedingly careful with age and in the process his nonfiction lost its razor edge. Or, he simply mellowed out and retired his samurai blade. (The last devastating critique he offered in print was in 1992—prior to that, in the 1970s.) It could also be that at eighty, with an established reputation and a certain responsibility for Jazz at Lincoln Center, he had more to lose than when he was relatively unknown at fifty. Also, the domestic issues facing the country in the 1990s were less contentiously argued than in the 1960s. At the same time, he seemed to become an even more freewheeling yet almost mystically serene and inspiring verbal communicator, when he entered a certain mysterious zone. He had no personal investment in organized religion (outside of its relation to history, art, and anthropology—from the perspectives of which he was deeply interested) or in any kind of mysticism, but his discourses often had a Zen-master-on-top-of-a-mountain quality. He was interested in ethical conduct and a fulfilling life, a vantage point from which to appreciate "the sweat on the wine bottle"—a detail from Hemingway's *The Sun Also Rises* that Murray used as a metaphor for "the blisses of the commonplace," a phrase he borrowed from Thomas Mann.

As mentioned earlier, in Murray's novels, his semiautobiographical protagonist, Scooter, finds a balance between his appreciation of traditions of orality and literacy. He is a natural "Schoolboy" (which will later become his nickname) with an easily facility for the study of texts. But he also relishes the African American vernacular. The section of *Train Whistle Guitar* in which Young Scooter's dual appreciation of traditions of orality and literary is explored is included in *The Norton Anthology of African American Literature* as "History Lessons."

Murray knew very well the tension, or productive interplay, between speech and writing (see his essay on Louis Armstrong in *From the Briarpatch File*). By turns an equally skilled writer and conversationalist, there was perhaps something of the eighteenth century about him. In a 1993 *Boston Globe* profile, writer Mark Feeney referred to Murray as perhaps the last nineteenth-century man of letters—and his meaning was evident—but perhaps Murray was also the first twenty-first-century man of letters. Peter Elbow argues in *Vernacular Eloquence* that standard written English is literally nobody's mother tongue: "I ask you to consider the possibility that we've been going through what is really a brief historical interlude during which the forces of standardization in written language have been peculiarly strong. The eighteenth century brought us a climactic frenzy of standardization and prescriptivism, and with it unusual resistance to spoken language for correct writing. In fact, the very concept of 'correctness' in language was an invention of the eighteenth century" (389–90). Of course, the arc of standardization and prescriptivism mirrors of the arc of capitalism and colonialism. But I suspect that Elbow would have been fascinated by Murray, an adherent of prescriptive correctness *and* vernacular literacy.

At the moment when English was being rigidly standardized, Samuel Johnson's speech thrilled the literati of London, to the point where James Boswell decided to devote his career to its memorialization. As Leon Edel put it, late-eighteenth-century London "seemed to echo" to the conversation of "that great ponderous figure." Yet Johnson, of course, was also a key figure in that process of standardization. Murray memorized many passages from *The Life of Johnson*. His conversation had a certain Johnsonian richness. Another figure from eighteenth-century London comes to mind when trying to describe Murray's speech. David Bromwich, in his biography of Edmund Burke, explains that the professional, seasoned note takers in

Parliament often had to give up when Burke really got rolling. "Their reports often stop midway in his speeches," Bromwich writes, "with a tactful compliment to the speaker's 'wealth and variety of illustration.'" I feel that many transcribers of an average day with Murray would have had to stop halfway as well. If Murray was on the threshold of what Elbow perceives as a cultural shift from prescriptive correctness to vernacular literacy, he also, from a certain angle, seems like a person from the last time that great shift took place.

It is difficult to write about a great talker. Saul Bellow tried in his 1975 novel *Humboldt's Gift,* wherein the narrator, Charlie Citrine, frequently, in the early chapters, tries to explain just what a phenomenal talker was his friend Von Humboldt Fleisher (a character based on Bellow's old and troubled friend Delmore Schwartz). Citrine notes: "His spiel took in Freud, Heine, Wagner, Goethe in Italy, Lenin's dead brother, Wild Bill Hickok's costumes, the New York Giants, Ring Lardner on grand opera, Swinburne on flagellation, and John D. Rockefeller on religion. *In the midst of these variations the theme was always ingeniously and excitingly retrieved"* (my emphasis). That was Murray all the way. Eclectic assortment of topics, with theme always ingeniously and excitingly retrieved. But Murray did not implode like Fleisher, who achieved atmospheric success in his twenties. As Fleisher rapidly declined from his early peak, Murray seemed to improve with age. Citrine goes on, a bit later: "To follow his intricate conversation you had to know his basic texts. I knew what they were: Plato's Timaeus, Proust on Combray, Virgil on farming, Marvell on gardens, Wallace Stevens' Caribbean poetry, and so on. One reason why Humboldt and I were so close was that I was willing to take the complete course."

Murray too had a complete course that one could take: Constance Rourke, Thomas Mann, Hermann Broch, Faulkner, Hemingway, T. S. Eliot, Stevens, Auden, Millay. Frederick Douglass: "the father of us all," as Murray would say (in the sense of his vision of American pluralism and composite identity). Melville, Twain, Henry James, James Weldon Johnson. In journalism: Joseph Mitchell, William Bolitho. Literary criticism: Erich Auerbach and Kenneth Burke. Philosophers such as Susanne K. Langer and Ernst Cassirer. Lord Raglan. Herbert Asbury. David W. Maurer. Now-overlooked French thinkers such as Denis de Rougemont, Paul Diel, and Roger Caillois.

On jazz: Andre Hodeir, Gunther Schuller, Martin Williams, Roger Pryor Dodge. Malraux's *The Voices of Silence*. He'd recommend contemporary writers and thinkers as well: Jed Perl in the *New Republic* and K. Anthony Appiah in the *New York Review of Books*. He routinely clipped and marked up their articles at eighty-five years old. His favorite contemporary writer was Joan Didion. I took the main course and the specific subject courses. But one aspect of Murray's genius was that he tailored his intricate conversation for those who hadn't taken any of his courses yet.

David A. Taylor, in his profile "Albert Murray's Magical Youth," observed Murray's discursive style on a 2004 visit, aptly noting that Murray speaks "in long, looping paragraphs—nets that each haul in a huge, wriggling catch." Murray's answers to questions he considered silly or simplistic—or ones he'd already answered in his books—could receive curt answers. But the bigger the question the longer it took him to answer because he had to answer as thoroughly as he could. Perhaps he was not quite casting nets, but rather fly-fishing, or approaching questions as a matador approaches a bull—taking his time, sweeping hither and yon, trying out different angles, making sure the answer was ready. Perhaps those metaphors are better because they suggest ritual—a topic with which Murray had a lifelong fascination.

One summer evening in 2003 I arrived at Murray's, along with Michael James (1942–2007, Duke Ellington's nephew who was like a nephew to Murray), to sit in on an interview that journalist Christopher Lydon planned to do with Murray for a radio show celebrating Ralph Waldo Emerson's bicentennial. Several writers were to be interviewed for their thoughts and reflections on Emerson. In this instance Murray cast a net appropriately enormous for the Leviathan-sized catch that is Emerson. Over the course of five or six hours, and covering the entire history of the world on a muggy Harlem night, Murray explained to Lydon why he appreciated Emerson up to a point, but only up to a point. It was extraordinary. I marvel at the memory of it. This was Murray's approach to education through speech—thorough, richly contextualized, and without shortcuts (time permitting). He does not quite stretch out like that in the interviews in this book. He was always conscious of his interviewer's time. Murray's thoughts on Emerson never aired.

As Murray's writing became more guarded and his spoken discourses became more cosmic, it sometimes seemed as if he were changing careers: exchanging late-twentieth-century writer for wisdom-keeper-of-the-ages. I should note that Murray bristled at the idea of being described as only or mainly a dazzling raconteur. In an unpublished 1996 interview not included in this book he said, "You know, I jump on the table and start lecturing if somebody says 'it was an honor to talk to Mr. Murray, who is a wise griot in New York.' I don't buy that. We're talking about illiterate people, man. I'm supposed to be the ultimate in literacy. Don't reduce me, man, in the age of the personal computer. Your thoughts are gonna be appropriate to the time of the griot? Get with it, Hoss." A little while later in that same interview he expounds upon the idea of a colloquy as the ideal relationship between a writer and a writer's personal library. Albert Murray University was also an ongoing colloquy, but following Murray's formulation below, it was a colloquy composed of colloquies, with many small wheels working within a larger wheel—perhaps like the gears in a watch. After explaining "the relativity of originality, individuality, and stuff like that," and explaining André Malraux's "museum without walls," he said:

> You gotta be careful about what you think is new and what's
> not new, what you think experimentation is about and all
> that . . . each statement, if it's effective, becomes part of an
> ongoing dialogue with the form . . . so it is really a colloquy,
> not just a dialogue. It's all these different voices. There's a
> poem by Auden in which he talks about who's around him as
> he's writing. He's got all these different people in the room
> right there watching over him—these are his books—and as I
> say, we enter a colloquy. All these voices are talking about the
> human proposition.

Statements like this have been made by various writers, perhaps most famously by T. S. Eliot in "Tradition and the Individual Talent" and Italo Calvino in "Why Read the Classics?" But Murray's specific use of the term *colloquy* is important in his formulation, with its suggestion of the transformation of writing into a kind of speech, a voice in a writer's head.

Murray was, of course, correct that he should not be referred to as a griot. But the fact of the matter is that toward the end of his public life, he polished much of the élan out of his nonfiction while reaching new heights of verbal discourse—but it was a discourse *informed* by a vast library and by his own oeuvre. The events of October 2004 illustrate this. In October 2004 he published his final work of nonfiction, the essay "Jazz: Notes toward a Definition," in the *New Republic*. He began working on it in January 2003, with me typing his handwritten drafts into his laptop (bought for him by Wynton Marsalis a year earlier) and him instructing me how to edit it on the screen. It went through countless drafts in our weekly or biweekly meetings. Murray wrote it with the intention of celebrating the new home of Jazz at Lincoln Center in the Time Warner Center at Columbus Circle. (Murray was a founder of what became Jazz at Lincoln Center in 1987 and was still a very active board member in 2004.) He hoped that his essay might be published in the *New York Times Magazine* along with photos of the new, architecturally stunning home for jazz. Well, for whatever reason, it ended up in the *New Republic* with reference to Jazz at Lincoln Center omitted. The content of the essay is fascinating and important. The style is just fine, but nothing special—not when compared to Murray's writing in the 1970s. It is a major statement toward a definition of the art form he devoted much of his career to explaining and promoting—and it's also, frankly, kind of on the dull side. It was honed and polished to be just that way. (For another 2004 example along the same lines, see his "Biographical Sketch of Count Basie" in this book.) Murray revised it many times before submitting it. The published version is almost exactly how he wanted it to be (minus one missing sentence—restored in this book). I think I must have known the essay by heart at one point, so perhaps I spent too much time with it to comment objectively—but it's simply not comparable to his earlier essays in terms of style. To be clear: it provides indispensable information. It engages in debate and counterstatement, but that is mostly buried and implied.

On October 14, 2004, Murray was on a panel at the Whitney Museum for the opening of a major retrospective of his close friend and collaborator Romare Bearden's works, which first opened at the National Gallery of Art in Washington, D.C., the previous fall. His fellow panelists included the art historian and former commissioner of New York's Department of Cultural Affairs Mary Schmidt Campbell, photographer Frank Stewart, and the exhibition's curator, Ruth Fine. But they allowed the panel to be Murray's show. He was eighty-eight years old, after all, and the person the packed crowd (sold-out crowd?) really came to see. And his discourse was spellbinding. He ranged from the achievement of Bearden to the achievement of humanity and his belief in its universality and continuity. Audience members were rapt. Some exclaimed to one another "Thank God this is on tape"—as big, fancy cameras were trained on the stage. The Whitney's then-manager of public programs wrote to Murray a few weeks later: "Please know that your comments . . . won't soon be forgotten (and we of course have the tape to prove it)." (The tape has yet to be located.)

I recently asked a fellow student of Murray's, Lauren Walsh—an accomplished writer and professor (and contributor to this volume as translator of Murray's Morocco talk)—if perhaps I was misremembering that evening at the Whitney. She replied: "That's one of the times that comes to mind when I think of how I was bowled over by his amazing speaking (narrating, teaching, improvising . . .) abilities. I had experienced those abilities in person, but here he was doing it in front of an audience. I found it spellbinding, in fact." It was as if he was communicating from some higher plane of consciousness and clarity or something. This was his fourth-from-last public speaking appearance, but the rest were nothing quite like it, as his health began to decline and his physical discomfort increased. And so in October 2004 it was as if Murray had made a transition: his writing and speech had fully swapped places in terms of their immediate impact. His novel *The Magic Keys* was published in 2005, but it had been in the works for a decade and was more or less finished before he began "Jazz: Notes toward a Definition." Some might say that Murray was always a magnificent talker. Yes, without a doubt. Perhaps no person in history, backslapping politicians not excluded, was more comfortable or smooth in myriad social settings. Ellison wrote to Murray in 1952: "I was talking with Bellow and he told me about you in Paris. He was both amazed and amused over your ease of operation. I said 'Who, him? Hell, man, the world is his briarpatch. If he didn't understand me he will when your book comes out.'"

Despite his pain at that time (he often said, at eighty-eight, that he was trapped between those "two eights knocking together") and his famous cantankerousness with regard to stupid pundits on television or in print, in the zone of ideas he'd achieved a kind of serenity. It was a little otherworldly and it was glorious to observe, as he could make others feel serene as well. One of the radio talk-show callers in Murray's interview with Susan Page in this book refers to listening to Murray, whom the caller knew in the Air Force, as an "island of civility." Numerous published pieces reflect this impact on interviewers— on wily old professors and career journalists alike.

The night at the Whitney was special, but Murray thrived in informal settings. His setting of choice was his own living room. Numerous interviews and profiles not included in this book attest to warm, challenging, and inspirational aspects of an afternoon listening to Murray riff. Sanford Pinkser's essay "Afternoons in Albert Murray's Living Room" is a good example of such a piece, as is his interview with Murray in Murray's *From the Briarpatch File* (2001). Sentiments such as "I couldn't believe so many hours flew by" and "I didn't want to leave" are typically seen in published interviews or profiles of Murray.

In this book, the piece that most closely approximates a typical afternoon's tour of the Cosmos Murray in Murray's living room is Greg Thomas's 1996 interview. This interview does not stay as close to the subject of music as most of the others (though Murray's commentary on music here includes examples and comparisons he makes nowhere else), but free-flowing discussions never did. Murray would range from music to literature to visual art to history, anthropology, engineering, architecture, politics, cooking, sports, and then back to music. The world illustrated jazz and the blues and the blues and jazz illustrated the world. Greg's interview is, after all, a structured interview. It wasn't pressing "record" on an afternoon's visit, as is my 2006 interview in this book, but even that has a theme, as I was then beginning to work on what was to become *Rifftide* and was eager to discuss Jo Jones. And so, while Greg's piece is reflective of so many afternoons at Murray's, it is also more formal. I'm not sure if a tape exists of a purely informal session in which Murray just riffs at the height of his powers.

Murray and Jazz at Lincoln Center

During most of the years these interviews took place, Murray was working closely with Jazz at Lincoln Center, which he helped to found along with Alina Bloomgarden, Wynton Marsalis, Stanley Crouch, and Gordon Davis in 1987 as a classic jazz series at Lincoln Center. A certain amount of context should be provided here, as Jazz at Lincoln Center is a topic that comes up often.

Jazz at Lincoln Center became a full constituent of Lincoln Center for the Performing Arts (along with the Metropolitan Opera, the New York City Ballet, and the New York Philharmonic) in 1996. As Murray notes in his lecture at St. John's University (in this book), the idea grew out of classic jazz programming that he worked on alongside Martin Williams at the Smithsonian in the 1970s. It had other antecedents as well, such as Barry Harris's Jazz Cultural Theater. Jazz at Lincoln Center was not created in a vacuum but was part of a movement toward jazz repertory. Serious attempts at creating permanent jazz repertory ensembles began in the 1970s, notably with George Wein's New York Jazz Repertory Company and Chuck Israels's National Jazz Ensemble. The idea was revived a decade later by the American Jazz Orchestra (1985–92), founded by Murray's friends John Lewis and Gary Giddins along with Roberta Swann at Cooper Union, and the Carnegie Hall Jazz Band (1992–2003), led by Jon Faddis and cofounded by George Wein, who was also on the board of Jazz at Lincoln Center. Jazz conservation orchestras arose when they did because they were urgently called for.

There seems to be some confusion in the historical record about what his actual role was, so I'll try to clear it up. Murray was an active board member of Jazz at Lincoln Center from 1996–2005 and received its Ed Bradley Award for leadership in 2009. He became a director emeritus in 2011. In 1991, Murray received the Directors Emeriti Award from Lincoln Center, honoring "extraordinary service to Lincoln Center in a volunteer capacity." Board members George Weissman and Nathan Leventhal wrote in their letter to Murray: "The volunteer award is not usually accompanied by a cash gift. We have made an exception in your case because of the unusual depth of your participation in our daily activities. You have not only allowed us to benefit generally from your wisdom and guidance but have also helped, in a very tangible way, to shape and support Jazz at Lincoln Center." Nothing should be read into that—Murray did not need the money and in fact, he donated it back.

All jazz is modern. That is a mantra of Jazz at Lincoln Center, and it is true. Semantic confusion can arise here because at the moment when other art forms began to go postmodern, in the 1950s and 1960s, jazz proceeded along a similar formal or structural route, but because there was no jazz prior to the advent of modernism in the other arts, what was really "postmodern" jazz (compared to its analogues in the other arts) began to be referred to as "modern" jazz. In the 1980s, renewed interest in achievements of the 1920s, 1930s, and 1940s began to be labeled "postmodernism." Postmodern paths taken by other art forms have often not proved to be lasting, making the experimental and cutting edge now seem like a relic firmly rooted in a certain moment.

There is an idea, widely entrenched, that Jazz at Lincoln Center was or is focused entirely on the blues and the big bands, but this is not historically accurate. The coffee-table book *In the Spirit of Swing: Twenty-Five Years of Jazz at Lincoln Center* (2012) contains a timeline beginning with what was initially called Classical Jazz at Lincoln Center. Its first concert ever, on August 3, 1987, was a tribute to women in jazz ("Ladies First"). After that there were tributes to Thelonious Monk and Charlie Parker. And that was it for 1987. The next three years featured tributes to big bands and their leaders—Tadd Dameron, Duke Ellington, and Benny Carter—alongside tributes to Jelly Roll Morton, Billie Holiday, Max Roach, Jackie McLean, and Bud Powell. Jazz at Lincoln Center has never been predictable, but it has been consistent. Murray remarks in an interview not included in this book:

> The objective of Jazz at Lincoln Center is to present jazz
> as a "fine art" and not just a "pop" art. Critics are not going
> to criticize anyone if they play Bach instead of Aaron Cop-
> land, just because Copland is more recent than Bach. To
> me, that's crap, that's adolescent. Certain music forms are
> not sufficiently developed and sophisticated. There may be
> something that people are excited about, but the background
> that is brought into it must be worthwhile, other than per-

sonal preferences. . . . If you stopped jazz with World War
II, you would still have a body of classic American music. If
you stopped . . . at 1941 you would have a form of American
music that qualifies as "fine art." Just as if you stopped docu-
menting music at World War I, you would have a great body
of classical music as "fine art."

Jazz at Lincoln Center has endeavored to conserve all jazz. Murray
notes that its critics often operate on teleological assumptions that are
not as frequently brought to bear on European art music. It is a peculiar American insecurity that decries the preservation of American
art forms.

The debate around Jazz at Lincoln Center in some ways echoes
the conflict between André Malraux and Maurice Blanchot in the
mid-twentieth century. Malraux—one of the most important thinkers, for Murray—theorized the "museum without walls," based on the
technological innovations for image reproduction that enable anyone
to now live in terms of all the art in human history. Blanchot did not
agree—he felt that art should not be removed from its original context. Jazz at Lincoln Center added a permanent live-performance dimension to the musical "museum without walls." Some of its critics
thought it was taking jazz out of its context, but as certain contexts no
longer exist (Storyville in the 1910s, Harlem in the 1920s, Kansas City
in the 1930s, 52d Street in the 1940s)—just as the court of the Ester-
hazys no longer exists—it creates new contexts for ultimately timeless
sounds, while often contextualizing each work during each concert.

These interviews are not about defending Jazz at Lincoln Center
per se—they are about much more—but Murray does defend Jazz
at Lincoln Center throughout the book, as criticisms were swirling
during those years that the interviews took place. Today it is well
established and doesn't really need defending. But in its earliest days,
Murray was a formidable intellectual champion of it, along with
Stanley Crouch.

A Note on the Prose Pieces and Photographs

I have thus far focused on the interviews. A word on the prose pieces
is now in order. This book contains the first public, nonfiction statement Murray ever made on jazz or any other topic (not counting his

1948 M.A. thesis on Ernest Hemingway and T. S. Eliot as a public statement) and also includes his final published nonfiction statement ("Jazz: Notes toward a Definition," discussed earlier). In 1956 and 1958 in Morocco, where he was stationed as a captain in the U.S. Air Force, Murray gave a series of talks sponsored by the U.S. Information Service. They were written and delivered in French (which Murray could speak at a fast clip). One version is included in this book. In between 1958 and 2005 he wrote many essays and reviews, included for the most part in his other essay collections. But in this book there are some overlooked gems. The only liner notes he ever wrote—for soundtracks to Alvin Ailey Company performances—are included here. This book also contains two pieces Murray wrote as forewords for very different sorts of musical stories, William Zinsser's *Mitchell and Ruff: An American Profile in Jazz* (1984/2000) and David "Honeyboy" Edwards and Janis Herbert's *The World Don't Owe Me Nothing: The Life and Times of Delta Bluesman Honeyboy Edwards* (1997). In each of these pieces Murray meditates on the responsibility of the as-told-to writer, especially if the writer is white and the subject is black (or if there is any idiomatic difference between writer and subject). Murray's ultimate take on ethnic difference is that it is akin to geographic distance. He wrote in a late notebook entry: "My so-called blackness should be considered as a matter of idiomatic variation, much the same as is William Faulkner's southerness, or Fitzgerald's mid-western Ivy Leagueness, or Hemingway's mid-western internationalism." In each foreword Murray praises the white writer for making the proper idiomatic adjustments. Murray's essay "Comping for Count Basie" (in *The Blue Devils of Nada*) and his review-essay "Louis Armstrong in His Own Words" (in *From the Briarpatch File*) are his most significant meditations on as-told-to biography as well.

It is almost as if Murray was destined to work in the field of as-told-to autobiography. As Dan Morgenstern wrote (quoted earlier), Murray was not just a dazzling talker, but an equally gifted listener. In 1972, following the success of *The Omni-Americans* and *South to a Very Old Place* (and four years before Murray was invited to work with Count Basie on his autobiography), he was invited to ghostwrite Hank Aaron's autobiography as Aaron closed in on Babe Ruth's home-run record. This invitation came from Aaron's baseball agents.

Murray took two meetings with them in New York, but ultimately declined the offer. (He published three books over the next four years, so it can be surmised that he was perhaps too busy.) Had Murray written Aaron's book, his career might have proceeded on a much different trajectory. Lightning struck again in 1976 when Murray's friend, the composer, songwriter, and music historian Alec Wilder, turned down Willard Alexander's offer to be Count Basie's as-told-to writer. Wilder suggested Murray. That led to Murray starting a book with Jo Jones, which surely would have been done by Murray had Jones not died in 1985, just as Murray was finishing up Basie's book. The tapes Murray recorded with Jo Jones ended up in *Rifftide,* edited by me and published by the University of Minnesota Press in 2011.

And so, partially owing to the knock of fate, which was occasioned by the feeling out there that Murray would be a good listener—and through a hundred other twists and turns—Murray's work with Jo Jones led to me, and to the good folks at Minnesota putting this book out. Murray helped others tell their stories, and now we're rescuing a thousand of Murray's riffs from obscurity.

Murray spent a lot of time talking to students and acolytes—teaching, educating, enlightening, critiquing, correcting, edifying—time in which he could have been writing more books. It is thus fitting that another book came out of so many afternoons during which he was essentially devoting to educating and improving others—because he certainly didn't have any special desire to talk (he never talked frivolously) and run a complex educational program. Plus, aside from sharing his valuable time with young people, he also talked to lots of peers and friends closer to his age: Ralph Ellison, Romare Bearden, Sidney Offit, Elizabeth Hardwick, John Chancellor, Herbert Mitgang, John Lewis (the pianist), Arthur Altschul, John Hollander, Mary Hemingway, Paul Resika, Avery Fisher, Martin Williams, T. J. Anderson, Louis Auchincloss, George Wein, Alexander Eliot.

Murray didn't have to talk to students, professors, or admirers because he got a kick out of it, or something like that. He saw it as his duty. He loved writing at his desk. He loved spending time with his wife, Mozelle, and daughter, Michele, and being home for Mozelle's gourmet dinners. He loved reading and listening to music. He liked watching golf and baseball on television. He was a skilled and enthusiastic amateur photographer.

Albert Murray not only talked music, but he captured its creators on film as well. In *Trading Twelves,* he and Ralph Ellison discuss cameras at length. In a 1970 faculty questionnaire from Colgate University, where he was O'Connor Visiting Professor of Literature, he listed photography as his hobby. Two of Murray's photographs are in the permanent collection of the Metropolitan Museum of Art, as they were used as studies by Romare Bearden as he composed The Block, a monumental collage in the Met. They were donated in 2005 by William S. Lieberman, an influential curator at the Museum of Modern Art. Both are titled *View of a Harlem Street* and were taken from the balcony of his Harlem apartment.

All of the photographs in this book are by Murray. For the most part they were taken at the Newport Jazz Festival (possibly in 1962) and during Duke Ellington Orchestra recording sessions at the famous Radio Recorders Studio at 7000 Santa Monica Boulevard in West Hollywood in 1960. Murray was a frequent guest at Ellington's recording sessions over three decades and on several occasions Ellington gave him free rein to photograph the band at work in the studio. This book contains a selection of those photographs. Many excellent photos made for a difficult selection process. I made the selections based partially on the aesthetic value of the photograph, but often on whether or not it features a musician who either is mentioned in the text or was otherwise important to Murray. (At some point, perhaps by the 1990s, his interest in taking photographs waned.)

I claimed that Murray was one of those "great masters who have shown mankind / an order it has yet to find." That's from a poem he knew by heart. Yet, unlike many of those great masters, he was not "hunted . . . out of life to play / at living in another way." He led an exemplary life. It wasn't perfect and he wasn't perfect, but my goodness, he sure made the most of the time he had. Books, music, art; food, wine, clothes; friends, family, conversation—he had the best the twentieth century had to offer. He took time to notice the sweat on the wine bottle, knowing it was nothing and that it too would quickly pass. He was generous with his time and his vast knowledge, with his humor and his friendship. Here, in this book, a very special and in-depth cross section of his wit and wisdom—through the prism of music—is now available to the world.

MURRAY TALKS MUSIC

"Art is about elegant form"
Interview with Wynton Marsalis

In April 1994 Wynton Marsalis interviewed Albert Murray on tape at Murray's apartment. Marsalis was and is one of Murray's most careful and serious students. They first met circa 1981. Since 1987 they had been working closely together, along with Stanley Crouch and others, to establish Jazz at Lincoln Center and plan its programming. Marsalis's deep knowledge of Murray's thought leads him to frame questions that allow for Murray to answer their critics and critics of Jazz at Lincoln Center. Marsalis is acting as a sort of home-run derby pitcher here, serving up questions to which he already knows the answers in general outline, while encouraging Murray to aim for the fences with his answers. There is a certain polemical angle to the interview but, ultimately, more than two decades later, it has transcended many of the controversies of its moment (some of which take on perennial incarnations anyway), and rises to become perhaps Murray's most comprehensive interview.

WYNTON MARSALIS: Mr. Murray, I know you often make the distinction between the blues as such and the blues as music. Now, this is something that a lot of times is not understood. I know for myself that I really didn't understand it. I thought that if you played blues it meant you had to be sad or you had to pay some dues, so I'd run outside looking for a car to run over my feet, or look to get shot or stabbed or something so I'd pay enough dues to be able to play something with some feeling. But after I met you and had the opportunity to come into contact with your philosophy, it really illuminated for me what the objectives of blues musicians are.

ALBERT MURRAY: Well, the objective of the blues musician is to get rid of the blues; is to stomp the blues and of course you stomp the blues not with utmost violence but with elegance. The more elegant you can be, the more effective you'll be at getting rid of the blues. Because it's a matter of having the blues on the one hand; that is, feeling despondent, feeling sad, feeling melancholy, feeling defeated, feeling out of it. That's having the blues, that's having the blues as such. Whereas blues music has to do with playing the blues. It's the right word for music because music is an art form. You can't get to art in any reenactment—you have a ritual, you can have religious reenactment and so forth, but when you get to the playful reenactment, you're on your way to fine art, and that's the most *effective* way of dealing with the basic existential problems of human consciousness, and good feeling.

WM: Now, when you say reenactment, what exactly do you mean?

AM: Well, that brings us to the natural history of art, or aesthetic statement. Underneath all art is the reenactment or the repetition of the basic survival techniques of a given group of people in a given place, time, and circumstance. When they go over that, when they practice it, we call that ritual. You see? From ritual you get a mind-set which helps you to continue. You build up a pattern which adds up to what you're conscious of, which adds up to your perception of reality. Now, this is so important to people that some cultures have that reenactment, or that repetition, or that rehearsal—it's like rehearsing the survival technology, the food-getting or life-saving technology. It's so important that they have it supervised! When you supervise it very carefully it becomes a religion. You see? But they also reenact it by playing around with it—and that is when we are on our way to art. Because play, although it may be supervised too, leaves a lot of space there. It really has tolerance; it really has a little play in the repetition of what you're doing. Although you have a referee, or judge, or umpire—in certain games—and certain games have rules that are supervised and some have not, there is always room for individual options as to how you would repeat this. And it's that type of playing around with the options that leads us to art. And it's out of that particular basic human activity that art comes.

WM: So you're saying that blues music comes out of this desire to affirm things in cultures and to repeat, rather than hang out in the bar and grill on Friday and Saturday night with a beer in your hand and recount the woes of how your old lady treated you. What you're saying is that actually that might be one part of the blues but that isn't an attempt to deal with these situations.

AM: Well, we can reduce it. You wake up in the morning and realize that if you really look hard at what some of your possibilities are, life is a low-down dirty shame that shouldn't happen to a dog. You could either cut your throat right then and get it over with, or you could try to pull yourself together to be ready to stomp at the Savoy by 9:30. What is likely to help you to do that? Not money, power, all those things. Getting your head straight will help you to do that. And that's what the function of all art is. And of course, blues is an art form, and that's what it can do for you. It keeps you from giving in to the melancholy, or the sense of defeat, or the sense of uselessness that you have. You get it together so that you really want to do something elegant *yourself.* You're *inspired* to dance, to get with it, to get it on, to be yourself, to be with somebody else. You see? But the other thing about that, you know, is that the blues lyrics spell out a tale of woe, and the music counterstates it. "She's lean, mean, and ugly, and got three left feet, but I love her just the same." So the contingencies of romance are always being dealt with. You're spelling out the negative aspects not just to wallow in the negative aspects but in order to realize what you have to confront in order to survive. You don't kid yourself about the fact that life is rough, and you accept that life is rough—that means you accept the necessity for struggle, and that makes you stronger.

WM: That means you would probably tell a younger musician or the person who's interested in playing or listening to the blues or enjoying the blues that you don't have to create a situation where your wife has to leave you, or where you get shot or something, to get in step with the blues idiom statement.

AM: That's a very big fallacy in dealing with art. You see, art is a matter of mastering the devices of expression. Just because you suffer doesn't make you an artist. It's the mastery of the means of expression that makes you an artist. People say, well, Bessie Smith sang the blues because she suffered and this and that. Why is she always suffering in the twelve-bar chorus? You know what I mean? [laughter] Twelve-bar chorus, eight-bar chorus, four bars. Art is a stylization of raw experience. It is not like cinema verité or something like that. It's how you stylize it into aesthetic statement. We could say that art is a means by which you process raw experience into aesthetic statement. Then, when you get the aesthetic statement, that feeds back into general human consciousness and raises their level of perception of their possibility in the face of adversity.

WM: That leads us to a discussion of the form of the blues and the importance of form in art in general.
AM: Right.

WM: Because in the twentieth-century discussion of art there is always the question of form.
AM: Yes.

WM: Is a work of art just the fact that you've done it, or are there some objectives, some things that you are trying to achieve, some standard by which things can be measured or judged? And if there is a standard, or a primary objective, things that are quantifiable, what are these things in blues music statement?
AM: Well, you know, one of the basic fallacies with so much twentieth-century art journalism is that they confuse art with rebellion and revolution. Art is really about security. The enemy is entropy, the enemy is formlessness. Art is about form. Art is about *elegant form.* If you're going to be just for tearing down something, that is as ridiculous as trying to embrace entropy, then you're gonna embrace chaos. If you want to try that, go down to the waterfront and try to embrace some waves coming in. You'll do much better trying to surf on the waves. You've gotta be elegant to surf. You go out there and hug those breakers coming in, that would be exactly the same thing as hugging a monster from the depths of the earth, or hugging a dragon and whatnot. They are always defeated by what Thomas Mann calls "life's delicate child." And man prevails through his style, through his elegance, through his control of forces. Not through his power, but through his control. People who confuse art with attack forget that

what art is mainly concerned about is with form, and adequate form, and the artist is the first to know when a form is no longer as serviceable as it was. You see? *And that's what innovation is about.* He's trying to keep that form going and he finds it necessary to extend, elaborate it, and refine it; to adjust it to new situations. That's what innovation is about. It's not to get rid of something simply to be getting rid of it, or to turn something around. It's to *continue* something that is indispensable.

WM: You know, many times when the word *art* is brought up in a discussion it is used to discuss something that you're not interested in or to make something you are interested in uninteresting. It's used as a form of intellectual browbeating, a way to make someone feel as if they're excluded from something. How does the discussion of art as a thing, like *art,* how can that be applied to something as down-home, and essential, and functional as the blues?

AM: Well, when you're dealing with art you're dealing with a process of stylization, a process which changes your experience into style. There are degrees of skill and sophistication that are involved in the processing. And I think of it in terms of three levels of sophistication or three levels of control. The folk level of control, which is more or less traditional, which you pick up or what's handed down. Folk art is basically illiterate. It doesn't have to be written and whatnot. It's simply passed on traditionally by word of mouth and so forth.

WM: Now, you don't mean that negatively, right, when you say illiterate?

AM: Definitely not. Definitely not. There are some statements in some after-dinner remarks that I made recently that you might want to read into this before it's over.[1] It could be very authentic, very profound, deeply moving, you get huge goose pimples, and all of that. But the control and the range is going to be limited. You see? The person might do that in one key or two keys and not be able to name the keys. He could be completely illiterate, but it could be very moving. He would have greater control if he were literate and had the same feeling. The next level of sophistication or degree of control would be pop art or pop fare, which can take the option of being illiterate *or* literate. The highest level, the ultimate extension, elaboration, and refinement of this process of stylization from raw experience into aesthetic statement would be the fine arts level, where you have the optimum or maximum control. He could make a statement in many keys, so he's able to deal with a wider range of experience, and he can deal with a greater range of subtlety in the expression. The level that has the broadest appeal would be the pop level. But the thing about the fine arts level is that it's always there and people can be conditioned, and can be trained to expand their appreciation of it. Now, that's what frightens people sometimes, that they have to expand themselves, that they have to put themselves out to expand from the pop level to the fine arts level. But if they don't move, they're missing something that's available to them if they're simply oriented to it.

WM: But what about the widely held belief that all of jazz is just a high grade of folk music, essentially, and literacy actually destroys the musicianship and the real authentic blues feeling in the jazz musician?

AM: That's ridiculous, and it has to do with the perception of black experience in America by people who can't help but try to condescend to it. You see? It's ridiculous to think that a man who can play an instrument, who can play in all keys and has heard the music of the world, is gonna keep himself on a folk level, as if all literacy is around you and you choose to be illiterate. That's a condescending attitude and it's somebody else trying to define what these people do. Why should Louis Armstrong not be the best trumpet player that he can possibly be? Why shouldn't he master the horn? He went beyond what anybody else in any other art form was doing—*with the trumpet.* You see? That's a human option. It has nothing to do somebody trying to make a racial or an ethnic ideology—that has no place in a real discussion of art, except that it reflects a certain attitude toward black experience in the United States. But the artists take care of that, because they're going to continue to grow and expand. You just hope they don't get lost with some cockeyed theories on the way.

WM: We were discussing a moment ago the conception of form and the blues. What are the objectives of the musician, or the person who is performing blues, in the context of the form? You have the twelve-bar form, the traditional form that is laid out. What do the musicians do with this form?

AM: Well [laughter], they do anything that they're capable of doing with it. It's a basic frame of reference, it's a point of departure, it's a benchmark, I mean, they can come back to it, it's a mooring, it's a basic map. But they can extend, elaborate, and refine in accordance with the requirements of their sensibility. The more of the world they come in contact with, the more they can put into this form. And this form is the basis of their identity, you could say.

WM: You could say that form of the blues is the basis of the identity of the jazz musician?

AM: The jazz musician is a man who approaches all music as if he's filling the break on a traditional twelve-bar blues stanza. He starts out and plays a whole song as if that's the break, you know, and he's always being informed by the changes that he's playing within.

WM: When you say "the break," what do you mean by that?

AM: Well, that's the interruption of the established cadence or momentum, and so forth, of the statement.

WM: So if I'm saying, [scats "Ornithology"].

AM: Then, the pickup! You've got the break, then the anacrusis, right? Or the pickup.

WM: The *and.* So, what you're saying is, how that musician articulates their identity when the time stops then they attempt to make the same type of statement when everything is going on.

AM: He can hear the whole thing in terms of that. Like Charlie Parker is hearing "How High the Moon"—he's playing the obbligato.

WM: When you use the term "extension, elaboration, and refinement"— can you break down each of these terms so people can really understand what you're saying?

AM: Any element in any system could be extended; you could get more out of it than simply stated flatly.

WM: Like Duke Ellington's version of "Daybreak Express," for example [contrasts folk blues guitar and Ellington's piece].

AM: Or you could do it like Count Basie does it, simply by going back to the locomotive onomatopoeia, that you find in your street corner guitar, you know, a guy strolling with a guitar. [contrasts this with Basie]. That's simply refining the beat. He doesn't extend it or elaborate. Duke would extend, elaborate, and refine. But Basie can do it just by refining it. Refining the basics that make blues music swing is the Basie trademark. He doesn't ever have to get away from good, solid twelve-bar blues played with a stomp-type overtone. Whether he's gonna shout it, whether he's gonna stomp it, whether he's gonna swing it, or whether he's gonna jump it, whether he's gonna go up tempo, whether he's gonna have a down tempo—it's gonna be basically that locomotive onomatopoeia that you can go right back to the folk-level blues and do. That brings us back to that folk-art thing. A guy strolling with a guitar is not gonna play "Track 360," or "Loco Madi," or "The Old Circus Train Turn-Around Blues."

WM: But what about those who say that this type of sophistication corrupts the real meaning of jazz music?

AM: They want you to stay in your place, man! [with intensity] *Ain't nobody gonna keep me in my . . . I define my place!* Jazz musicians define what jazz is and what it will be. It's the creative artists that do it, nobody has any business *prescribing*. Let's get to this. The function of the critic is first to mediate between the unfamiliar statement and the uninitiated listener, viewer, reader, or whatnot. It's not to prescribe what somebody does—that destroys the creative process! That means you commission him to do what you want him to do. That's ridiculous. That has nothing to do with the aesthetic impulse that makes an artist an artist. The first function of the critic is to mediate, that is, to make an unfamiliar statement accessible to the reader, to the listener, to the viewer. You follow me? Now, once it's made accessible, he take over from there, he can decide whether he likes it—

WM: When you say "he" you mean the listener or the reader?

AM: The reader [of the critic]. He can say "I like that, I see what he's doing." Or the person might take the view you just expressed and say "I don't think they should be doing that, I don't want to listen to it, I want them to go back and sound like they've just come out of the cotton field. I don't want them to sound like they're walking down Broadway"—and they're gonna take all these sounds like

Duke heard in "Main Stem" and put them into music. And anybody knows you're jumping more to that music than you're jumping to Leadbelly—there's just more music there. Then the second function of the critic could be to help decode what is strange. That is part of making the statement, or his approach to the statement, accessible to the uninitiated. He might then venture to say how well this is being done, provided [laughter] he knows enough about what it is that's being stylized. What we get too much in jazz journalism is somebody who presumes to tell us how well the musician is playing something and he doesn't even know what the musician is trying to play. He does not know the raw experience that he's processing into art and yet he's telling you whether or not it's successful. And if you ask [the musician] what was that he was doing, and he says, well, that was an Amen-corner moan that he put in the trombone section—he [the critic] wouldn't know that, yet he'll tell you how well the trombone section played. He doesn't know enough about what is being stylized, the raw experience. You can see it being transformed into aesthetic statement. But, you see, criticism has gotta be based on taste. Now, that's something else that frightens the hell out of people. Talk about art frightens people? If you talk about aesthetic taste, they really become hysterical if you don't watch out. But it turns out that taste in the arts is pretty much the same as it is in the kitchen and in the dining room! It's the sense of the optimum proportion and process-ing of the ingredients in a given recipe. In other words, you've got to know a lot about the blues. You've had to have heard a lot of the blues on various levels to develop taste to say this is about right: it's brown enough here, we stirred it enough here, we've left it in, we'll serve it at this temperature or that. That comes from a lot of experi-ence with the whole process of moving from the raw experience to the statement. If you have that, then you could venture to say: "This is ef-fective. This could be a model for somebody else who wants to get to this. This tells us a lot about what this form is like. This has achieved something here. There is a form there."

WM: You know many will say it doesn't really make sense to talk about music one way or the other. To speak about music in general is a waste of time—

AM: I wouldn't agree with that. It's possible to make it accessible to people who otherwise would not appreciate it. I mean, that's what education is about. They're against education if they're against that.

WM: Two basic elements of the blues—the devices that are used—incantation and percussion, like the train [train whistle sound, train on tracks sound]. What are the functions of the melody and the rhythm in the blues? How are they combined? Is one more important than the other? Does the melody come out of the rhythm? What are the relationships?

AM: They're interwoven, so I don't want to separate them. You see, it's like, in, say, traditional European music, the rhythm is sort of like a framework that you put it in, but the music which evolved into the blues [was oriented to] dance-beat elegance. Now, the thing about African music and African dance is that it uses, probably, more of the body than any other dance. A total-body response is being evoked, you know, is being stimulated by that music. When you translate that to the American scene it becomes American music, it's no longer African music. It's a *disposition*. What you get is a disposition to make percussive statement when you make music because you're making dance statement. The drum which was a talking drum in Africa becomes a locomotive beat in the United States because that's a sound on the landscape. And art comes out of where it *is*; it isn't something that goes back to ancient times necessarily. It's a part of the basic equipment for living, for coming to terms with the situation in which you find yourself. I think what was most appealing to an African-derived musician would be beat of the locomotive.

WM: You're talking about an African-derived musician in America.

AM: In America! Oh, definitely! Only in America, because nowhere else would it add up to the blues, because the other elements in the culture would not be synthesized—there wouldn't be the same elements that would go into the synthesis.

WM: So, Mr. Murray, let's say you're in a time when the expression that's found in jazz, the type of adult expression, is no longer prevalent. It's not really viewed as being important in the overall culture. Why would it then be important for the general populace to be informed of the music or for the aspiring musician to know the particulars of this music, if they then have to go out of their time frame? It's not that they have to completely go out of it because they still would be dealing with things in their immediate environment, but it's not a thing that is celebrated so it's a thing they have to go out of their way to learn.

AM: It depends on how serious the artist is. If he's a true *artist* he takes his profession as seriously as a priest—as a poet-priest-medicine man. He provides basic existential equipment for living. And he's gonna try to do the best there is—he's gonna read the actuality of his time and determine what is needed and he's gonna devote himself to that. He's not just out for popularity—that's a bastardization of his calling, if you consider it a calling. Any artist is always carrying on an ongoing dialogue with the form that he's practicing in, and the things that are there that mean something to him. And each time he adds something, each time he comes up with something valid, it *alters the total emotional scale of that form.* So, constantly he's going back to find out. He doesn't want the important things to be forgotten. He knows that continuity is what he's about.

WM: Can you give me an example of an artist who would exemplify this?

AM: Well, Duke would be a perfect example of that, as easy an example as you could find. At the turn of the century when American musicians of *our stripe* were concerned with working in larger forms, they had come up with ragtime; they came up with the blues. See, between the 1890s and, say, 1915, you had gone from the stranglehold of the Strauss waltz and the three/four music-hall popular music to the fox-trot, to the four/four, to the one-step, to the two-step, and whatnot. See, by 1909, certainly by 1910, W. C. Handy had codified the folk-level blues and put it in the public domain so that more sophisticated musicians could look at it and go to work on it. By the way—and don't let me lose this thought—when they got to the break, W. C. Handy and these people used to call that "the jazz." "Hey, who's got the jazz on this?" They used *jazz* almost interchangeably with *ragging.* You had ragtime by the 90s. But that spirited interpolation that you found— they'd say, Who's gonna rag on the break? Who's got the jazz on this? These words came in in various ways. I'm not saying that's the pure meaning of it. When you had these changes, each one was a sort of fad. It became the big, popular thing at that time. Whether it was rag-time at the turn of the century, then the fox-trot came in, which was the basis of popular song. Then, by the time you get to 19'9 [1909] you get the "Memphis Blues," you get the "Beale Street Blues," you get the "St. Louis Blues." You've got another musical form there, and you've got the basis of the contemporary popular song—moving away from the operetta which was dominating the conception of popular music. You move on up to the twenties and all this break filling is becoming something on its own. So, by the time you get to the twenties, they're playing the fills! You get down to New Orleans, you've got a whole group of guys—they're all playing the fills!

WM: They all play as if they're playing on the break. Everybody's playing their own personality, they're all taking chances, but still the form remains.

AM: The form is there. Certain people were operating on a popular level—they would move with each superficial change. For other people, these were fundamentals being added. So, to a man like Duke—he's never gonna give up ragtime!

WM: You don't think that's being old-fashioned?

AM: Nobody called Monk old-fashioned. And Monk is Duke. And Duke is ragtime. You update. The best-dressed people don't change their fashion every year. They're looking for validity. They're looking for truth. In statistics we would say: reliability, validity, and com-prehensiveness. That's as applicable to aesthetic statement as it is to scientific statement. A serious artist knows when he has a value and values are things that you protect. And you keep looping back. You don't want to lose something. A guy may come up, and he's ex-ecuting very fast, but his tone is—somebody's gonna insist on some tone! There's no reason to get rid of tone simply because a guy is clipping at another velocity. Is he adding something to music or is he taking it away from it? There's no reason he should give that up. It's back to the business of being an ongoing dialogue with the form.

WM: Your playground would be the world that you live in and all the different things that influence you, but in addition to that, also the history of your art form, and all of your art, all of the music, not just jazz music or American music—

AM: Everything you hear is processed into your musical statement. See, the *world* is your *oyster.* You use everything that you are capable of using. You make it a part of your identity. Nobody establishes that. They don't know what you're gonna be until they go through the experiences that you go through. You make your identity out of the experiences that you have. If somebody's going to legislate what you're going to be, you're talking about totalitarianism, you're talking about something other than freedom.

WM: What about the conception that jazz music is always new? You'll hear this over and over again, that jazz music's function is to be new, every day.

AM: Those are people who don't know anything about jazz. They just have some theory about modern art. But let's talk about that, what in the United States they call the avant-garde. These people don't even know what avant-garde means. Avant-garde means shock troops, explorers, and whatnot. You can't be a pathfinder unless you have a turnpike or superhighway coming behind you. Stanley Crouch and I were talking about this some years ago. I was going into the military basis of the metaphor. The avant-garde is expendable to bring the main body of the troops up. So, when the main body comes up to the beachhead, the avant-garde is dead. They're in the veterans' hospital, or they're back on the home front. They don't even get to meet the local girls! The whole idea of putting the avant-garde on the beach was to bring up the main body. If the main body doesn't come up, they can't be called the avant-garde, they'd be called what Stanley fed back to me—that's the Lost Patrol. People around New York write is as if you can spend twenty years on the beachhead and then you retire to the veterans' hospital or somewhere from the beachhead. Then you didn't do anything because you did not establish the beachhead. If you want to talk about one *indisputably avant-garde musician,* you say: Louis Armstrong, because everything that came after him was modified by what he did. He wasn't out there being a revolutionary; he was just trying to learn to blow his horn, and get as much music out of that horn as possible. And he hypnotized everybody. That became the once-upon-a-time when everybody said:

that's me too. You see? That's what the avant-garde functionally really is. But if you can write articles where the whole thing is to be new—that's back to embracing chaos. We want a bulwark against entropy. Things are constantly falling apart; we want something to hold on to. We don't want to become so conservative that we become reactionary and we become hysterical if something is gonna change. We know that we've gotta change with the times, but we've gotta have some basis for the change. So, tradition is that which continues. It is not that which freezes.

WM: It's the fundamental aspects of things which allow you to change and retain your own identity.

AM: Absolutely.

WM: I always tell teenagers, "You don't want to rebel out of being yourself. You rebel yourself into being something else that doesn't even relate to you."

AM: That's exactly right.

WM: What about this question of swing? Does something have to swing in order for it to be jazz? What is the importance of swing?

AM: Well, that goes back to the question about the percussive beat. The whole business is to engage as much of the body into the response. If you've got an art form that's going to address itself to more of the total person than anything else, I mean, why should you ever want to get rid of that? To me, there's no greater human achievement, so far as personal well-being is concerned, as the ability to swing. I would never get rid of swinging.

WM: What is swing?

AM: Well, it's that impulse that makes you want to dance! That's easy enough!

WM: Is there any way for you to quantify what swing is?

AM: We don't want to get too scientific about it on that level, but musicians certainly know when a given, say, melody or melodic line has something added to it which makes it more danceable, or makes the impulse to dance stronger.

WM: If you were to go to a dance contest and you saw like fifteen couples dancing . . .

AM: Mmm hmm.

WM: . . . it's apparent to you what the top two or three are. It's because of the elegance of the motion, the groove of it. Can the same thing be applied to music?

AM: Well, I think so. I think that's a rough analogy that could work. You can look around. You can *feel* it in the audience. That's when the communication between the audience and the musician is greatest, which is why jazz musicians should always have some experience playing for dancers. His idea in a concert hall should be to get the audience as close to the response he would get in a dance hall as he could possibly get. That's what Basie would play. He'd say, I want 'em to pat their feet. If you can't get 'em to dance, you can at least get 'em to pat their feet and move their head. You may get the musicians up there dancing. If you don't think they're swinging, look at the musicians' feet. That's what would Dizzy used to say, when everybody was getting all abstract about bop and Dizzy would say, "I'm always dancing!" Then you had that great line, one of Dizzy Gillespie's greatest lines: "Dancing don't make you cry." Beat that, man.

WM: What you're saying is that's the essence of the blues statement.

AM: That's right!

WM: We've had that definition backwards. Most people tell you, "The blues, aw man, that's sad. I don't like the blues because it makes me sad," when in actuality the blues is supposed to make you happy.

AM: That's right. They play the blues when they're gonna get it on— gonna have some barbeque, a guy's got his best perfume, he's got his shoes shined, and got his favorite trillie [woman] right on to him, or he's trying to get to her. The worst thing in the world that could happen to you is if you're in the wrong place when the band goes into a dance groove and somebody else has got your girl. I mean, you're moving beyond purification, you know what I mean.

WM: Oh yeah, I understand.

AM: Actually, a dance, a Saturday-night function, is a purification ritual where you get rid of the blues. And as soon as you get rid of the blues, it becomes a fertility ritual.

WM: Uh oh. Watch yourself.

AM: The union of lovers, which is the salvation of the species!

WM: That's what we talkin' 'bout.

AM: How 'bout that?

WM: There it is. We're treadin' on holy ground now.

AM: If it's not sexy, forget it.

WM: I hear that. And understand it well. And understand the importance of it. I had a question about sex and the blues. We're speaking about blues in the context of romance, rituals of courtship, levels of sensual engagement—things that attract most musicians to music anyway. When you're a musician, mainly, you want to get a girl from playing. If you're a female musician—well, I don't know. I haven't spoken to any female musicians about what their original impetus was for playing. But I know most of the male musicians, they say, "Yeah, we saw the musicians, they had the girls, so we wanted to play."

AM: Well, let's remember that before the instrumentalists took over, they were working for people like Ma Rainey and Bessie Smith—and they were hot mamas. There wasn't any way you were going to get away from sex—they were earth-mother hot mamas. Louis sort of wiped them out, took over from them. But any time he got a chance, he would say "hot mama," because he still remembers Trixie Smith, Ida Cox, Mamie Smith, and all these people. You can't get away from that aspect. And this is profound. You go to remove the menace, that invisible menace that we call the blues—that monster, that entropy. But then you go to continue the species—you have the union of lovers, which is the end of *all* stories. You see? The fertility ritual is as important—it's what it's really about—to clear the atmosphere of menace so the species can continue.

WM: What about many who would say that the primary sexual statement of the blues is tawdry? It goes with the houses of ill repute—

AM: They're a bunch of idiots. They act like they've never been to school. What were they doing when Sophocles and Euripides and Aeschylus were making things like *Oedipus Rex, The Agamemnon,* and all that? They were drinking wine! They were getting it on! These were bacchanalian festivals. I don't know what schools exist for if they can't learn a simple thing like that. When we get into the medieval period, you get another thing, that's another outlook on life that came with that. But the classics, the so-called classics, have to do with the bacchanalian festival.

WM: What would you say the fundamental attitude of the blues, if we could say something like this, would be toward the engagement of a man and a woman? What is the basic stance that the blues takes toward this?

AM: Pas de deux! I mean, it's a duet. It helps them to choreograph their duet more effectively. It puts them in a better mood for it and it actually gives them lessons on how to do it. It gives them accents, you know, here and there. And it teaches them what ecstasy sounds like maybe even before they know what it feels like.

WM: Uh oh!

AM: Without romance, forget human beings! Unless you're gonna go back to a poem I've been playing around with recently, that I read when was I was college, by Edna St. Vincent Millay, and she says at one point, "whether or not we find what we are seeking / is idle, biologically speaking." But I don't buy that. I want some romance. The union of lovers is what romance stories make possible. A tragedy happens is when we don't have it. When it's missing it becomes tragic. What we want is continuity. Without the union of lovers there is no continuity, there is no future.

WM: What about the whole thing that's been said about how blues music inspired promiscuity, and the downfall of Western civilization, and uh—

AM: [Laughter]

WM: And all these type of statements that we've heard many times?

AM: These are post-Puritanic statements. If you know the history of the Western world, you know there are always ups and downs and so forth. If somebody thinks of what happened during the medieval period as immutable and anything that's changing from that is the downfall, that's the way he looks at it. If you want to say the Middle Ages declined—they were also elevated into the Renaissance period. So, you had a breakdown of any number of values that people thought were absolute—but we know they're not absolute. Their conception of the world was completely naive compared with what we know about the world today. Many values that were established back in that time are still being clung to, but they don't stand up in the face of what we know about biochemistry, what we know about particles and waves, what we know about the relativity of actuality. You see? A person is taking a very narrow and uninformed view of what the world is. You have to have that transitional period in which established values are being challenged. But look at how much continues. And we have the *means* to continue it. Look at the phonograph records. Look at the reproduction of art. Look at the innovations in communication and transportation. You know, that business of Malraux's Museum without Walls. Now we live in terms of *all human experience,* as people one thousand years ago couldn't do. I wouldn't call that the downfall of Western civilization. It will be superseded by something richer, greater, and even better for the human proposition. But you pay a price for everything too.

WM: Don't you think the belief that everything is always in decline is just part of that natural pessimism? There's always a belief that the end is near, and these days are always much worse than the days of yore—

AM: Oh yeah, I think so. But the spirit of jazz, the spirit of the blues and jazz, is always to counterstate adversity and negative feelings about the outcome of things. This is a thing I've tried to work out in my writings. Whereas the great art forms of the past have dealt with these aspects of human life—like Greeks had separate forms—Greek tragedy, Greek comedy, Greek satire. To me, jazz is a form which includes all of that: it's tragedy, comedy, melodrama, and farce. So, in my book *The Hero and the Blues,* the ultimate thing is straight-faced farce. That is, life is a low-down dirty shame that shouldn't happen to a dog, entropy is always threatening you—how do you get with it?

You have to have a slapstick behavior for slapdash situations, which means: you are ever trying to maintain that dynamic equilibrium. That's the *fate of man.* Jazz is the music that does this. Jazz provides the basis for that type of choreography. And it's based on that blues awareness of it. Duke will play, say, "Mood Indigo" and will put you in the mood: this is how it feels, how it sounds when you're sad. But when the bass starts bumping up and whatnot, all of a sudden people will start pulling off their clothes if you don't watch out! The train starts moving and you're into a fertility ritual.

WM: So, this could also be a description of swing?

AM: Oh, yeah!

WM: When you speak about an equilibrium—

AM: A *dynamic* equilibrium.

WM: A rhythmic attitude toward change—things change but you still can get in sync with them.

AM: It's resilience. You know that quote I love so much from Constance Rourke—"to provide emblems"—let's say, "to provide the musical equivalent of emblems for a pioneer people who require resilience as a prime trait." I can't get any deeper than that. That's what this music does all the time, which is why I think, up to now, Duke is the quintessential American composer.

WM: How did jazz music change? When people stopped dancing to the music, let's say around the mid-1950s—I mean, the younger people, not the people who grew up dancing. What type of effect did that have on the performance of musicians who didn't grow up playing in dances?

AM: I think it distorted the view of a number of them. It's like, the intrusion of politics and sociology into something—they thought it was improving their social status or something like that, which is not what art is concerned with in that sense. It's concerned with your existential—your *essential* well-being as a human being, not your social status. That could be a part of an individual's ambition, but it's not the most fundamental part. When they were faked into that—"We want more respect, we wanted to be treated like concert hall musicians," and so forth—this was part of a social struggle that destroyed a lot of artists' aesthetic sensibility. It became something else. They wanted to be part of a social and political revolution. They simply bootlegged what was happening in jazz to say it was a part of something that it was not really a part of. Take a guy like Charlie Parker—he loved playing dances, with Jay McShann and this sort of thing. He really didn't go all the way to the concert hall. He just had a lot of time he could spend in jam sessions, which is a semi-workshop situation. The challenge of the horn itself moved him away from having to satisfy dancers. He got personal problems—he never really got back to that. Personally, I don't see how any musician that's really ambitious could stay away from having a big band. Ultimately, he wants a richer palette to work with. Well, Parker's personal problems precluded his going into that. People who were latching onto the postwar emphasis on the "new thing" got caught up in that. And then it got connected with the civil-rights movement and they went that way. Meanwhile, this other stuff wasn't dead. Count Basie was making more money—and so was Louis Armstrong. None of those other guys made the money or had the crowd that Count Basie, Duke Ellington, and Louis Armstrong had. As popular as a concert venue called Jazz at the Philharmonic was—those guys were mostly swinging. It was never dead. You get economic factors coming in—using a large number of combos to play big dances and that sort of thing.

WM: In what other American musical forms can you hear the influence of the blues?

AM: Well, of course, in popular music. In rock and stuff like that you find it. You also find it in country and western.

WM: In what way?

AM: Well, the percussiveness of country and western. They like percussive stuff. You know what I mean? And they like riffin'! They like up tempo. There's just another choreographic style that they bring to it. It's another perception of elegance. It's as if they rate enthusiasm over elegance, whereas in our idiom the enthusiasm has to be controlled by coolness, too. The more enthusiastic you are, the more you want to come across as being laid-back—but it's gotta be poppin'! Underneath being laid-back, it's gotta be poppin'! And that's the ultimate in elegance. That's your bullfighter—here's a ton of destruction moving toward you, and you're just gonna move over just a little bit. Of course, as a result of the visit of Dvořák over here in the 1890s the so-called concert-hall-oriented composers have been influenced by the so-called folk music of America, coming out of the music of the slaves. Meanwhile, what we've gotta remember is that the slaves were making the most effective *synthesis* of all the musical material of the United States. They were making the American synthesis. They were not shackled by pieties which they had brought because they didn't have any pieties to bring, coming from so many different cultures and idioms in Africa they couldn't bring *one*. And there's no such thing really as an *African* thing. Certain dispositions were similar but the languages and so forth were different. But over here there was sort of a unified sensibility. There was a sort of aesthetic nationalism which evolved as a natural thing—in the South, mainly.

WM: You're saying they were able to address all of the elements of music that were around them and synthesize this into one thing that had the true feeling of the national character.

AM: Exactly. They made the American synthesis. They didn't have as big a struggle with the pieties that already existed. A guy out in Kansas City somewhere could hear a fugue and say, "Hey, I like that, this is going this way, that's is going that way, when we get here I'm gonna have a break, and I'm gonna have a gui-tar, right here." It's just another device for making music. Like a bunch of things in a tool kit.

WM: How do the jazz composers use the blues? If we could pick one piece by Duke Ellington and point out different influences of blues idiom statement, what would be the composition?

AM: Well, man, what about "C-Jam Blues"? You can't get any simpler than that. You start out with a melody which is as noble and more swinging than Beethoven's Fifth? You ever think of that?! [hums opening]

WM: [scats opening of "C-Jam Blues"]

AM: See, there's nothing inherently superior in Beethoven's phrase over Duke's phrase—and Duke's is more challenging musically. Underneath all this there's that twelve-bar chorus. It's like a ring game in one sense. He takes a series of solos—the whole composition is going to be a string of solos, *each one beginning on the break!*

WM: Which version are you talking about?

AM: The RCA Victor version, on the Blanton-Webster band CD. When Duke moves out, then the reed section picks it up, and if you don't listen carefully you think he's still playing piano [scats the different parts of the tune]. And then here comes Ray Nance [scats]. He finishes the solo with the rhythm behind it. Look at all these devices being used! Each person comes in there, has so many bars, states his identity, and gets the heck out of the way and moves along. It's just like the commedia dell'arte, all these characters. We've got Ray Nance, we've got Lawrence Brown, we've got Tricky Sam, we've got Ben Webster, and then we've got the out chorus. That's a composition that's as pure as a diamond. Everything in that record is in place. You've got a perfect example of jazz composition. You've still got your locomotive onomatopoeia; you've got the solos with the train whistle, so you never get away from the train whistle guitar. You see? You've got swing, you've got individuality. Everything is in that three-minute piece. And it's pure blues. Most people say that's just a swing number—that's blues.

WM: How has the blues influenced vocalists? We know a lot of times the instrumentalists imitate the vocalists.

AM: The instrument is an extension of the human voice. But in the natural history of the blues from the 1920s to the 1940s, by the time you get the arrival of Billie Holiday, or the primacy of Armstrong, by the time Armstrong gets through the thirties, he extends the human voice to a point that the vocalists begin to imitate the instruments! And Louis was doing that himself. It was going both ways at the same time. I think you can find what you need to know in the natural history of Louis Armstrong. And when he moved into the field of popular music, reinterpreting, creating a revolution in the way people sing in the United States, from the way they were singing in the 1920s and in the teens to the way they were singing after he started vocalizing, you could see that effect. Louis could extend Bessie and people like that. Then he had his own things that he was doing which put him right to the edge of scatting and all that. Then by the time you get to Billie

Holiday and Sarah Vaughan, they're coming out of the instruments. What could you say about Sarah Vaughan? She's made by instruments. Or Ella, by that time.

WM: What we see is the constant call and response, the constant dialogue that takes place on all levels of jazz music.

AM: Exactly.

WM: There is always the instrument speaking to the vocalist, the vocalist speaking back to the instruments. The dialogue with the form. The form's dialogue with the history of form.

AM: And the singers and the musicians never really stopped dancing, remember that.

WM: What about the influence the blues has on instrumental soloists, like somebody like Sweets Edison or Ray Nance, or Louis Armstrong himself?

AM: It's underneath that at all times. It's the human voice that does it. The trumpet's always going to extend that. The trumpet is the first violin in the band, right? Somehow or other in the evolution of American sonata form, or sonata instrumentation—that is, the fully orchestrated blues statement—who's the man? Who's the man with the bow? The trumpet man!

WM: Say it again. There he is! Well, you know one of the great things as a jazz musician is to have the opportunity to cut some head—or sometimes you get your head cut. That's not quite as great, but it's fun to be in the battle. We always say we *play* jazz. If you play basketball or you play sandlot ball of any sort, you always keep score. Nobody wants to play if there's no score being kept. Win or lose, you still come out, because you just want to play. Can you tell me about any great musical battle that you witnessed or heard? Whose head got cut? What their attitude was toward that cutting?

AM: Let us bring another concept in here from my little book *The Hero and the Blues* and that is the concept of *antagonistic cooperation*. Sort of a contradiction in terms but it adds up to a mnemonic device which is very useful. If you don't have adequate opposition, you don't develop. To be a great champion you have to have great contenders.

To be a great hero you have to have dragons to kill. To be a great general you have to have great battles to fight. So, at the same time everything is being improved by this contention that we have, that can come into the arts. To come back to play there are four categories of play which are useful to keep in mind when discussing aesthetics. One is competition, another is make-believe, another is chance, and the other is vertigo—gettin' high, man, bringing it on up to a point where it knocks *you* out. Competition comes into the jam session situation. Make-believe is where you can evoke things. Chance is if you can do this, you can do that—you go into what we call gratuitous difficulty. You can play high C? Well, how many can you play? When you gonna get to "Swing That Music," man? How many notes you gonna hit on "Swing That Music"? That type of thing. You've got all these elements operating where you can add up to art. Then if you can knock yourself out—obviously you're trying to knock them out—that's an indispensable element of aesthetic play too—you get high. Like Michael Jordan. You see the guy shift the ball when he goes up there? You gasp when you see that type of thing.

Well, one of the most famous cutting sessions—it's somewhat apocryphal and there are various tales about it—is supposed to have taken place in Kansas City, when Coleman Hawkins came to town with the Fletcher Henderson band. And of course Kansas City was tenor territory. Texas and Kansas—tenor territory! And the local guys like Herschel Evans and Lester Young and various other people were there. Herschel was a great admirer of Hawk. Lester, of course, was always independent. He liked him too, but he was always doing his thing. As Buddy Tate was telling me one time, Lester would say, "I *love* Herschel, I love him, he's my friend, but he love his horn and I love mine." So he's gotta do what he was gonna do. Lester's always off to the side doing something. And they tell this story about how they met Hawk. These big bands would go in and all these guys would be down there with the horns to get the chance to rub shoulders with these giants. This is how the whole tradition developed, and developed such high musical standards. That's why the precision in those sections and those ensembles was so great, because they really learned their craft. They don't do that in conservatories to the extent that it takes place in these Renaissance-like guilds. It's like the goldsmiths in Renaissance Italy, that type of thing. Hawk was the master, he had just about invented—see, Mr. Sax had invented the saxophone, but the jazz musician found out what to do with it. These guys were practicing this stuff, so they want to cut him. Just like Duke and these guys in Washington were waiting for the stride piano players to come to the Howard Theater. So, Hawk came to town and they start playing, and Hawk sent one of the guys back to his hotel to get his horn. "I better get up there with these kids. They trying to show me stuff. I better show 'em who the master is." Basie was telling me, "I ain't never seen Hawk do that! He sent for his horn!" Some people say Hawk got tangled up with those guys—and couldn't leave! Fletcher went on to his next gig, maybe St. Louis or wherever it was. And Hawk was from St. Joe, you know. Hawk had to burn his car to catch up with Fletcher 'cause he got delayed trying to blow these cats out. And they were playing as much out of admiration for him as they were out of any antagonism. But it was an antagonistic cooperation. Basie said, well, they tell all that stuff about that, but man, "you gotta do something to cut Hawk, 'cause when Hawk got up there and started calling for all them hard keys, that eliminated me and about three-fourths of the rest of the guys." Mary Lou Williams said they came and got her. She was one of the people in town who could play those hard keys. But all that illustrative of the educational significance—and you've gotta find the university or conservatory of jazz where it exists. And it existed in places like that. It existed in apprenticeship to the big bands.

WM: What about those who say they don't recognize the significance of this—the type of the training inherent in this type of activity? They feel that jazz has to come from the street. Or the fact of Coleman Hawkins being able to play in all these keys not reflective of some level of education, it's just something he naturally can do.

AM: Nobody in a conservatory could teach you how to do that. You know that. You know that Horowitz can't play ragtime. It's too difficult. We know that Scott Joplin was perhaps the most brilliant student of Chopin's piano literature in the United States and he knew what to do with it to make it his own. These guys who came through conservatories can't play ragtime to the satisfaction of somebody who has valid taste in ragtime. It's a gap between what the facts are—it's a culture gap, you see, between what formal education is and what the realities of education really are. And that causes a lot of confusion. This is what we've been trying to do—trying to convince people that you can approach jazz with the same level of intellectual abstraction or sophistication that you bring to the other music. That's what I claim for you, Wynton. I was saying, well, from the feedback I get from Wynton, I gave him some notion, some vague notion, that he could approach Louis Armstrong and Duke and these people with the same level of intellectual sophistication as he approached Haydn or Mozart.

WM: You certainly did. And I really didn't think that, to be honest with you, even with my father being a jazz musician. Not because I didn't feel the music was serious, but because there was no outlet for that type of expression that wasn't pretentious to me. But since we're on that subject—all of our efforts are geared toward our listeners. Can you give listeners any pointers to let them know what they should be trying to do to get more enjoyment out of jazz music?

AM: The first thing they should realize is that the person is dealing with *your life*. Art presents the life of human feeling, how it feels to be a human being in this time, this place, and these circumstances. The music comes out of stylizing the raw material of experience, to make it into a form that elevates your conception of life and possibility. It's always trying to give you a superior form, something that raises your horizon of aspiration.

WM: Many people say it should reflect today's society.

AM: It should counterstate the problems. It's getting rid of the blues. It should bring a form superior to the chaos that's around society. Art is a secular companion to religious devotion. It's just as profound. It's basic equipment for living. So you listen for yourself and when you find yourself responding, it's because the musician is getting to you and you say "Oh yeah, this is it!—oh lord, am I born to die?! Why can't this happen over and over? I'm gonna *buy* this record and play it!" Time and time again, if the record is good enough, it will continue to dispel the blues. You go back to "West End Blues," and this guy [Armstrong] comes in there *beginning* with a cadenza, right? And you say, hey man, *what a piece of work is man*. Listen to this guy soaring like this. They didn't even have people in outer space when he wrote that solo. He was in outer space! That whole business of horizons of aspiration is what the music was about. It's just as functional on that level of elegance as it is when you're playing march tunes, when marching into battle. You're just marching into battle on a more elegant beat and a more complicated battle, because it's a battle of the spirit. That's why I wrote that phrase—"when Louis Armstrong came to town, to Paris, as if atop the glad-wagon, and pointed his trumpet up, he could hold the blues at bay, stone-frozen in place like the gargoyles on Notre Dame." They'll be up frozen until he leaves town. They come back every day, we know that.

WM: Amen.

AM: But a masterpiece in the blues, like any other masterpiece, can dispel them time and time again. Who's gonna get rid of that? Who's gonna call that old-fashioned? A person who can say old-fashioned but can't say permanent and can't say lasting and can't say timeless, is in bad shape.

WM: Uh oh.

AM: 'Cause the artist wants to be timeless. And even when he's got something new, he wants that to be timeless. Don't forget that Miles was kidding. Miles was a big put-on when it came to talking about things. "Well, Miles, all you're gonna do is your latest thing, you're only gonna play that? Should I go home and throw away all my old records? I don't need to listen to *Kind of Blue* anymore, I don't need to listen to 'Freddie Freeloader,' I don't have to listen to 'Bag's Groove'?" He would know better than that. "I don't have to hear Dig anymore, right, man?" He would never really say that. And that's terribly important. The superficial approaches really confused people. Once you develop a taste, you're gonna hold on to your records. Or if you even make a record, that means you want something to last.

WM: What about the influence that the blues has had on the American theater?

AM: Well, ever since the early twenties, when Sissle and Blake brought *Shuffle Along* to Broadway, the use of popular music coming out of ragtime and the blues has been highly perceptible. By the time you get to the twenties everybody's been influenced by that change that

took place from the waltz beat to the four/four. By the time you get to
the twenties you get DeSylva, Brown, and Henderson and all these
people writing. You've got Vernon Duke, you've got the Gershwins.
All this is directly out of what the black musicians started doing before 1912, before 1910. When Will Marion Cook back in the 1890s did
Clorindy, or the Origin of the Cakewalk, I mean, he really was estab-
lishing American musical theater that supplanted the operetta and
the music-hall music which was imported from Europe. By this time
we had a whole generation of songwriters that dominate the world!
Cole Porter, Vernon Duke, the Hammersteins, the Gershwins, Walter Donaldson, all these people. They're coming out of what Shelton
Brooks and Fats Waller and all these guys—they'd sell songs all the
time. The blues has had definitive influence on the American theater.
If we go back again to the 1890s when Dvořák pointed out—Dvořák
who was over here to establish an American conservatory and to en-
courage people to deal with vernacular materials and try to process
them into fine art—one of his key people was a guy named Rubin
Goldmark, who became a professor of composition at Juilliard, and
two of his students were Aaron Copland and George Gershwin. They
started out dealing with what he called Negro folk melodies and everything else that Negroes were playing. Aaron Copland went his
way to try to make a European concert hall–type music out of vernacular materials. But Gershwin was hanging out on 135th Street!
And he was hanging out with song-pluggers, with ragtime piano
players, with stride piano players, and his first efforts were always
to incorporate this type of music in what he was trying to do. And
he became a peerless popular songwriter, one of the greats. And his
stuff feeds back into jazz. "I've Got Rhythm"—you know, you can
just name song after song by Gershwin that's very close to what he
was picking up from James P. Johnson and other piano players he
hung out with. They were raising the level of musicianship, always.
If you're talking about Duke, you're talking about a guy whose first
devotion was trying to get that keyboard straight in terms of ragtime.
But through Willie "The Lion" Smith, James P. Johnson, Sissle and
Blake, the stuff that was done by Fats Waller—the Broadway musical was transformed.

WM: Why would you say that jazz is a quintessential American form of expression?

AM: It's the most universally affecting synthesis of American expression in music. I just wrote the other day: when Louis Armstrong came to be known as Ambassador Satch, and when that got all tangled up with the fact that he also claimed to be born on the Fourth of July 1900, nothing could be more appropriate because Armstrong's music came to symbolize for the world the American attitude—the affirmative American attitude toward experience—in a way that went beyond the festive reiterations of Fourth of July firecrackers. If you heard Louis Armstrong opening with "Indiana"—in Turkey!—I mean, it would be like the "Star-Spangled Banner." It would move them more to say "Oh, America's a wonderful place." So Louis Armstrong really supplanted "Yankee Doodle Dandy" and Uncle Sam as the symbol of improvisation, of continuity. When the music does that, it's gotta be quintessential. Now, when we say something is *quintessential* we mean that *fifth essence*. There are four essences, you know: water, fire, earth, and air. But that fifth essence is that *spirit* which makes life meaningful. That's the quint-essence. When he says it's a quintessential music, it means it's a music that pulls it all together. It makes the "St. Louis Blues," really, in effect, as much a national anthem as the "Star-Spangled Banner."

Note

1. Murray is referring to his essay "Art as Such," published in his essay collection *From the Briarpatch File* (2001).

"Finding ourselves in the role of elder statesmen"

Interview with Dizzy Gillespie

Albert Murray interviewed Dizzy Gillespie for Andy Warhol's Interview *magazine in late 1985. The interview took place at Gillespie's home in Englewood, New Jersey. A much-abridged version of the interview was published in* Interview *in April 1986. This is a very special document: two American innovators in different art forms, born a year apart, now nearly seventy, and engaging in an in-depth and substantive discussion of jazz and culture. It should change misperceptions and assumptions about Murray's attitude toward bop, which is often conflated with Ralph Ellison's. Murray expertly guides the conversation from Gillespie's youth all the way through 1985, covering many of the major facets of Gillespie's life. The text here is based on an anonymous for-hire transcript from 1986. I retyped and corrected it, incorporating a few changes made by Murray. The University of Minnesota Press republished Gillespie's 1978 memoir* To Be, or Not . . . to Bop *in 2009.*

ALBERT MURRAY: Well, most of us who were born in the teens are somewhat astonished to find ourselves in the role of elder statesmen. I know there's a record album of yours from a tour where they call you "world statesman." You were much younger then than you are now. I remember getting that record when I was in the Air Force and I was in Morocco. You were making a tour to various places throughout the world at that time for the State Department. Well, they were talking about diplomatic statesmanship. Who would have thought in 1935 when I was finishing high school and you were in about the tenth grade or something—

DIZZY GILLESPIE: I was coming out in 1935 too.

AM: Yeah, you see? Who would have thought that in 1985 we would be finding ourselves in the role of elder statesmen—

DG: Wo-o-ow.

AM: Responsible for several generations younger than we are? I thought we would talk on that level this afternoon, about some of the things that have to do with the human content of the music. Everybody talks about the trouble they've seen and that type of thing, but anybody who's heard the music of Dizzy Gillespie does not have an image of a gloomy person. They have an image of him as something entirely different from that. I have a book called *Stomping the Blues,* and I'm sure that anybody thinking about Dizzy Gillespie and the blues would say, "Blues come messing around with Dizzy Gillespie, he'll kick 'em in the butt. He'll bop 'em. He'll riff 'em outta here." In other words, the word *Dizzy* does not suggest silliness to anybody. It suggests high spirits, it suggests energy, and it suggests playful elegance. Now, that's a big load for you to carry, but you've carried it with everything for years.

DG: Yeah, that's a hell of a load to be carrying around with me. It is rather strange to remember some of these things that happened during the formative years of the evolution of our music. I can remember a time . . . A guy named Harry Lim used to give jam sessions down at the Village Vanguard. This was in the late thirties, because I came to New York in 1937, I was one of the boys from that moment on. When I would walk in the place they would say, "Aw, here comes that wrong-note trumpet." Musicians, especially horn players, were not too adept at harmony. They didn't follow harmony too much. They were . . . saxophone players were booters—boot, you know, trumpet players were screamers and riffers—they made big riffs, a lot of riffs. So when this music came on the scene, in the development of this music, if you played a chord that was a flatted fifth, they'd call that a wrong note. I can remember, and I just laugh, because at the time it finally developed into a music where the younger guys were coming up and were talking about the flatted fifth, they would play all together in the key of the flatted fifth. Suppose they were in C; they would be playing it F sharp. So it really gives me great pleasure to know that our music is still evolving now, and I hope I can be a part of it until I get out of here.

AM: Well, the interesting thing, back to that theme of being an elder statesman, a living legend and so forth, is that we're elders but not old fogeys. Nobody regards you as an old fogey, an old fuddy-duddy, or an old codger. I know how much Wynton Marsalis, for example, admires you and thinks about you.

DG: We have some interesting conversations sometimes.

AM: Right. He's already rated as one of the top two classical trumpet players in the world today, but he wonders if he will make it into the top ten jazz trumpeters. That type of thing is very, very good. Let's just go back a little bit before. We both came up from the South, as it were, spent our early years in the South, so we were listening, since we were approximately the same age—I've got a couple years on you—to the same type of thing. Let's look at some of the content that you're actually making variations on later when you began to do your own thing in music. Back in the late teens and early twenties, do you sometimes recall the tunes that were very, very popular? Just the pop tunes first, and then we'll get to the other tunes. Like, you know, "California, Here I Come," "Linger a While," stuff like that.

DG: "The Stars Fell on Alabama." [laughs]

AM: And the songs you sang in school, like "Sweet and Low" and left-over songs from World War I; "Pack Up Your Troubles" and things like that. Some of those others, "Hindustan" stuff like that—

DG: "Limehouse Blues." "Nagasaki."

AM: "Nagasaki"!

DG: I got a story to tell you about "Nagasaki," though. This is before I came north. I went to school, up through the first two years of high school, at a place called Cheraw, South Carolina. I remember I was maybe about eleven or something like that. It was a public school. They had two schools there. They had a Presbyterian school, Coulter Memorial Academy, and this was run by Dr. Long. I was going to the public school, which was rather small. The state bought them instruments, and so they started passing these instruments out. I was little. The bigger guys got what they wanted. The only thing that was left was a trombone, so I grabbed the trombone, and when I grabbed the trombone and learned how to play a chromatic scale, I could not reach further than the fifth position. There were two more positions down there; I couldn't reach. [laughs] Then I learned how to play . . . This teacher, Miss Alice Wilson, was very talented. She used to write songs. I don't think she could read music. As a matter of fact, she couldn't read music. She played in B flat all the time, so I learned all of my songs in B flat. We had a little minstrel show where we had some dancers and singers, and then we had two guys on the end called Mr. Interlocutor. He'd jump up and say a joke and sit back down, and somebody'd start dancing. We played for them. Well, this went on for a couple of years, and I was still playing in B flat. A guy named Sonny Matthews was a very good musician. His mother taught the piano, so he knew how to read music. He left home and went up north. In fact, he went up north—Charlotte, North Carolina. [laughs] That was called up north.

AM: From Cheraw!

DG: From Cheraw, yeah. So he went up north. He came back home to visit his family and someone was telling him about this little Gillespie boy that played the trumpet. He said, "Go get him. I want to see what he can do." So they went and got me, and I was playing this raggedy school horn. I went down there and I took out the horn, played a couple of notes. He said, "Okay, what do you want to play?" I said, "Well, what do you know?" That was the epitome of . . . I don't know what you'd call that, because here was a guy—

AM: Arrogance.

DG: Arrogance, that's right. He said, "Do you know 'Nagasaki'?" I said "Yeah, yeah, I know 'Nagasaki'!" So he sat down to the piano and started playing in the key of C. I could not find *one* note that went with what he was playing. I was so embarrassed. I cried. I packed up my horn, and I was determined then. I said, "It must be something else besides B flat." So after that, there was a guy named Norman Poe who took up the trombone—he was a tall guy; he had long arms. He learned how to read music from another guy, named Ralph Cole, and he'd bring the lessons over to my house and my trumpet, and I would play along with him. I don't think he could read the treble clef, so I learned how to read the bass clef. [laughs] So, after learning how to read in the bass clef for a while, we started getting little stock arrangements, and I learned how to read music *after* that, and then I got a scholarship to Laurinburg Institute, which is one of the finest black schools in the country now. They don't feature music too much, but they feature sports. They have basketball players. Basketball players that went to Laurinburg Institute were Sam Jones, Charlie Scott, Jimmy Walker, Wes Covington, who was a baseball player, several others. I can't remember the names, but they were the ones that went on. So finally I stayed in Laurinburg for a couple of years. I finished Laurinburg Institute, and my family in the meantime had moved to Philadelphia, so I moved to Philadelphia in 1935. Then I stayed in Philadelphia for two years and came back to New York in '37.

AM: Now, it was before you went to Philadelphia that you were taught by Shorty Hall, wasn't it?

DG: Shorty Hall—

AM: From Tuskegee.

DG: Yes, of course. Shorty Hall didn't have too much time to spend with me because he had to teach all of the younger musicians how to play. When I went there, I could play. I could read music. I was the leading trumpet player at Laurinburg Institute when I went there, because the trumpet player whose place I took was named Isaac Johnson. He was the son of the dean, and he went to A & T College.

AM: Yeah, in Greensboro, North Carolina.

DG: Yes, and then Frank MacDuffy, who was a trombone player . . . Two of us went to Laurinburg. Norman Poe, the one who taught me how to read . . . Both of us went, so we were the nucleus of the band. So Shorty didn't have too much time to teach me too much, because he was so busy with these younger musicians that had never played before. I had a lot of experience with him because I heard him play a lot, and he was one of our masters. As a matter of fact, he played during the World's Fair in Chicago back in 19—

AM: '33?

DG: No, this was before. This was before, because I was still at Laurinburg. He was in college in Tuskegee up until about 1930, and then he went north and played with Speed Webb. But when he was there he was the soloist with that bad Tuskegee band. Also my coach—I played football, too—Mr. Smith, was the center on that bad Tuskegee team that had Ben Stevenson on it.

AM: That's right. He was the center. So we had two Tuskegee graduates at Laurinburg. That's interesting. They used to have battles of bands, especially dance bands, between Tuskegee and 'Bama State, back during those days, just as they had the marching bands competing and the football teams. They had the dance bands, and of course it was the 'Bama State Collegians and the Tuskegee Melody Barons. The guy who was sort of the student concert master for the 'Bama State band, as Shorty Hall was for the Tuskegee band . . . You know they had a student who would lead the cheers and so forth and lead the band when the cheerleaders were out in the stands. It was a guy named Carl "Mike" Thompson, a trumpet player, and he came to my high school in Mobile. He was the bandmaster down there. He came down there in the early thirties. Shorty Hall was succeeded by Ralph Ellison, the writer, who was a trumpet player and music student at that time.

DG: I didn't know he was a trumpet player!

AM: Right, at Tuskegee he was two years ahead of me, and the guy who succeeded Carl "Mike" Thompson at 'Bama State was Erskine Hawkins. So this stuff really sort of ties in interestingly, because one was unaware of various things that were connected during that period. I want to talk about some other things that were part of your musical experience growing up. Of course you remember the old T.O.B.A. theaters and the T.O.B.A. circuit and the acts on that.

DG: Oh, yeah!

AM: Who are some of the people you remember? You remember Butterbeans and Susie?

DG: Of course. Butter and Susie were both great friends of mine—

AM: I mean, as a kid. Is that right? That was in later years, but as a kid you knew them growing up, right?

DG: Well, in South Carolina . . . I knew them from 1937 on. We'd get the *Pittsburgh Courier* and we read about all the people that were playing around, but as a personal touch I learned all of these people after I had come to New York. As a matter of fact, when I was in Philadelphia, they'd come to Philadelphia.

AM: What was the showcase theater for T.O.B.A. in Philadelphia? Do you remember?

DG: Lincoln. Abraham Lincoln. [laughs]

AM: Right. But you remember various other theaters, because they're legendary in our experience, in that circuit?

DG: The Howard Theater, the Royal Theater in Baltimore. Howard Theater in Washington.

AM: Right. Bailey's 81 in Atlanta?

DG: Well, when I went south, we usually played one-nighters. We played some theaters with Cab Calloway, but this was in 1939, '40, '41. I didn't know any big cities in the South because as soon as I got out of high school, up north I went.

AM: But you were aware of the tours, people like Ma Rainey and Bessie Smith—

DG: Yes, I knew about them too.

AM: Any number of musicians who were a little bit older than we are actually spent a lot of time on the T.O.B.A., touring, as I said.

DG: Yeah. Well, I almost ran away from home to join a minstrel show. The minstrel show was where they did the show in the tents. I almost left home to do that, and I almost went with King Oliver, but I went to Philadelphia instead. My friend, a trombone player, went with King Oliver and I came north.

AM: Yeah, well, those bands made that circuit in those days.

DG: Oh, yes, they stayed out on the road all the time.

AM: All the time, and I mean great, legendary names you grew up knowing about, like this guy Dorsey who used to work for Ma Rainey. Fletcher Henderson used to work with Bessie Smith. But as a very young man, say, the age you were in 1923 or '24, you already knew about Bessie Smith.

DG: Oh, yes. 1924 . . . I was seven years old. I knew something about them in 1924, a little bit, a little bit. When I first started learning about bands, I knew the bands that went down south to play the dance halls, like . . . I'll name you some of them: Capital City Aces from Raleigh, Kelly's Jazz Hounds from Federal, Carolina Cotton Pickers from Charleston, Belton's Society Syncopators from Florida, Smiling Billy Stewart from Florida, Jimmy Gunn from Charlotte, Bill Davis from Charlotte. And I was little. Around when I was about thirteen or fourteen, I was a little guy, and I'd go to all the dances with my older brothers and sisters. They'd tell the leader, "Hey, we got a little brother that can play." They'd put me on a box and let me play the trumpet. I knew some of the arrangements that they played.

AM: Do you remember the Sunset Royals?

DG: Sunset Royals! Oooooo, they were mean.

AM: Yeah, now, a number of those cities down there had their like resident maestros. You know, if you came out of Mobile, you had worked with Papa Holman—

DG: I know him too.

AM: You *do* know him? He came out of Birmingham. He worked with Fess Whatley.

DG: Fess Whatley was at Alabama State.

AM: Yeah, well, and Birmingham later on, like the territory band working out of Birmingham.

DG: Yeah, yeah. Everybody was talking about him.

AM: And Milton Larkin in Texas. You had all these people around like that.

DG: We didn't know any bands from California or anything like that.

AM: Oh, no, until the radio came in and started getting those networks. Then we would hear about Les Hite.

DG: Yeah, that's right. I worked with Les Hite, too.

AM: What we used to do was stay up late at night and get those national hookups when radio first came in, pick up Duke at the Cotton Club, and the guys at the Grand Terrace, and then all out to the Cotton Club in California.

DG: And the Savoy Ballroom.

AM: Oh, yeah.

DG: That was my favorite. That was my favorite trumpet player, Roy Eldridge. He was playing with Teddy Hill's band then. I said, "I want to play like that!" That was my idol, my role model.

AM: About how old were you at the time?

DG: When I first heard Teddy Hill's band, it must have been around 1933, so I was seventeen . . . [counts] I must have been around seven, eight years old, but I was just listening then, I wasn't playing anything at that time. I can remember when I went to Laurinburg Institute in 1933. How old was I then? I was sixteen, I believe. I used to listen to Teddy Hill at the Savoy Ballroom on the lady's radio, next door. We didn't have a radio.

AM: Exactly! I used to go down to the corner, like, the corner drugstore or something like that, or the corner delicatessen, and go in and listen. That late stuff, if you could stay up that late, the late broadcasts used to come in like that. Well, how old were you when you became aware of Louie, for example?

DG: Louis Armstrong . . . I didn't become aware of Louis too much until I moved north, until 1935. I went to see his show. He fascinated me, man.

AM: What was your involvement with phonograph records?

DG: I didn't have no records.

AM: Is that right?

DG: I didn't have any records. I didn't have no Victrola. Victrola! [laughs]

AM: Victrola! In writing the book which I just created with Count Basie, he was talking about waking up hearing the Blue Devils and thinking it was Louie Armstrong playing on the jukebox. I said, "It wasn't a jukebox. It was a Victrola, it was a talking machine, it was a graphophone."

DG: Graphophone! [laughs all around] You'd wind it up—

AM: And you had either the steel needles or those cactus needles. That was very fancy. Highfalutin.

DG: Mm-hmm. The lady next door had one of those.

AM: It had those little stacks of records under there, and sometimes they had that speaker, you know, like the RCA Victor Victrola, with the dog listening with his ear turned to one side. Those are common experiences which were really feeding a lot of things into our—

DG: You see, we . . . I personally integrated, like, white dances sometimes. I was a good dancer, too. They'd let me come to the white dance, and I'd be, like, on the periphery. At one point during the night they'd call this little dancer out there, and I'd come out and do my little dance, and they'd throw money all the time. Make a little change on the floor.

AM: Where were you when you first became aware of Ellington, and what did that mean to you at that time?

DG: I was in Philadelphia when Duke Ellington first came.

AM: You were fortunate, because you could hear it but you could also catch him at the local showcase theater.

DG: That's right. Yeah, man, I went to see Duke Ellington. Every *day* I was there in Philadelphia. Duke Ellington, Fletcher Henderson, Jimmie Lunceford. When I went to school in Laurinburg, Edward Wilcox, the pianist, his sister taught French at Laurinburg, So I went around to the Lincoln Theater and told the guy, "I know your sister."

AM: You were talking about the piano.

DG: Well, the piano is the key to a guy who wants to be an improviser, because you see all the notes at one time on the piano.

AM: Actually, when you began to supplement your work on the trumpet with the piano you were really taking a big step in the direction of being the kind of leader you became without realizing it, because you didn't have in mind that you were preparing for that, but the preparation was sort of taking place, wouldn't you say?

DG: Yeah, well, I would imagine so. To be a soloist, you need to know the piano because it is the key to improvisation. Not only that, but another major influence on my life was my first bandleader, the guy that was the leader of our little band in Cheraw. His name was Wes Buchanan. He played the bass drum, so rhythm . . . piano and rhythm was my thing. It has remained that all through these years. When I learned the music of Brazil, Cuba, the West Indies—those were the major three—I wanted to find out what they were doing with the *rhythm* first, because with my harmonic background there was not too much I could learn from them in the beginning of when I started listening to that music harmonically. *We* had the harmonics here, but they had that multirhythm. I was lucky to have embraced a rhythmic concept along with harmonics.

AM: It's so consistent with the central percussive nature of Afro-American expression in music, it seems to me. The piano is essentially a percussive-type instrument; the mallets are *hitting*. You know, you're not drawing a string across; you're *plucking* it. And the jazz musicians didn't rest until they started plucking the bass, and they played the big tuba like a percussive instrument.

DG: Uh-huh, that's right. It's like when I first heard Charlie Parker. I was very much fascinated by his percussive effect, more than anything else. How he *attacked* and where his *accents* fell. The first time I heard him I was with Cab Calloway. A little guy named Buddy Anderson introduced me to him and brought him to my hotel room. We sat up and jammed all day in the hotel room, and I was *very* much impressed by Charlie Parker because of his *percussive* effect on the music. Charlie Parker, I would think, was the architect of this music that we play, because style is the major thing. Everybody played the same notes but played differently. That's why I think Charlie Parker was the most important one of our crowd, because he gave us the style. You see, you can play the same notes that someone else plays and you don't play the accents in the same place. You don't even sound like him. But you can play something else that *you* thought of and play it with those effects on there, and you'll sound like the guy. So that is the most important thing, I think.

AM: Yes! It seems to me that the *quality* was already in our music to a certain extent, but they were not aware enough of it to manipulate it with the kind of control that you begin to do consciously. You see, a guy would *feel* up that way every now and then, but all of a sudden, it became a part of our technology because you could actually *know* where that stuff was falling.

DG: Charlie Parker was a great blues player, one of the greatest that jazz has produced.

AM: He had that foundation, and he could take off from there and go anywhere.

DG: *Yeah,* man, like one of those supersonic flights.

AM: One of the things that I remember, among all those wonderful things that I remember about you guys playing at the time you were playing, was that "Sweet Georgia Brown" that you guys did at Jazz at the Philharmonic, where you set it up and Charlie comes in and roughs it up, and you've got to come back and take another one. Then Lester comes in there, cools it down a bit. You remember that one?

DG: Yes, "Sweet Georgia Brown."

AM: That stuff was getting together at that time. In other words, people were becoming very much aware of it. It's interesting, I first became aware of you on "Disorder at the Border," with Coleman Hawkins. The next thing I got was "Salt Peanuts," or "Salted Peanuts," as the man on the record had it, and "Be-Bop" was on the other side of that. This was back during the war. Then the next thing was—and this was not just an individual with an individual style, but a thing that had sort of general implications—when I heard Howard McGhee playing on the first Jazz at the Philharmonic record. I said, "There's a guy up there in New York, a guy that used to play with Cab, named Dizzy Gillespie. He's influencing a lot of these younger guys these days, as well as the older guys. Howard McGhee is playing . . . some of his figures are Dizzy's figures."

DG: He was one of the boys.

AM: This is during the war and I was at Tuskegee. We used to go on cross-country training flights over the weekend. That meant a couple guys could check out an airplane. They could go anywhere, and it was chalked up as training. So these guys who lived in California would go out to California. They'd come back and say, "We saw these guys at Billy Berg's" or someplace like that. Or they'd come in to New York and run around Fifty-second Street and various places like that. They'd also bring back records and over in the B.O.Q.— the Base Officers' Quarters—we'd all play these records and discuss this stuff. You had a big following in the Air Force, down at the Air Training Base down in Tuskegee during the war.

DG: Well, out of the Armed Services of the United States, the Air Force was the most intelligent.

AM: Well, they thought of themselves as hip. They had a kind of mobility; they could follow through on their sophisticated tastes, you see. They could get to it easier than some of the other people, because every weekend, you had a plan to go somewhere if you wanted to. The planes were available. You had to shift around. There were a lot of pilots and so forth around there. But watching this stuff and checking the publications for those record releases—they were all on those kinds of off-labels for the most part in those days—

DG: A lot of times we weren't even recording. We had a band on the recording and then sometimes we were signed up with one record company and would make another record under another name. Try to find all those names that I made records under.

AM: Well, one of those things that was really close to home about abusing a state name was a record with John Birks on it. [laughs]

DG: Yeah, bebop style. Gabriel.

AM: Yes, that's right! I remember that.

DG: A lot of us did that. Charlie Parker, Charlie Chan.

AM: Yes. How do you remember getting involved in arranging and composing? I'm sure the piano had a lot to do with that.

DG: It had a great deal to do with it. I made my first big-band arrangement in 1935 in Philadelphia with Frankie Fairfax. In fact, the name of that was [singing] "Goodnight, My Love." I thought that was beautiful, a great song.

AM: Yeah, I remember that.

DG: Ella Fitzgerald played that with Chick Webb.

AM: Those songs I used to pick up out of those Hollywood musicals that were coming out at that time.

DG: That's right. I was in a musical.

AM: And the guys would take that stuff and give it a little more elegance, give it a little more of that percussive stuff.

DG: And then we did a lot of changing chords around. So we used a flat fifth. Instead of using a dominant 7 or a G 7th chord [going to C], we'd make the flatted fifth as a D-flat chord, and sometimes put two or three chords [before the resolution] . . . That's what they do in films. They do that in movies. They have carte blanche in movies, where they can write almost anything they want to write.

AM: Because for certain movies, they want certain sounds to go with it.

DG: Yeah, they can write anything they want! The movies really liberated a lot of the writers who had to stay within a strict modicum before the movies became music-minded. That helped a lot. Then, when I came to New York, there was a little slow time, and I became able to arrange. It took me some time because I never went to school to learn how to arrange, but I learned how to score. I wrote some arrangements for Jimmy Dorsey, Ina Ray Hutton, Woody Herman, Boyd Raeburn—white bands. The white bands were *anxious* to get some of this new music. One time Jimmy Dorsey told me . . . I brought an arrangement to him called "Grand Central Getaway" or something like that, an original composition. He said, "Kid, the next time you bring an arrangement, bring your horn with you." So I could show the trumpet players how to . . . [laughs] We were flying all over. I wrote the trumpet like he was playing one of our solos or something like that, but they got it.

AM: Well, they were very conscientious about that since you pretty much put down a lot of what you wanted to hear.

DG: Oh, yes, yes. We had a lot of fans amongst the white musicians.

AM: Yeah, I know. I was aware of that. Had you started that when you were still with Earl Hines? Did you do any writing when you were with Earl?

DG: I wrote "A Night in Tunisia" when I was with Earl Hines. Well, just before I was with Earl Hines. I was with Benny Carter, doing one of those little movies.

AM: One of those little . . . soundies?

DG: Soundie! Yes. I was doing a soundie once with Benny Carter and Maxine Sullivan. I used to always play around with the piano when there was a rest period or something. I'd go straight to the piano. This day I played these two chords, the two chords in "A Night in Tunisia." And they resolved into one another like that. From the chords I could see the melody, just from the chords, and I wrote "A Night in Tunisia" there, at the rehearsal.

AM: I'll be damned.

DG: Mm-hmm. I learned a lot from Benny Carter, too.

AM: Oh, yeah, a fine arranger.

DG: Much, much, much, much music. Much music that man has created.

AM: Other guys in the Hines band wrote things that had a kind of little emphasis that was some of yours.

DG: That was bebop. That was truly bebop. They had all the guys that were playing like that. Charlie Parker was in that band, and I was in that band, Shadow Wilson was in that band, Bennie Green was in that band, a boy named Crump, Tom Crump, another guy named Good. All these guys . . . Earl Hines was right there! It didn't change us at all.

AM: Sarah was in there!

DG: Sarah Vaughan, Billy Eckstine.

AM: There's a piece of his called "Scoops Carry Mary" that sounds like it was written by Dizzy Gillespie. Was a guy named Carpenter or somebody in the band writing? Who else wrote in that band?

DG: Richard Carpenter . . . He never wrote nothing, but his brother, Charlie Carpenter, was the manager of Earl Hines. If a guy would write a tune, sometimes it would wind up under Carpenter's name.

AM: René Hall? You know anything about him?

DG: He came in the band after me. He was a guitar player.

AM: He is listed as the arranger on "Scoops Carry Mary," but it's a bop piece.

DG: Oh, this band was the band before us. I can see my picture's not here with this band. Earl Hines always had some good bands. I notice here Truck Parham on bass; that was 1941. I joined Earl Hines in 1942, so this wasn't the band that I was in. I don't see hardly anybody there that was with the band when I got to the band. Ah, look at that. He's surrounded by girls. I know some of these chorus girls.

AM: Yeah, you probably got caught in some of that . . . Well, around "Second Balcony Jump" was—

DG: Joe Valentine! Well, when I was with Earl Hines, there was no recording.

AM: That's what I thought! That was [during the] recording ban [ban on recording during World War II]. There's one thing from '42 there; that's the "Second Balcony Jump." There's a Budd Johnson solo on there.

DG: Yeah, oooo! Was he a master! He was one of the greatest musicians that we have . . . "Topsy Turvy."

AM: Yeah, they play that thing. That was Cab's number, wasn't it?

DG: Yeah.

AM: But Walter Fuller sings the hell out of that thing.

DG: Yeah, yeah. "Deep Forest," that was his theme song. "Boogie Woogie on the St. Louis Blues"!

AM: Weren't you saying something when you said, "Play it the 1950 way?"

DG: Yeah, yeah!

AM: 1951 or something like that.

DG: "Jersey Bounce." Billy Eckstine, "Jelly Jelly."

AM: How early did you become aware of that band, let's say, from Philadelphia? That's when you really started hearing bands from all over, right?

DG: Trummy Young was with Earl Hines's band at that time, in 1935 and 1936. All the bands used to come through Philly; Duke, Cab, Fletcher, Jimmy . . . All of them came through at the theater, and Trummy Young, before he went with Jimmie Lunceford, with Margie and all that, Trummy was a featured trombonist in the band. He tried to get Earl to hire me, but Earl didn't do it. So Billy Eckstine brought me to the band, but that was after Trummy had left.

AM: That was a band, man. I saw that band. The guys say, "What's Earl playing now?"

DG: He had the first bebop band! He had the two leading . . . Charlie Parker and I were the two leading proponents of this music, and all the musicians in the band phrased like that, so therefore he had the first bebop band.

AM: But Earl was a pretty solid influence on a large part of the country because they were broadcasting out of Chicago. People were hearing that all through the South and the Southwest. That was the band heard most often on the radio. So that's why Budd Johnson and his guys from Texas grew up with an ambition to get in that *band,* man. Get in the Earl Hines band and play at the Grand Terrace, that type of thing. Those were great days. From Earl's band, the next band that was a bop band was Billy's band, right?

DG: We left Earl Hines. All of us quit at the same time: Billy, I, Sarah Vaughan. We all quit, and then Art Blakey came into Billy Eckstine's band as a drummer. That was the second bebop band.

AM: How did Basie fit into your consciousness? You were already a young professional before Basie came east. You were playing professionally in 1935.

DG: Yeah. I had an offer to go into Basie's band when he came to New York back in—

AM: 1936 and '37.

DG: I didn't come . . . My career went this way: I came to New York to play with Lucky Millinder, with Charlie Shavers, and "'Bama" Carl Warwick.

AM: Sweets had already gone to Basie at that time?

DG: I was supposed to take Sweets's place, because Charlie and "'Bama" and I were like one in Philadelphia. They got Lucky to say he'd hire me, so I came up to New York. Then I went up to the Savoy with them, and after I got here Lucky decided to keep Harry. That's pretty interesting. Count Basie at that time had a young trumpet player named Bobby Moore. One of his great solos was a number called "Out the Window." But they put Bobby Moore in the place for people's heads.[1]

AM: Institution.

DG: Yeah. Still now. Still there right now.

AM: Uptown.

DG: Bobby and I, our crowd, all of us following Roy Eldridge at this time—this is before Charlie Parker . . . Little Bobby, Charlie Shavers, little Benny Harris, Joe Guy, myself, those were the five trumpet players around New York. All of us were trying to play like Roy Eldridge. Basie heard me, and when Bobby got sick and had to go to this place, he offered me the job. I knew that I would be taking Bobby's place and I refused the job. Harry Edison took the job.

AM: What was your impression of the Basie band at that time?

DG: Jump. Oooh, everybody wanted to sound like Count Basie, Count Basie's band. Every band wanted to sound like Count Basie's band. There was a band leader in Philadelphia at that time called Bill Doggett. Bill Doggett was with Frankie Fairfax, and the whole band quit and went to Atlantic City to play at the Harlem Club. Bill Doggett offered me a job at that time to go down to Atlantic City to play with his band, but I didn't take that job. I just stayed around Philly, and I went with Frankie Fairfax's new band, which included Jimmy Hamilton. He was playing trumpet then, not clarinet. When he went with Duke Ellington, playing clarinet, I said, "What? Jimmy Hamilton?" Joe Trump, we called him, because he played the trumpet. I was surprised that he was playing—

AM: So you lost track of him when he was with Hamp? Wasn't he with Hamp?

DG: I don't think so. I don't think Jimmy Hamilton played with Hamp.

AM: He played with one other big band before that. I know Cab was with him.

DG: Maybe Eddie Heyward or something like that.

AM: Maybe he did too. That's right. Some other band he played with in there, because he'd had some writing experience—

DG: Well, he had to play with *somebody* before he went with Duke! [laughs] God maybe. You go with Duke Ellington's band, you better had been playing with *somebody*! Yessiree.

AM: So when you looked up and saw a guy playing another instrument with Duke—

DG: With Duke Ellington! He followed Barney Bigard.

AM: Right. I think they had Chauncey Haughton in there for a little while, didn't they?

DG: Well, Chauncey Haughton played with me with Cab Calloway.

AM: Is that right? I think it was shortly . . . There's some pictures of him sitting in there. I think he was on that other horn in there.

DG: Well, Cab and Duke were very close friends, and there was a time when they had some kind of gentleman's agreement like "I won't hire your musician and you won't hire mine." That's when Ben Webster was with Cab. When he left Cab, Duke wanted Ben very badly, but they had this agreement that they wouldn't hire one another's musicians. You'd never see a guy leave Cab Calloway's band and go with Duke Ellington.

AM: That's interesting. They finally managed to get Ben. That was something too. What was the emotional effect that, say, Lester had on you? What was your conception of Lester when he hit town?

DG: Lester turned saxophone players around! Up to that point, all the saxophone players were trying to sound like Hawk, but when Lester came with that breezy sound that he had, all the tenor saxophonists— you know, all the younger ones——

AM: Said that's the way to go.

DG: That's right. Took off. Especially the white boys.

AM: Oh, yeah. Well, the irony was if you just look at or listen to him at a superficial level without looking at the underlying dynamics, you realize how crazy Bird was of Lester too.

DG: Very much influenced by Lester, I'm sure.

AM: Right, but he's playing with all that other percussion stuff going too. It's so dazzling that you don't realize what's under there. They say that when Charlie was with Jay McShann and Basie would be broadcasting from somewhere, he'd say, "Well, I'm not making this set" and go listen to Lester with Basie.

DG: And they played different instruments. One played alto and the other played tenor. You hear him play tenor, he sounds very much like Lester. He played tenor with Earl Hines. That way that Charlie Parker . . . When they got me in the band, little Benny Harris was in the band and that was one of my followers. And Billy Eckstine was one of my great musical friends. Billy Eckstine told Earl Hines, "Why don't you get Dizzy? And why don't you get Charlie Parker too?" Earl said, "We have two alto saxophonists," which were Scoops Carry and Goon Gardner. They needed a tenor player. Billy said, "Buy him a tenor." They went and bought him a tenor.

AM: Well, Lester has a story where something like that happened. He was playing alto and the guy who was playing tenor would always give them a problem when they were getting ready to go off somewhere. You know how Lester would say it: *The guy's up there fixing his face, and we was down there waiting for him in the bus, so I said, Buy me one. Get me a horn. I'll play that motherfucker.*

DG: You know, Budd Johnson is one of the less celebrated musicians in jazz, but he was one of the greatest. He taught Lester how to read music.

AM: Is that right? He was telling me about those days.

DG: He came through Kansas City from Texas. It's strange. Budd Johnson's first job when he left home was in Kansas City, and his last job was in Kansas City. He died there.

AM: Is that so? Budd and I became good friends a few years ago when I got a group of Kansas City and Texas musicians to participate in a jam session for my publication party for *Stomping the Blues.*[2]

DG: Oh man, he was a master musician. We had a band together, you know.

AM: Yeah. He was doing all that fine writing for Earl—

DG: Yes, and Billy.

AM: And Billy, because he had *fun* with that.

DG: Yeah, oh, he could write too.

AM: You mention in the interviews[3] for the Basie book that when Billy was getting his book together he came by and Basie said, "Well, anything I got you want, just get it."

DG: Yeah, Billy told me the same thing when I got my big band. He said, "You can have all the music you want, *and* the stands." [laughs] "If you need some music uniforms you can have that too."

AM: Yeah, that's right. That was the point. You know, people don't think about that, but if you're really getting a band together to go out and play some dates, you gotta have all that equipment. I was very much impressed and gratified in the late forties, after you had established yourself as a major new force in jazz . . . There was the bop thing, then you and Charlie, then the next thing you did that really impressed very much was that you got a big band together, and started writing for that, and encouraging other guys to write. How did that happen? Did you have that feeling that you just wanted a richer, a big band?

DG: No, I was doing pretty good with a small group, and we had the same manager; Billy Shaw was my manager. He had my first big band, and he had a tour going down south with the Nicholas Brothers. So he said, "I want you to have a big band." We got Gil Fuller, the arranger, and Billy Eckstine gave me all the music I needed, the stands and everything, and we went down south with the Nicholas Brothers. It was a big flop, because the people down south were just used to hearing the blues and boogie-woogie and things like that and they weren't ready for us. They said they couldn't dance to the music. I'd tell everybody, "What do you mean, you can't dance to the music? What am *I* doing up there?"

AM: I wrote in my book that the guys could always make their *insides* dance even if their feet couldn't keep up with it.

DG: That's right! [laughs]

AM: But you always did illustrate the steps.

DG: I was always dancing to my music.

AM: That's right. Some of this stuff, the '47 stuff, you know, the big arrangements, "Cubana Be, Cubana Bop," "I'm Bopping Too," "Sweet Is Sweet."

DG: By Billy.

AM: Yeah? Dizzier and Dizzier and?

DG: "Dizzier and Dizzier" is Gerald Wilson. There's one of the great—

AM: Gerald did that too? Let's talk about arrangers.

DG: Well, he's the one that wrote that. There was some great arrangers out there in those days. Joe Valentine was the mainstay of Bill Eckstine's band. After Budd Johnson, actually, Joe Valentine came to the band.

AM: Tadd Dameron?

DG: Tadd. Oooo, yessir. Walter [Gil] Fuller was my major writer. Buster Harding was with Basie.

AM: Oh, yeah.

DG: And Cab Calloway, too. Any band. All of them had a major writer.

AM: Right, but you were feeding a lot of that new stuff that was so directly influenced, and then guys where I was were so thrilled when they realized. They said, "Do you know who's playing piano on that particular piece? That's Dizzy Gillespie!" They thought that was a really exciting thing because they figured that you played trumpet *all* the time, and you're falling back there *playing* it, too.

DG: Well, that's a compliment. As a matter of fact, I had to show most of the piano players what we wanted for our music. Our music didn't require oom-cha, oom-cha, oom-cha, oom-cha. Our music required bap . . . bap, bap, bap . . . yop, bap, bap. You know, it required punctuation, but before that time piano players were oom-cha, oom-cha, oom-cha. So I had to show the piano players that; I said, "Man, don't do that." I remember I played with Fletcher Henderson at several gigs around New York. I was at the Apollo with him, and my solo came. I stood up and started playing my solo, and Fletcher was playing oom-cha, oom-cha, and I said "Stroll 'em!" Stroll 'em means piano lay out—

AM: Right. He's the boss! That was the boss!

DG: Yeah, only I don't think he heard me, so he kept playing, so I just sat down. Let somebody else come in there and play. So he asked me, "What's wrong with you?" I said, "Man, I couldn't play behind that oom-cha, oom-cha. I play, you know, what I play."

AM: Both Duke and Basie had that way of comping, which was more like that than—

DG: More like that, but they were from that era. But Duke also plays like our era too.

AM: That's what I'm saying. They knew *that,* but their real way, the distinctive way of Duke's comping, was not just oom-cha, oom-cha, but he was doing this donk . . . donk, donk.

DG: Yeah, yeah, yeah, yeah. I loved playing with Duke, man. Basie plays the less as he can. I have a record with Basie called *[The Gifted Ones]* . . . Basie with a small group, Ray Brown, Mickey Roker, Basie. And Basie wanted to play as less as he can. He's *shy,* you know. So the day of the record date, I looked up, and there was a flute player with his flute on the piano. So I asked Basie, "What's this?" He said "Well, I thought, you know, maybe we need . . ." I said, "Basie, we don't need nobody. We do not need anybody. We can say enough here with us." This guy put his flute back, one of his musicians—

AM: Was it Danny Turner?

DG: Danny! Yeah! Danny had his flute here. And I said, "No, Basie. No."

AM: We got all we need.

DG: This is enough. He played majestically. Have you heard him on that album? I heard him play things I never heard him play before.

AM: He can hear, man.

DG: Ooo, man, I never heard him play like that before, man. "St. James Infirmary."

AM: Yeah, he could be touched. He'd get touched by other musicians.

DG: But he gave everybody else a chance.

AM: He'd pick up and respond. He didn't work out all that stuff ahead of time. He would respond to it. He was a counterpuncher. He'd be waiting for you at the next corner, see? I was curious about how Basie's arrival affected you, because with Parker you had that Kansas City input, and I thought of it as being that completely flexible 4/4 that never really was monotonous.

DG: No, no.

AM: Isn't that something?

DG: And Jo Jones with that ride cymbal? Walter Page walking up and down the bass? Shoot, man!

AM: You had plenty of room to do all kinds of things. Swinging little songs. That's great. What was your personal contact with Tadd?

DG: Tadd was very close to me. We—

AM: "Our Delight" and so forth?

DG: Yeah, we did a lot together. You know, Tadd took, like, a harmony . . . Tadd and I played piano about the same. Neither one of us was a real piano player.

AM: You had a composer's ear for the piano.

DG: Yeah, so Tadd took one of my arrangements and made a song out of it. You know "If You Could See Me Now?" "If You Could See Me Now" was taken. . . . You know "Groovin' High," that I wrote the ending, da-da, dee-de-doo-dee. Yeah, well, he took that and went "If you could see me now." He put my name on it, because he took that right out. We did a lot together, Tadd and I.

AM: I had that feeling.

DG: Yeah, we did a lot together, arranging tunes. We'd sit up making arrangements, both of us.

AM: That's great. Here's the other guy we've got to mention, trying other stuff into the new music. We've been talking this long, and we haven't said Thelonious Monk.

DG: Oh, man. Thelonious Monk is different. He's the most different one of that era. Monk was related to Charlie Parker as much as Charlie Parker and I were to one another. Monk was very, very deep, but I think I influenced Charlie Parker more than Monk, and I'm sure that Charlie Parker—

AM: Influenced *you* more than Monk.

DG: Yeah, yeah. But chord-harmonically, we used to exchange ideas. Monk is the first one to show me a minor 6 chord, and after he showed me that, I went crazy. I wrote "Woody 'n You." That's the first chord that we play. Monk is the first one to show me that, and I went crazy. I put that in a whole lot of my compositions. Recently, right now, that is very clear in my mind about that one chord, because it's something else now. You see, like a minor 6 chord with the 6 in the bass, that bass note looks like the tonic of the other chord, what they call it now. They call it that, like, an E-flat minor 6 with the 6 in the bass. That means the C is in the bass. Well, it sounds like a chord that's built on a C, but it's built on an E flat. They call it C minor 7 flat 5, they call it C half-diminished, but when I have to write that chord down for somebody, I write C minor, C minor 6, with the 6 in the bass, you put the bass note under there. If I run across it in my music, boom, and I see C minor 7 flat 5, I'd feel much more comfortable if he'd written E-flat minor 6, you know? I can pop it right away. That's a beautiful chord. Nat Cole was a great accompanist. He's proven it by accompanying himself. He's the best. He's the first one I heard play "How High the Moon," and I rushed up to Monk and showed him the note. That was one of our major tunes. I remember when I took that up to Monk.

AM: Yeah, Basie mentions something like that. Norman Granz was giving those jam sessions out in Los Angeles during the war, and he took him one night over to some place, some private home, and the house piano player was Nat Cole, and he wanted him to hear some of that stuff he was doing at that time. This may have been just before he first hit with the King Cole Trio.

DG: I was playing with Nat. When I learned "How High the Moon" we were playing together . . . King Cole Trio, Art Tatum, Benny Carter's band, and probably Billie Holiday. It was a whole lot of people. It wasn't paying no money, but there was a whole lot of people.

AM: It was a golden age, man. Those stars—

DG: That was great, and, boy, we had a good time down there.

AM: That's terrific. That's the excitement that was generated by that. See, the musicians were really getting to something different in the technology of expression. A lot of people were thinking of it in terms of novelty, revolution, and so forth, but I had the feeling that you were searching for *your* song and *your* statement in music.

DG: Another thing we can talk about a little bit too is classical music and jazz. Classical musicians don't know anything about an upbeat. The conductor, when he brings his hand down, that's one. One, you know. He has no beat for an upbeat. And we live on it. That's why we can play their music, and they can't play ours.

AM: Right. You start out with the conventional—

DG: Yeah, bap, bap, bap, ba-*dap*. Those were upbeats, instead of bap, bap, bap, bap. See, so that's why for one thing it's going to make music sound better and have more groove to it when classical musicians learn that there is an upbeat, which we feature in our music and they don't.

AM: That particular emotion comes from—

DG: Yeah, we are the sanctified church, we got that beat.

AM: In fact, when you look at Hamp, most of his gestures are up. It's a typical Hamp thing, like he's raising the mallets. When he's out directing with his hand, he's got that *up* thing that's going.

DG: Not only that, not only an upbeat, but we have a heavy downbeat, too. When we do *bap . . . bap . . . bap . . . bap,* that's a downbeat, and when we say one-two-three-four . . . bap . . . bap . . . bap, on one, that's a downbeat. But we got a very heavy upbeat; it's equal with us, when it's not with the classical performer. I have trouble playing with classical—

AM: It's like holding yourself in, right?

DG: Yeah, with classical conductors I have a lot of trouble unless they played jazz before.

AM: If you play with André Previn or Gunther Schuller, people like that, they already know the difference. They're sensitive to the difference.

DG: Yeah, but he understands me, but he knows that he's got a hundred other guys—

AM: Yeah, that don't!

DG: "You have trouble with him, with him too, with him too, yeah, and you have trouble with them too, with them too." Because he's got a hundred guys that's really for . . . We don't have nobody doing this stuff. We got to do it with ourselves! That's why I say I think jazz music is much more important than classical music.

AM: Yeah, well, you're getting into areas of expression and ways of reflecting life in the modern world which they're not getting. You've got cacophony, you've got dissonances which result into melodic sounds, harmonic statements and all, and it's all rugged stuff. They're just getting to that in, say, visual art. When you look out there now, you see a piece of sculpture that looks like the construction crew left something there, right? You look and see that rugged-looking stuff. It has a certain effect. You guys were always resolving or bringing in what Duke liked to call onomatopoeia, that is, you're imitating natural sounds, bringing them right into the music. That's the terribly important thing to realize if you're really going to put your human feelings at a given time and place into the music. If you're going to play on the technology that was invented in another time and that goes with horses and buggies going over cobblestones, that's one thing, but if you've got a guy gunning a Chevrolet or gunning a Cadillac or something, you've got to get that in there, so you've got those plungers, you've got those mutes. You've got a horn bent up, you've got all that. One of the things that is still interesting to this day is that what was most shocking about the arrival of what was then called bop was that it seemed so together, because for any critic to hear something new, he doesn't know whether it's hit or miss, but then he finds a consistency about it in that the person doing it has control of it and that there is a system involved. Then he's really challenged, because he knows it's not going to be a passing thing, that he's going to have to deal with it. Martin Williams, who's an old friend of mine, was telling me how when he heard this the first time, it was absolutely shocking that this new direction—

DG: A lot of guys in the Army, when they heard this—well, I mean, in the service—it really shocked them.

AM: Yeah, it wasn't that it was just different, but it was so together, it was so consistently what it was. It wasn't like hitting and missing. Some of those very first records that you heard had a symmetry about them that was—

DG: Thad Jones told me he was in the Navy, out in the islands near Hawaii, when he first heard "Groovin' High," I think it was, and he was in his bunk, and he said he fell out of his bunk. [laughs] And I said, "Yeah, well, I had to play some music that would make a guy fall out of his bunk."

AM: And Thad really picked up on that.

DG: Oh, man, man. I think out of all the people who know musically well like J. J.[Johnson], Thad, Mike Longo, the pianist, Frank Foster, Frank Wess, all those know what makes up the music. You see, they know what it takes to play the music like that.

AM: The thing about that, and that's why so many of those who can read also write well—

DG: That's right.

AM: Thad, Frank Foster. Those guys write well. Another guy in there who played with a little band—he was playing with that band—was Quincy, wasn't it? Wasn't he in the service?

DG: Oh, yeah.

AM: I know he wrote for it. He was also in the trumpet section. Well, that used to be a big thrill for me to see young guys playing trumpet with Dizzy Gillespie. That was a challenge for people.

DG: Yeah, well, you know, I was sort of like the new Roy Eldridge. Like Roy Eldridge was to us, we were to the next trumpet players that were coming along. Our music runs like that. King Oliver and then, after King Oliver, Louis Armstrong was the bellwether. After Louis Armstrong, Roy Eldridge was the leading trumpet. After Roy, me, and then Miles and Fats, and then Clifford Brown, and then Lee Morgan and Freddie Hubbard, and now this crowd of musicians, Wynton Marsalis, Terence Blanchard, Faddis.

AM: That's heroic action, you know, because what a hero does is set an example and push back the frontier. He's the one that goes out there and pushes back the wilderness. But Thad and those guys were equipped to make applications to the music; knowledge of the implications of the music made them able to apply it, so these guys could apply it to sixteen, twenty guys. What was your relationship with Quincy in his formative years? Quincy Jones.

DG: Well, Quincy was my straw boss. He organized the band. Quincy was also very much inspired by Gil Fuller and Tadd Dameron.

AM: Gil Fuller is on "Sweets for My Sweet" and all that, right?

DG: Yeah, well, that was my main man.

AM: "Things to Come"? Was he on that too?

DG: Yeah, of course. "Manteca," "Cubana Be," George Russell, "Cubana Be, Cubana Bop."

AM: John Lewis was fascinated by that. He did some writing and some comping on some of those records, right?

DG: Yes, he did.

AM: Speaking of the emphasis and so forth on percussion and so forth, we ought to mention some of our key percussionists, like Klook [Kenny Clarke]—

DG: Yeah, before that. Before that you got Big Sid. He was an inspiration of Kenny Clarke. Papa Jo Jones was his inspiration, but also Kenny Clarke. And there's Art Blakey and his inspiration of a whole lot of music. Philly Joe Jones and J. C. Heard.

AM: Who was drumming with Earl at the time you were there?

DG: Shadow Wilson.

AM: That's right, that's right. Now, before that there had been Alvin Burroughs and somebody else. That's why I mentioned the Basie-type influence in the music, because those guys dealing with that infinitely flexible Kansas City 4/4 and moving this stuff up to the high hats and dropping the bombs in the various places that went very well with the type of thing you were doing.

DG: Of course. One led right to another. It's always that way, it leads right to another.

AM: Have you heard the story about Elvin Jones being out in Detroit, listening to your stuff on records, before he had a big-time hi-fi system, and heard Clarke doing certain things? He tried to figure out how he was doing it. Some things that Klook was doing with two hands, like this, Elvin on his system couldn't hear him changing sticks, changing hands, so he learned to do it with one hand, some of these licks. He comes to New York to find out he was doing it wrong, but it turned out he was doing the new thing!

DG: Elvin was bad, boy.

AM: My God, that's a musical family, right?

DG: Sure is.

AM: Could you tell a little bit about John Lewis, for example, your first contacts with him? I was reading about how he had heard about you—

DG: When I came back from California in late '45, I had my deal to go in the Spotlight Club with Clark Munroe, on Fifty-second Street. Our name was going around a lot then, you know, bebop was really going around then. All the places on Fifty-second Street wanted to be bebop. Billy Shaw made a deal with Munroe that I could come in there for eight weeks with a small group, because we left Charlie Parker on the coast.

AM: Yeah.

DG: I had Sonny Stitt, Ray Brown, Al Hayes—but Al Hayes, I don't know, didn't come—Bud Powell for a couple of minutes, and then I had Monk. And Monk never did make time. He never did get to work on time, so I decided we needed a piano player full-time. Kenny Clark said, "Wait a minute. I know somebody. I know a guy that I was in the Army with would make a good addition to the band": John Lewis. That's when John Lewis came to the band.

AM: Right, and he's a very conscientious man about being on time. Well, that was one of the things that people always appreciated about you, was that.

DG: John Lewis is one of the most organized musicians.

AM: Well, people always respected your sense of responsibility too, about making the gig and being there. That's why I was saying nobody ever thought of the nickname Dizzy as implying any type of irresponsibility. It really implies high spirits.

DG: Yes, because I always made time. I was always one of the first ones there. Even now. My musicians look up, and I'm *there*. When they come in the door, I'm looking at them like this. I've been there warming up.

AM: That's right. That's the way Basie was, at least an hour beforetime. I mean, he wanted to *be* there. He'd start dressing and whatnot. The things that you started doing in terms of arrangement for your new band, how did you see that in the context of the stuff that Ellington was doing at that time? I think you had two different things. You had the general convention of what most people were doing, and then there was always what Duke was doing—

DG: Yes, well, I was always bathed in Latin music. I had the experience of being with Chano Pozo, who taught me a lot about African music, and then I discovered Brazilian music, the rhythm of Brazilian music, and I played with a West Indian band. I played with a Cuban band once; I played with Alberto Socarras. I played with his band. He's a flute player. I played with his band's maracas and trumpets. I played with the West Indian band a while. So my music has just always got the influence of some kind of Latin in the music. All my compositions, my arrangements, got some of that in it, and I *still* believe that the music of the Western Hemisphere one day will be unified. One day it will be unified. It's not there quite yet, but they're doing it. The rock-and-roll guys are doing it. They got jazz and they got blues and they got Latin in their music. I think one of these days the music of Brazil, the West Indies, Cuba, and the United States will be unified, and you won't know where they're coming from.

AM: Well, actually, back during the times when Handy was working on the "St. Louis Blues," when all that stuff was starting, it would have a tango or something in the first part. He was aware of that. He became conscious of that. There were several events—

DG: Duke Ellington, daaaa, da-da-da-da-da-da-da-da ["Caravan"]

AM: Yeah, he was aware of it. The whole business of the Spanish-American War and the Panama Canal stuff made for immigrants coming into New York.

DG: Yeah, they got some good music down there, especially the rhythm. Cuban music and Salvadoran and Brazilian music is closer to African music than ours.

AM: Well, it seems to me that [black Americans] were busy dealing with so many other kinds of really advanced music.

DG: Oh, yeah.

AM: You see what I'm saying? Dealing with Bach and Beethoven and English madrigals and Christmas carols, all the kinds of influences that our music had to assimilate in a sense to express what was going on in the United States. The beat is so independent of that. That's what's so interesting. Don't you find that very interesting—

DG: Oh, yeah.

AM: How much individuality, how much distinction this music has over that. Right in New Orleans, where you had the New Orleans opera house and you had all those different dances and so forth from France. They're there, but what dominates us is the Afro element that was flattened out in a certain sense for American usage and consumption. I think it's quite interesting. I was impressed when you actually put the bongo and conga in some of those pieces. Then I realized; I said, "Uh huh. Listen to that trumpet wide and up there. Those Latin American trumpets do that," you know, there's that trumpet way above all that stuff, way up in the sky and it sounds like it.

DG: Our music is a little different from . . . Up until recently, since the revolution in Cuba, the guys down there didn't have the facility for playing jazz like we play jazz. They were more rhythm. But now they got harmony and rhythm and everything. All kinds of Brazilian harmony. Boy, that's *bad*. Brazilian harmony, man, they surprise you when they resolve.

AM: Right. Have you listened to much of Villa-Lobos?

DG: I know of him, but I don't know his music.

AM: He was very much concerned with working folk elements directly into the music.

DG: Music and rhythm, he had both of them.

AM: Right. I mean, just as, say, Bartók, was working folk themes into the music he was composing, Villa-Lobos was working with that rhythm, with that rhythm you could not ignore. You had to deal with it in terms of the Brazilian basic statement, which was music. Now, I was curious about that, but it did occur to me when that rhythm started appearing in some of your releases, then that trumpet was up there riding all around. There was a difference, but it was up there. It made it make another kind of sense. So, what about your first trips to Europe? What was your reaction to that?

DG: My first trip to Europe—1937. They didn't pay me too much attention because they were after guys with the names.

AM: You were just energetic sidemen, right?

DG: Yeah. They've never forgiven themselves, because they say they could have recorded me over there for almost nothing. So right now they look at new musicians with different looks. They don't overlook anybody now.

AM: Yeah, they say, "We better get this in case it turns out."

DG: Yeah, bebop made them put a little thinking to it.

AM: That's right. Yes, I noticed that. As soon as David Murray hit the scene, he could get jobs all over Europe.

DG: That's right. He's in Europe right now.

AM: But then when you went back, of course, they were waiting impatiently because of all the news that had been coming out of New York, out of the United States, and especially Fifty-second Street. A lot of guys, as soon as the war . . . as soon as they could get over, those who were fortunate enough to get over during the war and those who came over right after the war—

DG: They was ready. They was ready to get there.

AM: Yeah, so what do you remember of your first tour after, you know, as the head honcho of bebop?

DG: Well, the next time I went to Europe, after '37, was '48, and they were ready. We were out in Paris. Our music was lost somewhere. Our whole book was lost, so we waited around, we got in there, and the music didn't come. So we sat up and played the whole concert without music. They never got over that. They still talk about 1948. I'm always running into somebody who says, "I was there at your first big band concert in 1948, and I never forgot it." The electricity of playing at that time . . . it was out of sight.

AM: Yeah, I remember reading about it, because I knew you were gone. I was in graduate school at NYU at that time, and so I used to hang out on Fifty-second Street. I'd go from the library and go by there before going out to Brooklyn, where my family was at that time. Then when they made that trip to Europe, everybody was waiting. They said that the French were impatient to hear this stuff.

DG: Yeah. The French were really engrossed in traditional jazz, except Django Reinhardt. But we were a big thing, man. They still remember that.

AM: A fine sense of accomplishment when you went back and all these people were so eager to—

DG: Sidney Bechet, Mezz Mezzrow, and all of them would go over there and play music over there. Ram Ramirez.

AM: Don Byas, was he there then, or had he gone back?

DG: He went over with Don Redman, and he stayed.

AM: Right, I know because I went over in 1950, and he was there then. Sidney was still there.

DG: Gil Coleman.

AM: And Roy was over there, Roy Eldridge. How many places did you go in 1948? Just Paris, or—

DG: I went from New York to Sweden.

AM: And then to Paris?

DG: Yeah.

AM: Oh, you did "Swedish Suite" for that?

DG: Yeah. Went to Sweden and Denmark, and then we came back to Paris. We got stranded. The guy ran away with the money. We didn't have no money over there. Billy Shaw had to come over and bail us out.

AM: This was where? Which town was this?

DG: Sweden. Stockholm. We had a big crowd up there, but there was no money.

AM: That happened to a lot of people, the guy ran off. One of Duke's guys ran off with some money once over there. You were saying you played your first concert in Paris with no music. Well, when Basie played his first concert in London, they got on the plane from the Blue Note and went over, and when they got there, they didn't have any music. So they played their first concert with no music. It's interesting how these things get repeated, isn't it? They said that they cut, boy. They cut it. They said, "That's all right, chief. We know it anyway." But that's the advantage of having a band full of musicians who are improvisers anyway. They set up the thing, and they're going to do something that makes sense.

DG: In our band, man, some of the guys never did know the music. They got put to work and just started. They knew it by numbers. Like one guy one time. We met a guy who was the composer of one of our tunes in the band. One of the guys said, "There's the old 2–0-1!" Everybody knew who he was talking about.

AM: That's funny. The guys, especially guys like me, know the name of it, how to play on the name, and all that, and you go up to the guy who wrote it and you say, "That's so-and-so's tune." That means the guy that has the main solo in it or something like that. "Let's play Harold's tune" or something like that. But the book becomes familiar like that to people.

DG: Oh, yeah. All I do is name a number, and nobody had no music in front of them.

AM: When you were out front calling, I mean, when you were out front directing, you'd simply call it by number.

DG: By number, yeah. 16.

AM: Have you seen Jacquet's new band?

DG: I understand it's terrific.

AM: It is.

DG: J. C. Heard has got a big band.

AM: He has? Where is he?

DG: Out in Detroit.

AM: Yeah, Detroit's a strong city for music.

DG: He's got an all-white band except for two guys, him and the piano player.

AM: They drive it away, right?

DG: Yeah, they hit it.

AM: But old Illinois, boy, he's got an interesting mix of guys. Rudy Rutherford is playing the clarinet and—

DG: I saw them in Detroit. I went by to see them.

AM: They played in Lincoln Center. They played on Basie's birthday last August, and it was a wonderful program. They guys had so much spirit. They were great. Illinois is getting to be a better and better bandleader and entertainer every day, because he used to do that stuff. He was always fun, but now—

DG: Singing?

AM: Doing the Louis Armstrong! He's singing, dancing—

DG: Everything.

AM: Yeah, and playing those solos.

DG: And the bassoon.

AM: That's right. He'll play "The King," which he did for Basie. Did Lucky Thompson ever play with you?

DG: When I went to Billy Berg's, Billy Berg thought that we needed more bottom. He hired Lucky Thompson to play with us. Charlie Parker, Milt Jackson, front line, and Lucky Thompson. Then Al Hayes, Ray Brown, Stan Levy. Lucky's a marvelous musician, but he was so concerned with how people were fucking over him, you know, the booking agents and everything like that. So he moved to Europe, and he took that to Europe with him and then he ran out over there. He came back, and now I think he's down in Alabama someplace. I haven't heard of him. He's not doing any records or anything. He was playing some kind of saxophone before Coltrane.

AM: Right, yeah, he was a good student of his horn. There's no question about that. Maybe we can end this by saying something about the state of music today and what it looks like to you.

DG: I think that our music is in great hands now. Our young musicians are studying. They're studying harmony at the conservatories. They're learning the instrument. They can go in a symphony band and play. They're really . . . I'm positive that our music is in very, very, very good hands, and they're creating.

AM: And they have a new respect for the background that they came out of.

DG: Of course.

AM: They're much more aware of . . . One of the questionable things that bop first had on the first guys was they thought they could forget everything. They forgot you guys had come through all that and were working on top of it. You see, Monk and all those, you could play any of their solos that you wanted to. You *knew* what Roy Eldridge was about, you knew what Louis Armstrong was about, so when a guy came up and thought all he had to know was what Dizzy was about or what Charlie was about, there were some other things that he may have missed that Dizzy was about. But nowadays, with all that other formal training and so forth, they have a respect for Sidney Bechet and whatnot. When they listen to that stuff, they don't think it's quaint or whatnot. They think it's solid music and they play off it. Like that group—you must have heard the Dirty Dozens Brass Band—

DG: I played with them in New Orleans a couple of weeks ago. I had a good time.

AM: They remember that music is good-time stuff.

DG: Yessir, they play bebop, old-time, in-the-middle-time, Coltrane, everybody. They play everybody.

AM: They're coming out with a stand-up drum, a marching band drum, and they're up there playing bebop riffs and Coltrane sheets of sound and everything else. I think that's quite an interesting thing. So you feel that the recapitulation of all that stuff puts us in good shape at this time to keep the whole history and tradition of people intact?

DG: Yes.

AM: Because they're aware of the historical resonances and that it's not a matter of just getting rid of the past, but of applying the past—

DG: To the future.

AM: Exactly. And with all of the new techniques.

DG: Tack it onto the future.

AM: That's right, or extend it into the future.

DG: That's right.

Notes

1. In Ira Gitler's *The Masters of Bebop: A Listener's Guide* (2001) there is a citation from the March 1, 1940, issue of *Down Beat*: "former Count Basie trumpeter Bobby Moore judged insane at Bellevue" (89).

2. Murray's publisher, McGraw-Hill, threw a "Kansas City Jam Session" at its headquarters in New York on November 30, 1976, to celebrate the publication of Murray's *Stomping the Blues*. The jam session featured Budd Johnson, Eddie Durham, Buck Clayton, Oliver Jackson, Mary Lou Williams, Bill Pemberton, and Doc Cheatham. In 1978, Doubleday Books threw a giant party to open its newly renovated bookstore at 724 Fifth Avenue in New York. The party was covered by the *New York Times,* which reported five hundred people in attendance, including many of the most prominent people in the literary world and in New York society. The press release for the event says: "Music will be provided by a group of six famous jazz musicians gathered by Albert Murray, author of *Stomping the Blues.* The leader is Budd Johnson, outstanding tenor sax man since the days of Earl Hines' Grand Terrace Orchestra in Chicago. The group will include Buck Clayton, trumpet; Candy Roth, trombone; Leonard Gaskin, bass; Eddie Lock, drums; and Cliff Small, piano."

3. These interviews between Murray and Gillespie are unknown to the Murray estate and are probably no longer extant.

"How did Basie come by the name Count?"

Interview with Dan Minor

Murray interviewed trombonist Dan Minor (1909–1982) at Minor's apartment in Harlem on October 27, 1981. Minor was from Texas and played with the Blue Devils in Oklahoma City, Bennie Moten in Kansas City, and, as will be seen here, with a bewildering array of other bands before joining the Count Basie Orchestra just before it gained national prominence. He played on many Basie records and later played with Cab Calloway.

Murray conducted this interview as part of his fact-checking process for Good Morning Blues. *The interview is in a somewhat unusual format and may seem odd at first—indeed, it starts slowly—but it evolves into an enjoyable back-and-forth and even finds a kind of poetic rhythm as it goes on. It is a glimpse into Murray's rigorous research program that resulted in* Good Morning Blues *becoming one of the most historically accurate of jazz autobiographies.*

A lot of the material here is really insider-minutiae regarding the intricate history of the Blue Devils–Moten–Basie continuum, but as such it gives a flavor of the musical maelstrom that the big bands in the Southwest and Midwest inhabited while hinting at just how chaotic that vast musical laboratory was, especially in the early years of the Depression when bands would occasionally get stranded mid-tour. At the same time, it's curious that these Southwest bands seemed to have spent so much time touring in the Northeast—suggesting complications to geographic narratives of development and subsequent influence (though there was undoubtedly a Southwest style). Parts of this interview are slightly mundane, but perhaps they are so mundane as to be enjoyable. Note the circular structure of the interview, as it begins with and then pivots back around to the crucial moment of the

Basie band's big break and its departure from Kansas City for points
east in late 1936 to become a band of national prominence.

ALBERT MURRAY: You were there when they had the farewell party on
Halloween night [1936]. That was a Saturday night, then that next
Monday night you played your last gig as a union band. You went on
first because Duke was playing. Do you remember that? You played
the first set before Duke came on, and then the bus was parked outside
and you guys got on the bus. Duke came outside and shook Basie's
hand. Then you went to Chicago.

DAN MINOR: Went to Chicago.

AM: 15th and Paseo or something was the ballroom. 'Cause you had
packed, and had everything on the bus before, then you played this
gig, you went on first. This was the first time Ellington had played a
dance on that side of town.

DM: George Lee, he was playing there too. I know we left and went to
Chicago, into the Grand Terrace. We did some broadcasting.

AM: Then you worked your way east, because you knew that your next
big gig was Roseland for Christmas. But you played, maybe Buffalo?

DM: Oh no, we played—we went up towards Maine and come back.

AM: In one of those places—Basie thinks it was Buffalo—you ran into
Mal Hallett. Remember Mal Hallett?

DM: Yeah.

AM: That is, that you guys had a little battle of the bands.

DM: Basie, I think he got the wrong guy. Uh, [the guy] he got a funny
trumpet—in Michigan he always played. All the students were root-
ing for us to play when this other band would play. So this guy, he
took out maybe four or five hundred-dollar bills and started wiping
his face with it. I can't think of the damn guy's name!

AM: A white guy? A white band?

DM: Yeah!

AM: Well-known guy?

DM: Yeah!

AM: Clyde McCoy?

DM: I don't think it was Clyde McCoy. We played with so many different bands.

AM: You think he's a little bit confused on the Mal Hallett thing?

DM: It wasn't Mal Hallett. It wasn't Clyde McCoy. Or was it Clyde McCoy?

AM: These were the hotel-type bands, right?

DM: Yeah. I think we played in the town where the Michigan college is—Lansing.

AM: Ann Arbor is where the University of Michigan is.

DM: Ann Arbor—yeah, yeah, yeah. Maybe it was Clyde McCoy.

AM: This is before getting to New York?

DM: This is after New York.

AM: If that's true Billie was probably in the band by that time.

DM: Oh, Billie Holiday? Yeah, she joined us in Pittsburgh. Her and Ed Lewis.

AM: Jo and these guys kind of flipped out in Pittsburgh, right?

DM: Uh huh.

AM: Who sent for Ed? Who told Basie to send for Ed Lewis?

DM: I don't know. Maybe John Hammond. Maybe.

AM: So that's when he came in.

DM: Him and Billie Holiday joined the same night.

AM: The other guy went to Pittsburgh—Freddie. "Fiddler" was still there, but—

DM: Freddie Green—Yeah. Well, John Hammond put him in there.

AM: I know. He'd given him an audition at the Roseland.

DM: He had an audition down at a little club called the Black Cat. Him and another guy named Bobby Moore.

AM: The trumpet player.

DM: Yeah, Freddie and Bobby Moore came.

AM: He took Carl's place, right?

DM: Yeah.

AM: And the other guy took Joe Keyes's place.

DM: Ed Lewis. Him and Billie Holiday joined the same night.

AM: Is that right?

DM: The way Ed tell it, he was in the room practicing on his horn and Billie Holiday heard him and she knocked on the door and asked him where was he working. He told her, "Well, I'm joining Basie tonight." She said, "I'm joining tonight too."

AM: I'll be darned. They sent for her then. Because when you were opening at the Apollo she was on the program. Billie wasn't listed, but she got the write-up.

DM: Yeah, she joined us in Pittsburgh. She was a nice girl. Just like one of the boys.

AM: So Ed was in the band when you opened at the Apollo. Because Ed and Bobby Moore were in that band. In March you were at the Apollo. And then you guys went to Philadelphia. Went down to Baltimore and Washington. Earle [Warren] says he joined in Philadelphia.

DM: Earle was playing in Cincinnati. I don't know exactly what town he joined in.

AM: Now, when did "Fiddler" cut out? Did he cut out after Philadelphia or after New York and the Apollo?

DM: I don't know exactly when it was.

AM: I don't think "Fiddler" was that interested. He was more interested in playing that fiddle than strumming that guitar all the time.

DM: Yeah, yeah, yeah, yeah.

AM: And that sombitch was a good soloist! His solos went right with the kind of stuff that the rest of the guys were playing.

DM: He played with Andy Kirk for a long time.

AM: Do you remember the battle with Lunceford? Remember when Eddie Durham came back to the band, or came into the band?

DM: When he came back to the band?

AM: Well, technically it wasn't back to the band because he'd never been in the Basie band but he'd been with you guys in the Moten band.

DM: Moten, yeah.

AM: He says on that day, this was in Hartford, Connecticut, he found out that Jimmie Lunceford was on the same program—

DM: I don't remember that. I remember the battle with Chick Webb. I remember the battle with Benny Goodman in Newark. And Lucky Millinder in Baltimore. We went to Chicago in 1938. We had rooms together, the trombonists. The trumpeters had rooms together. The saxophonists had rooms together. Vic Dickenson, he was a character. Every day before the show he had to have a big drink and smoke him a little tea. So we was on the third floor. You know how they call us— fifteen minutes, five minutes. Somebody said Vic, where's your trombone? He had left it upstairs. He got to get the key from the doorman and run all the way upstairs and come back, and after the first eight bars he had a solo. Nothing came out that horn. [Laughter]

AM: Do you remember when Skip Munn joined the band?

DM: Skip Munn arranged for the band for quite a while. At the Sherman Hotel in Chicago he was arranging for the band.

AM: That was later, but the first time, the first little batch of things, Basie says he picked up in Indianapolis during that time because he was trying to cool the band down. They were so powerful when they went into the Chatterbox; they needed some hotel stuff. When did you leave the Blue Devils?

DM: Well, I went through the Blue Devils a couple of times. I left 'em in '29, that's when I went to the other territory. I joined this guy Ben Smith. I went back home after I joined Gene Coy's Black Aces—then I went back to the Blue Devils.

AM: When did you leave for the last time?

DM: The last time we were in, uh, Sioux City, Eye-way [Iowa], working in some park. That's when I joined Hunter's Serenaders with Victoria Spivey.

AM: You were not there when Walter Page cut out?

DM: No. Page was in charge of the band when I left 'em in Sioux City, Eye-way. [n.b. Ralph Ellison also pronounced it "eye-way."]

AM: Page left and joined Bennie. You both joined Bennie in '32.

DM: Up in Boston we kind of got stranded with Hunter's. On our way back to Omaha I ran across Alphonso Trent's band in Pittsburgh. We ended up in Memphis, working. That's when Bennie Moten asked me to join the band, but I had to give Trent notice. So I joined him in Houston. That was 1932.

AM: How did Basie come by the name Count?

DM: We used to call Fletcher Henderson the king, Duke the duke, and Earl the earl—so once in a while he'd say, "I'm the Count." But nobody paid no attention to him. So him and Ted Manning got into an argument one time and Ted Manning say, "You just about the raggediest Count I've ever seen!" [laughter] So we started calling him Count.

AM: This was with the Blue Devils?

DM: Yeah. Wichita, Kansas, I will never forget that. Everybody started calling him Count.

AM: Manning—what did he play? Tenor?

DM: Alto.

AM: He played alto like Buster. They had two altos?

DM: Two altos and one tenor. His name was Ruben Roddy.

AM: Ah, so Ted Manning and Buster were playing alto. Ah. That's an unusual voicing.

DM: Yeah. Ted was playing first also. Buster was playing third. And Roddy.

AM: But Buster was a solo specialist.

DM: Oh, yeah. Buster was a good soloist—clarinet and alto.

AM: You know, once Big 'Un [Walter Page] mentioned some guy named Turk Thomas.

DM: Turk? No, it was Kirk.

AM: Thomas?

DM: May have been. I don't know what his last name was or what his first name was. Been so long. That was 1927 or 1928.

AM: I think it was 1927. Basie and those guys—Gonzelle White's band—played at the Lincoln Theater in Kansas City on the Fourth of July.

DM: That's just after I joined the Blue Devils. I remember Gonzelle and guys on the street—they were ballyhooing for the show, you know. You knew if somebody was playing the trumpet like Louis Armstrong it was "Hot Lips" Page.

AM: Right! Do you remember how many pieces and what they were in the band at that time? Was it ten pieces, you think?

DM: No, it was eleven. With Rushing singing.

AM: Who were the trumpets?

DM: Hot Lips Page, Joe Keyes.

AM: Joe Keyes was in the Devils?

DM: I got him the job.

AM: I'll be damned.

DM: He was in Houston. I introduced him to Page. Two trumpets and myself in the brass section. You had Buster Smith—alto. Ruben

Roddy—tenor player. And the other alto player was Ted Manning. Page was playing bass—

AM: Right. Sometimes he would play baritone, too, right?

DM: Baritone sax. Basie. Ernie Williams was playing drums. And had a guy named Reuben Lynch playing guitar. And Jimmy Rushing was singing.

AM: Who else was on trombone?

DM: Only one trombone! Joe Keyes, Lips Page, and me—the whole brass section.

AM: You didn't see that picture they called *Last of the Blue Devils*? [1979 documentary]

DM: No.

AM: Ernie does a lot of talking in it. According to your memory, Basie joined in Oklahoma City?

DM: I'm quite sure it was Oklahoma City, 'cause that's where the headquarters was. Then we went to Texas.

AM: Do you remember, roughly, how long Basie was with the band?

DM: I can't remember. We went to Texas, then we went up to Kansas City. We came back and Basie, Basie stayed in Kansas City. We picked up a guy by the name of Charlie Washington that played piano. He was such a lush. Then things were kinda—not too good. I went back home.

AM: To Dallas?

DM: Yeah. I think I went to El Paso to join a guy named Ben Smith. We worked around Nebraska, South Dakota. Then I went back home and joined a band by the name of Gene Coy's Black Aces. After that, I went back to Page. I went back to the Blue Devils, 'cause he had a job at a rich ballroom. That's how we got back together with Basie. I left the Blue Devils in Sioux City, Eye-way. I left there with a band called Hunter's Serenaders out of Omaha. This girl, Victoria Spivey—remember her?

AM: Yeah! Mmm hmm.

DM: We all worked together all the time, in different bands. Lips had gone to Bennie Moten.

AM: Right. Basie and Eddie got Lips in there.

DM: Yeah.

AM: Eddie got Basie in there.

DM: Yeah.

AM: Bennie didn't know that Basie had been a Devil. Basie found Eddie could write. He joined as a staff arranger. When they got in there, making those arrangements, they started reaching for that *Devil's feeling.*

DM: *Yeah, that's right!*

AM: They got Lips, then they got Jimmy. I think Jimmy was the fourth guy from the Devils to get in there. They started finaglin' then. Every time they ran across a Devil they got him in there. Do you remember the year you came into Bennie Moten's band?

DM: I think it was '32.

AM: '32? That was near the end then. Were you in the band just before Eddie Barefield came in?

DM: Eddie Barefield, and I, and Ben Webster—I think they joined the band just before I did.

AM: Ah, I got it. You hadn't been there long when they made that eastern tour—when they went into Camden and did those records.

DM: Yeah, yeah, yeah. I was in the band the last time they were in the east. 1932.

AM: That's when they got stranded in Philadelphia.

DM: That's right.

AM: That's with the famous rabbit or cat stew or whatever it was around the table, right?

DM: Yeah, 1932. I joined them in Houston. I was supposed to join them in Beaumont but the damn train was late and I had to catch a bus. At that time Eddie Durham and I was on the trombones. And we had Joe Keyes, Dee Stewart, and Lips. And then they had Ben Webster, Eddie Barefield, and Jack Washington. Buster Berry. Page. Basie. And Mac Washington, playing drums. That's been a long time, man.

AM: It was just like yesterday to me. I was in high school at that time and I remember the Bennie Moten records. Now, that was a hell of a trip. Sam Stauffel or Steffel of Philadelphia impounded the bus and the stuff because they had borrowed a lot of money the previous year, as I understand it. Then another guy got another bus and took you over to the guy who cooked the stew—

DM: You make me remember a lot of things I forgot! Who was the guy's name that cooked that stew? Eddie Durham and I had a laugh a lot of times—you eatin' gravy without any meat!

AM: That was the trip when the band got stranded in Cincinnati. Not stranded, but guys started going home.

DM: I got one of the records here with me, from 1932. "Toby."

AM: Yeah! And one of the versions of "Moten Swing" is on there.

DM: Yeah.

AM: You got back out to Columbus, then you were scheduled to go into a theater in Cincinnati for Christmas and New Year's. Did you stay till after New Year's?

DM: I stayed. We made a trip down south. That's how we picked up some more guys. Jesse Washington, he was playing saxophone. His brother played banjo.

AM: Was this the same trip?

DM: This was another trip. We picked up another guy in Mississippi. He was like a white guy—I can't remember his name. We stayed in some town in Mississippi—Vicksburg.

AM: Do you remember some guy, some football player or something, in the Midwest, who helped promote some of those trips in there?

DM: Oh, yeah!

AM: Ross Conroy or something?

DM: From Cincinnati!

AM: Is it Ross Conroy or Conway or something like that?

DM: Yeah, Ross. I know it's Ross. He was an All-American. I think his name *was* Ross Conway.

AM: Some time in 1933 the Moten band split up. Being a commonwealth band, they had a voting thing, and they split.

DM: Yeah, that's right.

AM: And Bennie went over with George E. Lee to Club Paseo or Club Harlem. These guys put Basie in charge of the band that was left.

DM: 15th and Paseo where that club was. Now, what happened, we split up with Bennie. Some of the guys stayed with Bennie. Jack Washington, he stayed with Bennie. Herschel Evans, he stayed. We [Basie et al.] took Jesse Washington to Little Rock. Lester Young went down, and Buster Smith. Big 'Un. Joe Keyes. Lester got that telegram from Smack [Fletcher Henderson]. He didn't want to go. Lester wasn't drinking at that time. He was smoking his tea, you know. I told him, get on that bus. I thought if he got to New York and got straight he could get some of us straight. I took him down, put him in on the bus. Next thing I know Lester was coming back to Kansas City.

AM: Do you remember anything about what the issue was that caused the split in the voting? I mean, Basie's not gonna say but so much about stuff like that, but the more background I have I'll know more of the skirting. Somebody said somebody was running up a bill or something like that.

DM: I don't remember exactly what happened. I think things got kind of slow. And we [much of the old Moten band with Basie as the leader now] went to Little Rock, and Bennie got this job at 15th and Paseo. What the name of that club?

AM: Club Harlem. It was the same building that was sometimes called the Paseo Ballroom.

DM: Maceo Birch was emceeing there.

AM: Is that right?

DM: Where is Maceo?

AM: I don't know. I've been trying to find out! There's two people I want to get to. One is Snodgrass—

DM: Yeah, yeah! I've been trying to find out about Snodgrass and Maceo!

AM: I'm-a ask Jo tonight when I see him. I'm-a see Jo and Eddie tonight. Jo Jones.

DM: *Jo Jones?!* Oh yeah?! I haven't seen that guy in a long time!

AM: Come down to the West End on Tuesday nights! They come around.

DM: I heard a lot of guys come down there. I know Earle Warren had a band down there.

AM: Earle's in there from time to time. Dickie.

DM: Dickie was working with him. I haven't seen those guys in a long time.

AM: When you came back from Little Rock, some of the guys went back to Bennie. Did you go back at that time?

DM: Yeah.

AM: Basie and Jo stayed down there.

DM: Jesse Washington was the first one came back. Bennie sent him some money to come up. They didn't go all at one time.

AM: Big 'Un, I understand, didn't go back. That's when he went to Jeter-Pillars [orchestra in St. Louis]. Jo was telling me that Billy Hadnott was the bass player—

DM: Yeah, yeah! He played a three-string guitar. Hadnott! I forgot all about Hadnott.

AM: These are things you're not focusing on. You're not thinking about them all the time.

DM: He was in the band when Bennie died. We were in Denver.

AM: Jo joined the band just before they went to Denver. Basie was playing piano in Denver. And Bus was the nominal leader, but Bennie stayed behind to get that tonsillectomy [from which he died].

DM: Bus would've had the band if he hadn't have been such an ass when Bennie was the leader. That's when we decided to vote Basie the leader. That's how he got the band.

AM: Yeah, that was the first time, but Basie said, after that last band broke up after the death of Bennie Moten, that he was the first one to leave, and that's how he stumbled into the job at the Reno. Well, Basie got in there, after a little while, he started bringing in ex-Bennie Moten people. They weren't really so much Bennie Moten people as they were Blue Devils.

DM: Yeah. At that time I think I was in St. Louis with Jeter-Pillars.

AM: 'Cause you left the *Bus* Moten band and went to St. Louis.

DM: Yeah. 'Cause Basie and all us said we'd get a job, and if anything happen we'd all get back together. Jo Jones, he went to St. Louis. Page went over there and come back. And I went over there. And when Basie got this job to come to New York, that's when he sent for me. He came through there, 'cause he was on his way to Chicago to meet John Hammond, I think. And he came through St. Louis and told me about the job and wanted me to be in Kansas City at a certain time.

AM: Ah.

DM: Basie sent me a telegram after John Hammond had set up this thing with Willard Alexander. Basie got this contract to go to the Roseland. He sent me a telegram to give my notice to Jeter-Pillars 'cause he wanted me in Kansas City in two weeks.

"Human consciousness lives in the mythosphere"

Interview with Greg Thomas

I had known Albert Murray for several years before I entered the doctoral program in American studies at New York University. I called Mr. Murray on a spring day in 1996 and mentioned that I had entered the program—at his graduate alma mater—and was doing a lot of new reading. Subsequently, I wanted to get his take on some of the things I was reading, and I had some questions for him. He said, "Okeydoke, come on by." Visiting him was an exciting experience but never without a certain amount of trepidation. He could be testy and short if you hadn't done your homework. Yet he could tell I was a sincere apprentice writer, and he knew by then that I had studied his works, under the guidance of his protégé, Michael James. Murray's knowledge of the discipline of American studies was vast and relayed effortlessly. Knowledge about the early years of the discipline that was then being excavated was as fresh in his mind as the morning's headlines. I wanted to get clarification of his principles as I worked on my own synthesis of disparate materials in cultural studies and theory. As you'll see, he gave such clarification and more, as he ties music in with the discussion. —*Greg Thomas*

GREG THOMAS: At what period would you say the study of American culture per se—a stream of thought that you tie into—began?

ALBERT MURRAY: From the point of view of criticism I would think it started by the 1920s. People like Lewis Mumford: *Sticks and Stones, The Brown Decades.* The artists were doing it—Hemingway, Fitzgerald, Malcolm Cowley—those people became more American by going to Paris. They weren't running from American culture. That's what

Malcolm Cowley points out in his book *Exiles Return*. They got over there, they were on the Seine dreaming about "The Blue Juniata." Guys that didn't go were also interested in basic principles of literary criticism. Like Kenneth Burke, he stayed in New Jersey.

GT: You also have people like Randolph Bourne and Van Wyck Brooks.

AM: Yeah, but Van Wyck Brooks was at first lamenting it—there's a lot of difference between the Van Wyck Brooks of *The Pilgrimage of Henry James, The Ordeal of Mark Twain, America's Coming-of-Age,* and stuff like that and the Van Wyck Brooks of "Makers and Finders" [series of books]. What had come in between was Constance Rourke! There was a guy named Paul Rosenfeld. Waldo Frank. Lewis Mumford. Some guy named Weaver. They didn't discover *Moby-Dick* until the 1920s. Between the late nineties and the 1920s nobody cared about Herman Melville. You had people beginning to look. You had a self-consciousness on the part of intellectuals as well as the artists. The artists were ahead of them. See, Twain was already there. But they didn't appreciate Twain, and, you know, William Dean Howells and all these people. It came into a certain type of critical focus by the twenties. Meanwhile, the stuff was already there, so far as the arts were concerned. Henry James was over in London but he was an American. It was an American sensibility with all the refinements and so forth. But that is part of America—to be European and American and whatnot. But he was an American. In one of her books Constance Rourke points out, in *The American*: that's the moral of the thing. By the end of the thirties Van Wyck Brooks was into his romance of American literature: *The Flowering of New England, New England: Indian Summer, The Times of Melville and Whitman, The World of Washington Irving,* and *The Confident Years*, which brings you into the teens. He was fascinated by how this thing came together and made a beautiful—

GT: Tapestry?

AM: Story. It's the romance of American culture is what that is. "Oh yeah, Audubon—that is American culture." *The Birds of America*—that's where it is. Constance Rourke, she's studying the almanacs and stuff like that. It wasn't until after World War II that you could

actually take courses in American civilization. There was American
history, American literature, there were anthologies of that. We had
our classics: Longfellow, Holmes, Hawthorne, Emerson. And they
stand up. Longfellow slipped. We think of him as like, maybe kids'
stuff. Hawthorne is still adult. You wouldn't find a group of very
sophisticated literary critics having a big, serious seminar on "The
Song of Hiawatha." I mean, *I don't think so*, you know. Basically, you
think "Americans should have read that," but in grade school or high
school or something. That didn't happen to *The Scarlet Letter, The
House of Seven Gables,* and things like that. It didn't happen to Emerson's essays. F. O. Matthiessen calls it the *American Renaissance.*
Whitman was in by this time. Academically, we didn't get to it until
the forties or fifties.

GT: Put in the contribution of anthropology also. After all, Constance
Rourke was influenced by and was even friends with Ruth Benedict,
who was a student of Boas.

AM: The basic study of culture is going to always lead you to that.
Aesthetic extension of that would be how it looks in the fine arts. But
all these things are coming out of the way of life of the cultural config-
uration that you have in mind. That's where I started in the eleventh
grade when I discovered anthropology. I wanted to know "where did
art come from?" and "what was the function of art?" I could see these
things better when I looked at them anthropologically. I could see society on a simpler level. You could see where the fundamentals were.
You've got what the Marxists were calling the *superstructure.* You've
got the elaborations of it but you've got to look down in there and
see what's under it: *the ritual.* That takes you back to the primordial stage, to the real fundamentals. Other people get all extended out
there and they don't know what people are really doing. They just
latch onto what they know about it. They come in on the level of
the way of doing something—which, of course, is *convention.* Most
people experience life through the convention that they inherit. The
conception of the world and everything is the convention, it's the way
of looking at it. What enables you to find the convention, to isolate
and define it, would be the anthropological elementals. You know my
book *Stomping the Blues?* What is it about? It's ritual. The primitive
ritual; it's either a ritual of purification or fertility. You can't get more

fundamental than that. I define the blues in terms of getting rid of the blues, which is why everybody else is wrong, so far as I can see. Yeah, he may be talking about this, but what do people do at a juke joint? You don't go there to pray about "Oh, how terrible it is to be a Negro!"

GT: [Laughter]

AM: It has nothing to do that. The white folks didn't say, "Yeah, those poor Negroes." Bessie Smith went through a lot, but if she missed that note, it doesn't matter what she went through. A lot of people were worse off than Billie Holiday. But she mastered it. She can't just say "I had it in me"—that's bullshit—she's imitating Louis. It's derived from something. Art comes from art. Art does not come from life. Nobody looks out there and all of a sudden he's an artist. People say that, but they forget. You're an artist because there are artists. You join in the ongoing dialogue with the form. You can't get Charlie Parker, for example, until you get Kansas City blues, the Kansas City approach to blues. That's why he's up-tempo to begin with! If he was with the traditional down-home blues he wouldn't have been up there—he wouldn't have moved up to a higher interval. He's got to get to Basie and Young and Sweets and Buster Smith and he wants them to listen. He's trying to communicate! Here's Jo Jones up here [imitates up-tempo Jo Jones drumbeat] and he wants to swing up there. Anybody who doesn't know that doesn't know anything about Charlie Parker. Now, technologically, you could make him aware of conservatory abstractions, "Oh yeah, I could do this, I could do that"—to refine your mechanism, but those are just refinements. You wouldn't expect a guy to come out of New Orleans or the Delta or various other places and play up there where Charlie Parker. Once it out there, they're imitating him! They're not doing it because they're musicians, they're doing it because Charlie Parker was a musician. That's why you get Strayhorn—he's doing it because Duke did it that way. But because he's not Duke, he's gonna sound a little different. It's very easy to tell Duke from Strayhorn. So all this bullshit they got about Duke and Strayhorn—that's bullshit. You couldn't get anything in the band without Duke revising it. Then, he's gonna be playing it every night. It's his music. But you gotta see that dynamic underlying all of it. It's a combination of those things that you like, approve of, and attempt to extend, elaborate, and refine in your own way—*or* that you feel the necessity to counterstate, but it's still a dialogue.

GT: Right.

AM: You can say, "Well, Murray and Ellison . . ." Yeah, but Murray's over here kickin' Baldwin's butt! So Baldwin is influencing me as much as Ellison.

GT: Ooooh. Wow. I see what you're saying.

AM: It's a counterstatement. I wouldn't have said that [Murray's essay on James Baldwin in *The Omni-Americans*] if he were not there. What would I have said? I don't know what I would have said! I had some conceptions but Baldwin brought it into a sort of focus. I said, "That ain't the way that is. What is this? I can't stand that! I'm not a victim. I never felt like a victim!" I always thought I was smart, good-looking, and *promising*. That's what I always thought. That's what people always said. "Look at that honey-brown boy. He's so nice. He's so smart." That's the way I was brought up. In Magazine Point they were too ignorant to go around and say "We can't vote." Shiiiit. Didn't give a goddamn bout no fuckin' votin'! Like the Africans, "We're not free." They ain't never been free! Like the Africans in the Middle Passage? "Lord, we not free." When had they ever been free? Maybe one or two princes or something got captured from another tribe. Maybe chiefs or something like that—maybe they were free. But the rest of them? There's freedom over there? How could any of them be free? They didn't have that in Europe. They didn't have that in Japan. They didn't have it in India. They didn't have it anywhere but here.

GT: Could you go a little deeper into the concepts of folk art, popular art, and fine art?

AM: The three levels of sophistication or technical mastery involved in the processing of raw experience into aesthetic statement. That's a whole encyclopedia right there. Art is a means by which raw experience is stylized—goes through a process by which we mean stylized—into aesthetic statement. The style is the statement. In order to know what the statement is, you have to know what is involved in the processing. Involved in that would be degrees of the control of the medium that you're working in. Some guy comes up with a poem—but they don't know grammar, they can't pronounce the words, they don't know syntax—that's going to be folk level, man. A good example would be, somebody says [sings in blues cadence]: *You be my baby, and I'll be your man.* Not "If you will be my baby." That's folk level, we can tell. It's pronounced on a folk level. It can be very moving, very authentic—but it's limited. It's an acquired taste for a more sophisticated person, like a cruder recipe. Now, you get a guy saying [singing]: *Is you is or is you ain't my baby?* [1944 Louis Jordan song] That's bad grammar, but it's pop. You know that's not folk. The guy's kidding. "Are you or aren't you my baby?" That won't work. He wants to be very close to the earth. [singing] *Is you is or is you ain't my baby? The way you acting lately makes me doubt you is still my baby, baby.* The way you say "baby," that's some country shit. But you could do that in a fifteen dollar or twenty-five dollar cover charge place. These other guys out there strumming, that's another thing, they got a tin cup in the town square on Friday afternoon. Now, the ultimate extension, elaboration, and refinement would be: [hums Ellington's "Rocks in My Bed"] That's the blues on another level. Technically more refined. More complex, more difficult to play. More complete control over the means of expression.

GT: Some of what Rourke was counterstating was some of Eliot's elitist conceptions or I guess maybe the stereotype of Matthew Arnold's conception of culture. They also had a conception of, say, "fine art." But it seems to me that Constance Rourke was trying to privilege and focus on the folk form and the popular form.

AM: It's a dynamic that you want to get that adds up to Constance Rourke. What she discovered, as I understand it, was a principle for the definition of culture that was derived from the German philosopher Herder. It gave her insight into the fact that cultures *develop*. They come from the ground up, not from on-high down. Most people were lamenting that there was no high culture. You forget, these were barbarians—Europe in the Dark Ages. When you come out of that, they've got an art form. They've got the gothic cathedrals, they've got these goddamn *vitraux,* the stained-glass windows. They've got scholarship, although it's on sacred texts and so forth. Then, when they get to the Renaissance period, they rediscover Rome and Greece.

Then they have a broader context of what they're doing. These guys had been all the way from savagery all the way up to Praxiteles to the Parthenon to Sophocles and Euripides and Aeschylus, Aristophanes, Socrates, Plato, Aristotle—all these refinements. Then you had all these extensions of that because the Romans could reach over there and get it. The Greeks were still around, for them. Any great Roman family had a Greek master. And they went around acting like Greeks. Just like classy Americans acted British and would speak with a slightly British accent, like that Boston thing. Well, that's the way that I understand it—that educated Romans spoke like Greeks. Which makes all the sense in the world, doesn't it? One is able to look at it this way because of the dynamic that Constance Rourke revealed. Extension, elaboration, and refinement—it's not just bootlegging something in.

GT: Process, continuum.

AM: You can see it in Mark Twain! He's a half-assed newspaperman, he writes about what he knows about, he's writing a fairly simple report, but the storytelling thing takes over at a certain point—and he's into art! He made the steps. You can see it. Whitman!—you've gotta make it *out of* this and it's gotta be *like* this. So when you've got *Moby-Dick*—there ain't nothing over there like that. It's a novel, it's not *The Iliad* and *The Odyssey*. It's something else. It's a big, thick American book about process. When I was in high school there was nothing like football movies, nothing like college movies. This sweatshirt comes from the 1930s, man! You find that very pragmatic level of how things are done at a given point. *Life on the Mississippi*—how it is to be a riverboat captain. The romance of it. It's a very practical thing. What's a riverboat captain? But it's transmuted into poetry. What the hell do you get in the first 150 pages of *The Seven League Boots*? *Life on the Mississippi*! What you'd call the *Life on the Mississippi* dimension. Nothing can be more American than "How do they do what they do?"

GT: Would you say you have a cinematic conception at all?

AM: Why not? What else are you gonna have? You're not gonna read as many books as you look at movies or television. I was learning it as they were learning it. You've got all these things that would make a twentieth-century American sensibility, all these devices and techniques of communication. Since your medium is prose—it is language, not pictures—then you assimilate that. You can make the language do things that pictures can't do. "Deljean McCray, who was as cinnamon-bark brown as was the cinnamon-brown bark she was forever chewing and smelling like." You can't do that on film, except you could have her say it. But it wouldn't be the narrator saying it.

GT: Where does John A. Kouwenhoven fit? Because John A. Kouwenhoven is after Constance Rourke. Would you say he's a further extension and elaboration?

AM: He zoomed in on what was American about American culture. Nothing is more informative than the story of the George Washington Bridge. The key thing—this would be the more direct answer—Kouwenhoven focused very directly on the interaction of the learned tradition, or the imported methodologies and approaches with the native, vernacular, or homespun methods of doing things—and American culture emerged from that, in a context made for the perpetual experimentation on the frontier and in an atmosphere of free enterprise—or experimental attitude—that's the same thing. It's a very pragmatic thing. This goes with this, this goes with that. When they got to the I beam, they were gone. You're not gonna get a skyscraper until you get the I beam. They realized they were back to frame buildings again. But, they could make it a hundred stories! Because the frame is holding up the building, not the masonry walls. You see what I mean? They said shit, we can make this shit out of glass! It's pretty light going up there. What brought the primitive bridge back—you know, *the real primitive bridge with vines and ropes and shit?* The steel cable! You can't be more primitive than that. So you have these two uprights and the steel cable going through—this is the George Washington Bridge! They had discovered this with the Brooklyn Bridge, but they got all this gunk around it. "Gotta look like a bridge used to look in Europe." Then you get over here, and they ran out of money. They said we already got it, man. All you need are the uprights. *That's a pretty thing! Look at that!* That's like inventing streamlining. That's one of the key things of Kouwenhoven. He mentioned that in a letter to me. You know about me and him? You've heard of that?

GT: Could you tell me?

AM: [reads from March 28, 1984, letter from Kouwenhoven] "Dear Mr. Murray, a young admirer of yours—a writer (and sometime jazz pianist) named Tom Piazza (believe it or not)—brought me a copy of *The Omni-Americans* in the Vintage edition a couple of months ago. How I missed it in 1970, when I was still active, I can't imagine. But better now than never. It's a beautiful job: clear, wise, and forceful. (I wished I had had 'Getting It Together' under my belt in my last years of teaching—1970–75; it would have helped bring some courage to a head that was getting ready to quit.)

"And of course I am rewarded by your reference to my books. Thanks for what you say on page 185 especially. Few of the people who comment on my work seem to have any idea that it is the *interaction* of the vernacular with the cultivated tradition that in my view matters."

GT: Just to ask you about Ellison for a moment—the second novel—what he shared of it with you, would you say that it went beyond *Invisible Man* in achievement?

AM: It depends on what you mean by "beyond." It was a different kind of book. I don't know. I saw quite a bit of it but I never knew what the overall form was gonna be. I didn't have an idea of what the major climax would be. He read a lot of it to me and he sent me some drafts of certain sequences. But I wouldn't speculate. It had a lot of possibilities. More than one hundred pages of it was published. Probably quite a bit more than one hundred pages—but you couldn't make it out from there. The difficulty of bringing it off was not a matter of barrenness. It's not that he had a writer's block and he couldn't think of something to do. That's not it. He'd bring in a character, he had to justify putting this character in, and he would start inventing stuff to make this character fit into the place where he was gonna be. That frequently got out of hand. The guy would take over. I don't know for how long—weeks or months. All he had to do was get the guy from one floor to the other—pushing a medical cart or something in a hospital. The senator, who got shot with a zip gun, is on one floor. And Ralph decides to put Ezra Pound in St. Elizabeth's. So he got a guy named Sterling—Pound Sterling ["Clyde Sterling" in the 2010 published version]—a poet who'd been committed for insanity or something. So he wants to connect these two characters in some way. So he's got a guy pushing a medical cart. The guy becomes fascinating to Ralph. He grows into a big fat character—all he had to do was get the guy from one floor to another. You could just cut. It would be an indulgence to use five or ten pages to do that. He'd be lucky if it was thirty. More likely it would be seventy-five. So, it wasn't a conventional conception of a writer's block. The problem probably is that there was too much manuscript. I wouldn't be surprised if it could be well over a thousand pages of manuscript.

GT: Speaking of long manuscripts, what do you think of Leon Forrest's *Divine Days*?

AM: I haven't had time to read it. Ralph's reaction was that Forrest, you know, should have been more . . . coherent?

GT: Tighter?

AM: Tighter. But he was impressed with his imagination and his use of language. He was very favorably disposed to Forrest's ambition and his talent. I think he thought it should have manifested more of a discipline than it had—it was almost like indulgence. Ralph may have been aware that he had a similar problem—but he wasn't gonna publish it! He was a very sensitive type of person, to criticism—that just meant that he was a highly disciplined person. He wasn't defiant, he just felt very strongly about it and felt it was worth taking a chance on, and that he was right and other people were not. And you have to be like that to be an individual artist. You've gotta do it your way, in a way. Somebody may think they know what a novel is, but they don't know what *this kind of novel is* necessarily.

GT: I was wondering what you thought of Derek Walcott's work.

AM: In some ways he's an outstanding modern poet. That's because he plays in the same league as first-rate poets. He knows what that is about and he's trying to find his voice in it. But he doesn't shuck on it. He knows what contemporary poetry is. I'm not all that taken with it myself. I've wished I had time to do *Omeros*. But I've dipped into it and I know it's big league stuff. I saw a couple of his plays a long time ago. I know he's a real student of whatever he does. I think he wrote a play called *Dream on Monkey Mountain*. And then he did a thing called *Remembrance,* which I saw, with Roscoe Lee Browne in it, at the Shakespeare Theater. I don't know if he was being somewhat critical of himself for being too British. I get the impression that he wants to create an image of ambivalence because he doesn't know whether he's British or African. But he isn't African—he's West Indian. I didn't go through all the poetry. I have quite a bit of it and I plan to. I have a high regard for his level of ambition. But the thing I like best that he did is his Nobel lecture! *There* he comes up with a Caribbean identity that makes a lot of sense to me. "They're not us and we're not them, we're not African and we're not British—we're Caribbean!" You see? But you can take what Negroes are doing in education in one state and wipe out all the islands. There is more institutional educational achievement in *Georgia* than any of those islands. Tennessee? Texas? They achieved that beginning with Reconstruction. What the hell was Marcus Garvey doing over here? Trying to be a Booker Washington. He wanted to be the Booker Washington of Africa! [laughter] But then Walcott reveals the other dimension. I was really delighted that he accepted the challenge of Saint-John Perse. *Alexis Saint-Léger Léger.* He is *the* Caribbean poet—but he's a Frenchman! T. S. Eliot introduced his work to the world of English poetry. This is the kind of thing you have to deal with. [reads extensively from the poetry of Saint-John Perse]

GT: What about the work of Soyinka? Have you read or seen any of his plays?

AM: Did he give them in the early days of the Ensemble Theater?

GT: I'm not sure. He's another one who, with that training in Europe, tries to maintain a native African sensibility.

AM: I never developed much interest. I didn't have any cultural relationship. Since I'm not a racist, I wouldn't identify with that. I don't have any particular connection with Nigerian culture. If he had a bigger impact that was related to literature and not race relations, then probably I would have some interest. But because a guy's got nappy hair and dark skin . . . *I don't give a goddamn about that!* I was pleased to see that Walcott is aware of the *sweep.* You can *feel* the *epic sweep.* That's what you get in *Anabasis.* Perse's *Anabasis.* Walcott's got this big conception, a man-against-the-horizon-type thing, with desert and seascape. Vistas and things like that.

GT: Can you explain something you explained to me the other night when I asked you how did things go when you got that award? What's the name of the organization you got the lifetime achievement award from?

AM: The National Book Critics Circle.

GT: Congratulations again on that. You mentioned the mythosphere. What's the mythosphere?

AM: Well, it's the ideational equivalent to the atmosphere. You live in terms of ideas, notions, words, lies, truths, mistakes, anything—that makes up the mythosphere. The atmosphere is oxygen and this and that. Human consciousness lives in the mythosphere—that could be anything from mathematics to a flat-out lie. Anything that has to do with human consciousness. Today I have a problem with my leg because of the humidity and so forth—that's a physical condition of the atmosphere. The mythosphere has to do with the quality of human consciousness. The piece of paper says "We honor Mr. Murray for lifetime achievement in literature." To me, that says "Here's a man who's gonna do big-league stuff!" If you don't read books and you don't care about books, it means nothing to you. Here's where we go with that: the big problem in the mythosphere is that people mistake very flimsy constructions of publicity as the real mythosphere. Literary criticism helps your insight into these things. If you think of yourself as somebody developing a more sophisticated taste on a higher level of aesthetic profundity, you're more careful about what comes into your consciousness—publicity is not enough. You don't go out and read a book because it's number one on the best-seller list. There is a less sophisticated part of the mythosphere.

GT: That would be the pop level of the mythosphere?

AM: That's the level of sophistication involved in the response. It's just like the sensitivity of the body to the atmosphere.

"Hear that train whistle harmonica!"
Talk at St. John's University with Paul Devlin

Murray's talk at St. John's University in Queens, New York, on September 30, 2003, was his final college talk. He had given dozens of readings and lectures at colleges since the 1960s and, like many successful writers, had a busy college speaking schedule for most of his career. This is one of the few talks of his of which there is a record. (A talk from 1985 at Wesleyan University in Connecticut—a very different talk from the one here—is included in Robert G. O'Meally's edited volume The Jazz Cadence of American Culture.*) One of the things that makes this so valuable is the record of the musical examples Murray shared, along with his riffs on them. His introduction of himself and his philosophy is also outstanding.*

As far as I know, this is the only time he tried out "Jazz: Notes toward a Definition" on an audience. (The early draft he read to the audience is not transcribed here; the published version is included toward the end of the book.) This is perhaps the only place that he mentions two important books that influenced him: Klaus Mann's edited volume The Heart of Europe *(1943) and Porter G. Perrin's* Writer's Guide and Index to English *(1942). It is also the only place he discusses the extraordinary recording "Train Time" by Forest City Joe, a story about realigning railroad track in a hurry as a train is coming, interspersed with swinging blues harmonica.*

On a blazing, glorious Indian summer afternoon, Murray's talk attracted sixty to seventy people. It was officially sponsored by the English department and organized by me. I was then in the master's program in English. Stephen Sicari, the chair of the department, gave a brief introduction and then I read what was probably a much-too-long synopsis of Murray's books and ideas. One thing that struck me as I thought about this excellent day: 2003 was still very much part of the twentieth century technologically. Murray's musical examples were on disparate cassettes and I recorded the talk on a cassette player. Within a year or two, everything would have been digital.

PAUL DEVLIN: And so, ladies and gentlemen, without further ado: Mr. Albert Murray.

ALBERT MURRAY: Well, I get the impression from Paul that this is a very bright group of people, because he took you through twelve books in less than twelve minutes. [audience laughter] We were trying to decide how to use the time we had to get you acquainted with what I've been trying to do in my work and what I'm trying to achieve with it, that is, what I'm trying to communicate. This is the only way I have of dealing with chaos. Chaos consists not only with the environment as such but also the misunderstandings that people have trying to communicate with themselves. So, I try to deal with very simple things; back to fairy tales and the simplest anecdotes. But really, what I'm trying to deal with is *the blues statement* as a representative American anecdote: one little story, or one little joke, or one little image that encapsulates a whole lifestyle. On one level you're talking about American culture, American identity, American objectives; but you're always talking about *human* life—existence on earth and whatnot. So, universality: something which is, let's say, mathematically valid for everybody. That would be something that we call *the truth,* or a fact of life. I think of it as an adequate metaphor, that is, a representative anecdote. I use those two terms. So, the writer tries to create images which function to enable us to realize what we are doing here on this planet, to face chaos, to face nothingness, and whatnot. And my main metaphor comes out of the blues. It's central to what I've tried to do as a writer. I've tried to find that representative anecdote which is most applicable to the way life is lived in this part of the planet. So I have to know as much as possible, as much as I can, about how we came to be here and how everybody came to be wherever they are and why they do what they do as they do it.

Personally, it started with me when I was in the third grade and I discovered geography and a special teacher. Everything that has happened to me in school since that time has been an extension of what I discovered in the third grade—foreign languages, different customs. The little things that used to be on the bulletin board. Windows on the world: this is the way Filipinos are, this is the way it is in Switzerland, this is the way it is in Holland, the Earth is a part of a solar system, Mercator projections of the map, the various states. And there I was in Mobile, Alabama, and the Earth was mine! And it turned out that living in Mobile, which was a seaport town, you saw a great variety of people. Some lived there and some were coming and going from other places all the time. So, in school—and school was everything to me—I decided that was what I wanted to deal with.

My first hero was a man who traveled a lot, and his name was Luzana Cholly. He's the hero figure, or the epic figure, in my first novel, *Train Whistle Guitar.* I'll put a lot of things together for you to acquaint you with what to look for in these books. I've written twelve of them so far and I'm trying to get the thirteenth *[The Magic Keys]* ready before Christmas—that is, out of my house before Christmas, not necessarily into the bookstores before Christmas. What I liked about this character, whose name was Luzana Cholly—and incidentally, he was not from Louisiana, he was called Louisiana because he had been to Louisiana, and came back—but when I got further along, I realized it by the time I was in the ninth grade—that he was really Orpheus! I always used whatever I learned in school to try to come to terms with what was in my community. So, this guy comes up out of the railroad bottoms strumming a guitar, singing about places and adventure and whatnot. But every now and then he'd get the urge to leave town, so he'd sling the guitar over his should and grab an armful of *fast freight train* and be seeing the world. That was one reason I was so interested in geography by the time I got to the third grade. I called that novel *Train Whistle Guitar.* And I wanted the title to *sound* like a collage. Do you have *Train Whistle* here?

PD: Right here, but I don't have the first edition.

AM: Well, the jacket is a Bearden collage.

PD: On the first edition.

AM: On the first edition. Any type of aesthetic statement could be borrowed to get to our understanding and appreciation of life. So, when I knew that that was Orpheus, slinging his guitar over his shoulder and grabbing this armful of freight train, it made me want to see *the world*. As it turns out, in that particular story, he catches Scooter, who is the hero of the story, and his running buddy, whose name is Little Buddy, trying to hop a freight train to run away and see the world. He brings them back, as if by the nape of the neck, and as if taking them to the *schoolroom door* and saying "You have to do *this*, before you can take on the whole world." My education should have prepared me to exist anywhere, in the United States and in the world. The hero's name is Scooter and the troubles of the world he thinks of in terms of *the briar patch*, which is what everybody has to contend with. You can bitch about the fact that it's a briar patch, but all the briar patch is gonna say is "This is life, buddy, you've got cope, bitchin' is not gon' help!" You have to be resilient and you have to be creative. You have to *improvise*. And you can't improvise unless you understand certain dependable facts. Once you get that, then you can cope with the variations, and you see them as variations. So, my literary effort has been in that direction. The metaphor which was central for me was the blues. I used that as the basis for coming to terms with all the various things I was learning about the world at large. The whole idea was to be at home anywhere in the world, in other words: to be cosmopolitan, or, as we used to say, to be hip!

Since I thought of the world in terms of heroic action, my frame of reference was what Kenneth Burke calls a frame of acceptance, not a frame of rejection. These two frames are underlying all literary strategies for communicating how you feel or what you know. You either have the attitude that you accept the complexity of life as given, or you reject it by saying "Why should it be like this?" "Why I am sick? Why am I not rich? Why does it rain? Why does it snow? Why is it freezing? Why me? Why do I not have *mink*?" And you write like that. The form would be protest, satire. You reject the fact that life is a problem. On the other hand, Burke also identified the frame of acceptance. This is the way it is, so what are you going to do about it? You accept the fact that you live in a briar patch and you become *a swinger.* You get with it. You get the changes in tempo, you get the changes in the keys and all that. You commence sneaking right up on the artistic form that I have anchored my literary statement in, which is the blues. And the blues, you should know by now if you're this far in college, represents the second law of thermodynamics. That's what it is, for a philosopher and for a poet: *the tendency of all phenomena to become random.* So, the only way to get with that is to have an adequate *metaphor* that makes it make sense. So the central metaphor that I played with, as an Alabama boy, is *the rabbit in the briar patch.* Resilience, or swinging, is the ultimate achievement. The achievement of elegance is the highest thing that a human being can do. You come to terms with life in such a way that it becomes *pleasurable.* It's as simple as that. That's an oversimplification, but you have to read the books to get the details.

I wrote *The Hero and the Blues* to try to establish that affirmative outlook as a basic procedure for coming to terms with American culture. I had come to terms with American character in *The Omni-Americans. The Omni-Americans,* I can remember had two definitive sources. During the war I read a book called *The Heart of Europe.* It was edited by Thomas Mann's son, Klaus. It was a book of essays about what Europe was. And in that anthology there was an essay by Paul Valéry called "Homo Europaeus." He said *Homo Europaeus* was Greek logic, Roman administration and law, and Judeo-Christian morality. A few years later I came across a book by Constance Rourke, who is one of my patron saints. It was called *American Humor* but it could have been called *Homo Americanus. Homo Americanus* is *Homo Europaeus* shipped overseas to North America, put in the midst of this particular continent, and becomes modified by his environment in the following way: Homo Americanus is part Yankee ingenuity, part backwoodsman/Indian or gamecock of the wilderness, and part Negro. Constance Rourke at one point talks about how this differs from the Englishmen who came over—these guys were already in buckskin! The English were marching in their red jackets and so forth, and [the rebels in the Thirteen Colonies] were already part Indian, fighting behind trees. So, Homo Americanus was another form.

The captive African, he had to adjust *everything,* which made him the most flexible. He made *the* synthesis. He had to pick up another language, and he modified the language. Essentially, he became the first Homo Americanus. He didn't bring a language. He couldn't bring a religion. He actually came into being as an entity *here* and reflected everything else that was here. Jumping forward, what he *expressed* turned out to be the most comprehensive expression of America in an art form that is truly an American synthesis: and that's the blues, or jazz, and jazz is a fully orchestrated blues statement. So the rest of my books had to do with zooming in on aspects of this and clarifying the basic metaphor: The Omni-American who has to come to terms with life through acceptance. I just get a kick out of the fact that these are the guys who have the lowest suicide rate. They were too busy adjusting to be depressed. Duke Ellington said, Well, they [captive Africans] saw these strange-looking, hungry-looking people that were buying them and they thought they were buying them for food. So, when they got over here they found out they were not going to eat them—they just wanted them to work! They've found humor in the situation ever since. That sense of humor has always existed, along with a sense of elegance, which they brought with them— an orientation to turn all behavior into dance-beat elegance. They brought the tendency to play dance music, danceable music. So the beat that they got came from another source. The rhythm came from something that was in the environment [i.e., the syncopated rhythm of the locomotive].

Culture comes from your environment. It's not inherited in your genes. So many Americans still don't understand that. You don't inherit culture. Culture is simply *environment*. If you see that, then you realize what this other stuff means and how you combine it. Since I've brought you up to the point of music, and jazz, I have a little thing that I'll read to you and from there we'll go into a few examples and some questions. I've been working on jazz as a writer and I'm the board of directors at Jazz at Lincoln Center. I was one of the founders of it and it's essentially based on *Stomping the Blues*—a book of mine—and a thing that was worked out at the Smithsonian called Classic Jazz. Originally the program at Lincoln Center was called Classic Jazz at Lincoln Center and I was a part of five people who set that up.

Now, you stomp the blues to get rid of the blues. You don't stomp it with a hammer or bang it down. You stomp the blues with *insouciance*. The blues is a boogeyman. And if the boogeyman comes to get you and you don't pay any attention, that wipes it out. He can't stand elegance and insouciance. That's what jazz does. So, I brought a thing that I wrote to try to clarify some confusion that's creeping into Lincoln Center. [Reads draft of "Jazz: Notes Toward a Definition," then moves on to the part of the program with musical examples]

AM: Here's another way of looking at what jazz does. The first on the tape here is Dvořák's *Humoresque*. [Sings the melody] *Absolutely 100 percent* Saturday Evening Post, *200 percent square Americana!* Ofay for days. It makes Americans think of *pastorale*. Makes you think of Clover Bloom Butter, Will Rogers, and freckle-faced white boys! [audience laughter, as Devlin was a freckle-faced white boy] I recall in a gangster film: it's too hot in the city, so they go out, and they look in the valley, and the music score will be [sings melody of *Humoresque*].

[*Plays tape of Dvořák's* Humoresque]

AM: That's the way the symphony orchestras play it. Now [to Devlin], go forward to Ellington's. Now, what I used to do when I used to go to colleges was have somebody go to the dictionary and look up *humoresque*. And then, play the Ellington one. You'll see which one is playing *humoresque*.

[*Plays Ellington's version of Dvořák's* Humoresque *from Ellington's 1948 Cornell University concert*]

AM: If you look up *humoresque* in the dictionary you find "lighthearted." It's not that slow *pastorale*—that's the way all American symphony orchestras play it. That was Bavarian or whatnot, when they were moving around like that. That was an outing *over there*. The way the Ellington band scores it, you feel you're in the midst of skyscrapers, subway trains, and all the things in the United States. And it turns out, that's what it is: a joyful piece of music! OK, I want to get to the locomotive onomatopoeia. The next piece of music will be Honneger's Pacific 231.

[*While Paul fast-forwards the tape, Professor Granville Ganter says, "Paul, can I ask a question?"*]

GRANVILLE GANTER [to Murray]: You said you were very interested in Constance Rourke and her book *American Humor*—that you borrowed a lot from it.

AM: Yeah!

GG: Is there anything that you *didn't* want to take from her? You said you borrowed from her ideas about the different parts of an American person. Is there anything you didn't want to borrow?

AM: Basically, I got the overall description of American culture, and therefore American character, from her. But she pulled together all these other things I had out there. I had a background, before you get up to the point of reading books like that. There was a book called *The Roots of American Culture* that was after *American Humor.* She had done some other work in Americana. She *is* the touchstone for that, for me. So that put me on the way and brought together a number of other things that I had known. What she does in the book is she goes and discusses other forms of American art.

In other words, all the way back the Americans had been lamenting over the fact that they didn't have a high culture and all this sort of thing. Van Wyck Brooks got all tangled up in it. Hawthorne and these guys made their statements about it. The guy [Brooks] wrote some books: *The Ordeal of Mark Twain, The Pilgrimage of Henry James*—looking for high culture, so they could find out how to do it in America. Well, *she* . . . these names are slipping me now. But Constance Rourke got it from . . .

PD: Herder.

AM: Herder! She got from Herder that the dynamics went the other way. The extension, elaboration, development of the folk culture— the refinement of it becomes the high culture, what they call the high culture. I call it the most comprehensive or representative culture. It's the ultimate *refinement* of the *vernacular.* As you become more adept at it, you polish it, you develop it. The input, the thinking is more sophisticated, more profound. *When you hit that part of Rourke, there's nothing to reject!* 'Cause she puts Henry James in it. In spite all that running around over there, can you imagine somebody writing a book like *The Bostonians* in French, called *The Parisians* or something like that? She was very much aware of how that dynamic would work, or did work. The natural history of a so-called high culture, most representative culture: the most definitive culture would be through extension, elaboration, refinement. And you can see that in the recent development of jazz from the lower folk level. When [critics] say blues, they're often talking about *folk blues.* Guys can't spell their own name! But it's an authentic expression of emotion. You get goose pimples this big. They're playing in two keys and can't name either one of them. It'll still move ya! That's folk.

It's just like language. And I got this when I was a freshman English teacher, about *levels of usage.* [To Ganter] You remember that? Way back? Porter G. Perrin's wonderful book for freshman and sophomore composition? Folk, pop, and fine. Levels of language usage. I applied that to aesthetic development. The folk level can be illiterate. It's the least informed. But it's a true emotional response. It's a true representation by a person with that level of sophistication. You have the illiterate level, the vulgate, then the popular, and the classic or formal level. You do your thesis on that level. The newspaper is on the popular level. And you talk with slang and stuff, to your illiterate cousins, on the other level.

PD: We only have about ten more minutes in this room, so I guess we should skip Pacific 231 and play "Daybreak Express"?

AM: Does "Daybreak Express" come next?

PD: It's next, I have it set up [on the cassette tape].

AM: What I wanted you to hear was the folk level.

PD: We can do that next. We have time.

AM: OK. We're gonna do it backwards. We'll give you the ultimate sophistication of locomotive onomatopoeia. Then, we'll show you where it came from.

[Plays Ellington's "Daybreak Express"]

AM: Now that's a fully orchestrated jazz conception. Actually, the tune they're playing is "Tiger Rag." It's a ragtime tune called "Tiger Rag." But the materials that are in there—the locomotive onomatopoeia is the language of jazz. Now, we have a little time for the folk stuff that led to a sophisticated musician putting it in his orchestration.

[Plays Forest City Joe's "Train Time"]

AM: [while "Train Time" is playing] Can you hear it? He's working on the railroad! [long pause while the tune plays] That's an American folk song! Hear that train whistle harmonica! [end of tape]

"A real conservative? I'm not one. I'm an avant-garde person."
Interview with Russell Neff

This interview was published in Apprise *magazine in February 1990.* Apprise *is now known as* Central PA *(as in Pennsylvania). I found it among Murray's papers in a box of miscellaneous items (concert programs, unimportant form letters, programs from his speaking engagements). I don't know why it was not included in Roberta S. Maguire's edited volume* Conversations with Albert Murray *(1997). Perhaps Murray simply forgot about it. The end is especially important, as he explains his relationship to the terms* avant-garde *and* conservative. *His critique of "the rat race" and its negative impact on humanities education is prescient. This interview also gives insight into Murray's friendship with the great composer, trumpeter, saxophonist, and bandleader Benny Carter. At the time of this interview, Murray had traveled to Harrisburg to introduce Carter in concert—and attend the proclamation of Albert Murray Day in Harrisburg.*

I approached my interview with Albert Murray with more than my usual apprehension. This wasn't just another "chat" with a jazz musician, in which I could slide by with my usual stock of questions. Not only had Murray spent years with Count Basie, preparing the legendary bandleader's autobiography, *Good Morning Blues*; I was also aware of his reputation as a keen observer of and commentator on the use of language in the United States. To be expected to hold an intelligent conversation with the man hailed by the *New York Times Book Review* as "one of the foremost literary interpreters of blues, jazz, and improvisation" can be quite an intimidating prospect.

Therefore, I was unprepared for the friendly, personable man

who greeted me at the side of the motel swimming pool. In Harrisburg for the 1989 Central Pennsylvania Friends of Jazz Festival,
Murray later that evening would introduce old friend Benny Carter
to several hundred fans. Along with Carter, he would also receive a
proclamation from the City of Harrisburg declaring Albert Murray
Day in the capital city.

We adjourned to a side room for our conversation, which began
with a question about the basic tool of his craft, the English language.

RUSSELL NEFF: One of the things that I was particularly taken with in
reading some of your work is your use of the language, your use of the
tools of your craft. Do you feel that this is becoming a lost art, that
the young people of today coming up through high school and college
aren't as careful with their use of the language, aren't as creative
with the language?

ALBERT MURRAY: I think it's a danger. I think we're in danger of losing
this sort of command of language, and that means a loss of precision
in dealing with actuality, in dealing with the facts of life. And that
always puts us in trouble, puts our civilization in trouble. Because
actually, our technology is requiring greater and greater precision,
you see, with the computer. So if you put it in wrong, you're stuck
with it.

And yet we have the type of precision where we could pick up
the phone right here in Harrisburg, make a reservation to get on a
plane at 11:30 in Houston, Texas, on October the fourteenth, and it
will be all ready. That's the type of precision that we have.

We have a problem, and yet we exist in a time when it is so easy
to become more literate than human beings have ever been before . . .
what with radio, television, with movies, with computers, with the
language disks and so forth, unlike when I first went abroad thirty-
some years ago. I had two records, French language, a little Italian,
and whatnot. Now you can have a Walkman and have a complete
course in Persian, or something like that. Or Turkish. And you can
just walk around and absorb this.

So all of that makes for a greater precision and a more precise
articulation. But because of an oversubscription in our education system to material things, to the fast buck, to an acceptance of the rat

race, that type of thing, and an undersubscription to the humanities in education—you see, at the core of the humanities was language training. That's what you started out with throughout the ages—getting the words right, getting an adequate vision—because the richer your vocabulary, the richer your sense of life. And when the vocabulary becomes reduced, it's because our sense of life has become reduced, you see . . .

Most people now rely on clichés, unfortunately, though fortunately, most of them don't rely on social-science clichés, which are the worst. Because it gives you the illusion of thinking about something that you'll never know about. It's just another way of dealing with platitudes and unexamined assumptions.

So I think we certainly should be alert to the fact that we face a great danger of losing our way in the world as human beings, because we're losing the precision with which we could deal with the complexities of life. Life is not becoming simpler. And life does not become simpler as you get older.

RN: Do you feel that maybe some of this goes back to what I have been noticing, which is a lack of respect for tradition?

AM: Oh, yes. And that means losing your way. I mean, if you don't know where you're coming from, you don't know where you're going. And that means that you exist in a state of hysteria, you see. And a state of hysteria is tantamount to living in the void, in the hole.

So that brings us back to a basic principle of dealing with life that should underline all art forms. The motivating force behind all art forms is the absolute necessity for form itself, for a pattern. We're looking for the "adequate image," which is an "adequate pattern," or the "adequate direction," or the "adequate story" of our lives that we will live in terms of, the adequate thing to emulate in order to fulfill our potential.

I've said in several of my books, but mainly in *Stomping the Blues,* I've said one of the most symbolic things about jazz as the representative anecdote for modern life is that the "break" always reminds us of the necessity for heroic action. Because a break is that time of disjuncture when there's a cessation of the cadence which has been established. And then you're out there like a fish out of water.

Now, that's the moment of truth. That's the moment of greatest jeopardy. But it's also the time when you do your thing. You hear what I'm saying? So that it conditions.

See, that's why jazz is central, so central to American culture, because it is there, like all art forms, to condition us to do what we're supposed to do. Like an epic. An epic conditions you for heroic action. You are born to fight the dragon. You are born to turn back the enemy. You are born to slay Grendel in the depths, or to fight any monsters that want to take this over.

So you don't say, "It's unfair that I have to fight the dragon." That's life. Even if you're a Southerner and it's the Grand Dragon. It's life. So that the whole business of dealing with form, and knowing that you deal with form, that you have the greatest necessity for form at this disjuncture.

So in jazz, you say, "You take the break." Or I will go around in the street saying, "Give me a break." Means, give me an opportunity. The same word which means disjuncture, and in Viennese mythology, in psychoanalytic mythology, that was trauma-producing. In jazz, it's your time of opportunity. Your moment of truth.

So that means you're being conditioned to heroic action, that when the calm of the community is disrupted, or, as in Faulkner, it's sort of abrupted, by this monster that comes in, by this disaster that hits, that's when your mettle is proved. That's terribly important.

RN: I've seen that in news stories that I've covered over the years. It is the time of the greatest disaster, whether as here in Harrisburg in 1972, when we had a major flood, that is the moment that the community becomes a community.

AM: The concept that I use in my work, and I sort of spell it out in a book called *The Hero and the Blues,* and it's a concept that I appropriated from a friend of mine named Joseph Campbell . . . that concept is called "antagonistic cooperation."

That is, we're supposed to live as if the dragon exists in order to make heroes, just as plagues exist, and great medical disasters exist, to make great doctors; wars exist to make great generals, people who will be the saviors of the nation. When you get that view of life, you see, then you are conditioned to heroic action.

You see, one of the problems of welfare sociology is, it's as if the underlying assumption—and it's unexamined, I'm sure—is that you should remove all difficulties so nobody will have to struggle against anything. Do you hear me?

It's all right to have compassion and all that, but, buddy, somebody's got to have some experience of dealing with the problems in the boondocks. If everybody's going to be retired and playing on a golf course, they're not going to realize that when you hit the ball into the roughs, and you look up, and you see that—that might be a dragon seed, not the golf ball.

So if you're alerted to it, through combat experience in the boondocks or wherever, you're prepared for these difficulties when they arise. That's just an example of how I use the concept of antagonistic cooperation. You don't say, "Why should this happen to me?" You say, "What am I going to do about this situation?"

RN: That goes to the term that we hear so often in jazz—paying your dues.

AM: Yes. You know you've got to pay your dues.

To see that as a natural part of life is terribly important, just as to see that bad weather, that droughts, that famine is a strong possibility. That earthquakes might strike. That tornadoes strike without warning. Tidal waves, if you're in a certain place, are a likelihood. All of these things we have to keep in mind.

Today we have a richer conception of life, and we know what we can never afford to get rid of the concept of heroism, that antagonistic cooperation. If you have the attitude, "This exists to bring out the best in me," then you don't go around moaning.

That's why a lot of people misunderstand the blues, as I have written about it. They think the blues is a matter of hissing and moaning about, "Oh, isn't it too bad we're in there." That's not it. If you relate the situation, it simply is to remind yourself that life is a low-down dirty shame, but the objective is to stomp at the Savoy by nine-thirty that night.

You know, we're not giving up. It's not suicidal music. It's not self-commiseration music. It's not self-pity music. It's "face the facts" music. And one of the things that we have that's really dangerous among young people of our time—it's a weird thing—we see evidence every day of a lot of unearned cynicism. Here's a guy all angry and mad and so forth, but he's never had it any way except soft, had all kinds of things done for him. And here he is, mad with the world.

You know, that's really weird. That's self-indulgence. And it's a lack of imagination. I mean, bored, really is what they are—ennui, as the existentialists used to say. They don't know what to do with themselves. And maybe if they had had to struggle, at least in games . . . You say, "If you play the game, you play the game." You don't cheat. You don't do it, because then you don't get the benefit of the game.

RN: Many times one of the very common criticisms that I hear and read of an up-and-coming jazz musician is that he's a good technician, but either he doesn't have anything to say, or he doesn't swing. And it's essentially the same thing.

AM: Absolutely. See, swinging is just about the ultimate boon, you see. That means that's when your whole body now is involved with a sort of adequate story of life. In any field. You can apply that to any field. If you're in politics, and all you can do is recite, then it's like playing stock arrangements. You know what I mean? But if you can now apply all the things that you know to the dance that's being done, or the dance they want to do, or the dance you want to see done at a given time, then you're swinging.

This is what is native in America . . . an art form for a pioneer people who require resilience as a prime trait. Now, doesn't that tell you what the basic requirement for swinging is? It means you know all the chordal structures, you know all of the progressions, and you have a warehouse full of tools, and all this. Now, to swing with that, you've got to be improvising with it all. You've got to accept the fact that all of the knowledge that you have adds up to your being able to improvise.

Now, what does a scientist do? Exactly that. He knows all this stuff. He's got to have a PhD to get in the lab, right? Now he's got all this stuff, what is he going to do? He says, "Well, we're going to try this. We're trying that." He starts improvising. You've got this necessity for resilience. That's the American pioneer.

Jazz is an Afro-American form. Everybody identifies with it because it is an adequate metaphor for the truth of the American experience. Do you get what I'm saying? That's why everybody feels

"That's ours." And they identify with it because they're telling the story about America, the basic story of all Americans: you've got to be resilient.

If you've got it all nailed down, and you know where all the notes go, and you do all that, and all you have to do is have the director come up and tell you, "Do that," you're not dealing with American experience, you see.

You've got to deal with what John A. Kouwenhoven calls that interaction of a learned tradition with a vernacular or frontier tradition. You come out with another product, which is indigenous to the situation that it's in. And that's what art is. If it's not indigenous to that situation, it's just something you're going to borrow and see if it will apply. Nobody's going to knock Brahms and Beethoven and all that, because that's great music. But you've got to do something with it quite different when you take it out to Detroit or somewhere. In St. Louis, it's got to be a different thing.

If you're loose, you can [fluff a note] and Duke says, "I like that, play that again." The guy hit a mistake, he resolves it. The guy may come up and he didn't event intend to play that note, but Duke hears it and he'd say, "Hey, go back over that. Do that." And then out of this comes something else, because he's working on a broader scope than these other people.

But a person who's going, "This is the way it was written; this is the way it has to be played. This is it. This is that. And I know I'm a good musician because I don't fluff any notes," that's another tradition.

RN: But it's not our tradition.

AM: No, our tradition is swinging. But most of the musicians are so geared to their formal conservatory training, they feel lost if they can't get away from that . . .

As a writer, no matter what idiom you're dealing with, you want to use a standard notation, as it were, for standard words. Then the guy who's playing it knows what value to give it. It's like, you would say, "You goin' ta town?" You write, "Are you going to town?" Now, you might have to put a little signal in there somewhere to let the guy know that's sharp or that's flat, something like that, and then he will play it. But that's the way you do.

When you look at an Ellington score, you see notes written on the score just like that. But you don't play those like you play a score at the New York Philharmonic. They want those values just as they are written, whereas in this, the guy has up there: "Carney." "Hodges." "Cootie." "Rex." "Ray." That is another thing of resilience, of adaptability, of perpetual creativity, that is what is required of Americans. They know that life is not settled.

Now, we're talking about how this stuff really goes, how it fits into the culture, how it affects the culture. And the youngsters who think that if they can be sloppy, if they reflect their sloppy-headedness in their music, that that's being valid because they're reflecting it, miss the whole point. Chaos exists to be dealt with, not to be celebrated, because chaos is not good for anybody. So you've got to find a way to counterstate the chaos, so that even if you start out with a lot of cacophony, a lot of disjointed stuff like that, there's going to be some type of resolution somewhere. It may be a new type of resolution. It may not be resolved as Mozart would have resolved.

RN: But it will be resolved.

AM: It will be resolved, almost sure enough, but the guy's speaking a different language. Once you get to that language, you will find that he's dealing with form. One convention is superseded by another convention. It may be less or more. The great people, they're going to absorb that minor thing, for what it is, and use it in proportion as it's needed for the total tradition that we started out talking about. Because they know where they're coming from, they know that this is just something, another means of refinement of a certain aspect of it, and that it has to be absorbed into that ongoing thing in order for the continuity of human conscience. I mean, to be there, to be continuously fructified, or ennobling, or enriching. So it's a terribly important thing to see how all these things fit together.

In the arts, it's got to be that way. You've got to have some form. You've got to have some conception of the conservative.We like to think that people are conservative simply because they have found a certain security in the way things are, and they're not willing to experiment with it. But at least they're clinging to something that has worked. Now, there's a difference between that—to my way of thinking, there's a difference between that and being reactionary. See, if you're a reactionary conservative, that means you're against change. You see, a lot of people are slow to change until it's proved.

Now I'll tell you something that I was conservative about. Cash machines. You know, I want to write a check. And then they said, "Use your card, and you go to the cash machine." I was a little slow on that. Then I realized, you don't have to get in line, you can go Sunday morning, or Saturday, you can go at any time, and the thing would really do it – multiples of twenty, and it's perfectly fine. So, I was hesitant to do it, conservative in the outlook of going that far, but not reactionary. I didn't want to go find the guy who put that in and fire him or anything like that. A real conservative . . . I'm not one. I'm an experimental writer; I'm an avant-garde person who tries to keep his own values.

I remember a long time ago the saying was: "Be not the first. Do not be so eager to be the first by whom the new is tried, not yet the last, by whom the old is cast aside." You don't cling to it when it's already changed. You're not going to take the horse and buggy—I mean, unless you're from a certain part of Pennsylvania [laughter]—when you've got a pickup truck.

"The blues always come back"

Liner Notes to *Revelations/Blues Suite*, Alvin Ailey Dance Theater

These are the only liner notes Murray ever wrote. Michele Murray, the only child of Albert and Mozelle Murray, was a dancer with the Alvin Ailey Company in the late 1960s and 1970s. Judith Jamison, longtime director of the company, gave a reading at Murray's memorial service at Jazz at Lincoln Center. Prior to that, I did not know, until Michele mentioned it, that Jamison and Murray often talked on the phone. Through trying to learn more about Murray's associations with the Alvin Ailey Company, I discovered these liner notes through a Google search in 2013 (nobody had yet had the opportunity to go through Murray's record collection). I quickly bought the record online. For more on Michele Murray and on Albert Murray's relationship with dance, see the interview that Lauren Walsh and I did with Michele Murray, included in the edited volume Albert Murray and the Aesthetic Imagination of a Nation *(2010). A transcript of a conversation between Murray, Ailey, James Baldwin, and Romare Bearden is included in* Conversations with Albert Murray. *Michele told me that during the 1966 New York City transit strike, her father drove her and her Ailey colleagues (most of whom lived in Harlem) to their rehearsals at the Clark Center at Fifty-first Street, and then back home.*

Alvin Ailey Dance Theater Presents *Revelations/Blues Suite*

TWENTIETH ANNIVERSARY ALBUM, 1978

Liner Notes by Albert Murray

Albert Murray's Notes for *Revelations*

REVELATIONS is divided into three major sections: The music of the first section, PILGRIM OF SORROW, is a medley of spirituals reflecting oppression and expressing protest. The color theme is brown, which symbolizes growth from the soil. The second section, TAKE ME TO THE WATER, is a reenactment of the religious ritual of cleansing through baptism and the color is white, which symbolizes purification. The finale, MOVE, MEMBERS, MOVE, expresses the ecstatic element of the religious service. The color yellow is used in this section and it symbolizes the celestial majesty of the sun.

Section one begins with a group dance by the company to the spiritual "I've Been Buked." Physically, it is a sculptural dance influenced by Rodin's *The Burghers of Calais* and various works by Henry Moore. It is a statement about escape and there are bursts of anger, rage, and fear; there are also gestures of reaching and aspiration. "Didn't My Lord Deliver Daniel" is a dance based on percussive movements and expresses a kind of internalized anger, a resistance to the isolation of the individual. "Fix Me Jesus" is a duet which begins with the idea of weight and of falling and then slowly becomes a dance about rising. Idiomatically, it is a dance of instruction, a dance of follow-the-leader in which the dancer symbolizing the pastor gives the word to his flock as symbolized by the infinite.

Section two, *Take Me to the Water,* begins with the "Processional," which consists of four acolytes, the mother of the church, and two initiates en route to the baptismal stream, the site of cleansing. One of the acolytes clears the way by sweeping the earth with his branch and sweeping the air with his white cloth. The rhythmic chant serves as a vamp to "Honor, Honor" which is the prayer before the immersion. Then comes the main ritual of self-cleansing. Not only are the worshippers "Wading in the Water," they are in a sense becoming one with the natural element of the water. "I Want to Be Ready" features the person who has been baptized and cleansed and the dance symbolizes the precarious balance involved in maintaining a state of grace. Choreographically, it is an étude based on Lester Horton's theory having to do with rising and falling and balancing.

Section three, *Move, Members, Move,* opens with "Sinner Man." The trio of male dancers is meant to suggest three men who are guilty in the eyes of the Lord and are trying to escape from the voice of judgment. "The Day Is Past and Gone" is a solemn prayer-meeting hymn that brings the congregation back together once more for Sunday Evening Service. As the worshippers assemble, greet each other and take their seats their mindfulness of the dignity of the occasion is obvious, but so is their earthy exuberance and their irreplaceable sense of style as elegant as it is robust. The third dance in this section, "You May Run On," is the service in progress. There is no dance figure representing the preacher; his sermon, however, is contained in the lyrics of the song which is based on various biblical texts applied to local community particulars, perhaps the very same particulars the members seemed to have been gossiping about even as they made their ever so dignified entrance. The fans and gestures of the members indicate that along with their concerns about liturgical purification they are well aware of what is being signified about the behavior of certain backsliders in the church community. "You May Run On" modulates into the joyful noise of "Rocka My Soul in the Bosom of Abraham," which is the universally infectious out chorus of the suite. This is the highest form of self-expression that the members reach in the church. The dance consists of ecstatic movements—movements of stomping and handclapping, of shouting and general rejoicing. The choreography suggests the improvisational solo call and ensemble response. It is at this point in the actual down-home church service that some members may become so possessed by the Holy Spirit as to do the holy dance and speak in unknown tongues. It is the earthy expression of the most profound affirmation.

Albert Murray's Notes for *Blues Suite*

"Something Strange," which serves as the overture to BLUES SUITE, is, like "I Cried," a traditional lament that bemoans the presence of the blue devils and the low-down feeling they always bring. The lyrics are the grieving victim's attempt to spell out the cause and effect of his affliction. This type of music, which as a rule is performed far more often by itinerant folk guitar–style strummers than by dance-beat-oriented honky-tonk piano players, has unmistakable overtones of the aboriginal chant and down-home field holler.

BLUES SUITE, which has been in the repertory of the Alvin Ailey Company since 1958, opens with "Good Morning Blues," a traditional twelve-bar folk ballad. The time is early morning and the dancers represent people who are waking up once more into a world of torment and trouble. The very atmosphere is oppressive.

The specific setting is a honky tonk or juke joint and the opening movements are intended to suggest a very intense human response to a gloom-ridden environment. There are waking and stretching movements which express rage, anger, frustration, loss, longing, and also yearning and also determination. These are the actions of people who are trying to extend their world, to stretch out into another perception of themselves. It is as if they are fighting their way free of an entanglement. At first it seems as if each individual thinks his troubles are unique, but as the dance progresses there comes an awareness of a common ground of commiseration. Hence, the ensemble climax.

The music and lyrics of "Mean Ol' Frisco" expresses the longing for a lost love who has left town by train. The train is the instrument of deliverance from one life to another. The movements of this section, however, come out of the choreographer's memory of his childhood in Texas during the Depression where young men with all their belongings waited beside the railroad tracks for the express train to Chicago, Kansas, Detroit. The lyrics refer to the train as being mean (i.e., cruel) because it took the lover's sweetheart away. But it is also mean because of the risk to life and limb involved in the task of snagging or hoboing on a train which to their minds is as huge as a fairy tale dragon and moves as fast and with almost as much destructive force as lightning.

In the blues idiom (and in the down-home Afro-American church, too, for that matter) the freight train is not only a concrete phenomenon and a very practical means of free long-distance transportation, but it is also a metaphorical phenomenon which the fugitive slave rode from the House of Bondage to the Land of Freedom. Incidentally, the wide use of railroad imagery in church music seems to antedate by many years its use in blues music.

The setting for the "House of the Rising Sun" is the caged-in atmosphere of the sporting house premises above the honky tonk, and in the movements of the trio of prostitutes expresses feelings of lost direction, another situation where they would be free to give their love instead of having to sell it as a means of subsistence.

"Backwater Blues" is a twilight pas de deux which also takes place upstairs over the honky tonk. Two lovers re-enact the long-standing love/hate flirtation ritual which is their prelude to what is a bit of time playing games of one-upmanship with each other, but such is the nature of their dalliance that, as always, they end up in each other's arms.

"In the Evening" is a dance for three men, each expressing his solitary response to his aloneness and his search for personal meaning. The time of this action is after the day's labor is done and the search is not only for sensual pleasure and diversion but also for a higher reason for being.

"Yancy Special," "Going to Chicago," and "Sham" all deal with the evening festivities. The setting is the dance floor of their honky tonk, where the very names of the steps make clear the blues are dragged, stomped, swung, shaken, bumped, snapped away, shouted, strutted, shimmied, and otherwise attacked not only with resolution but also nonchalance and with elegance withal. All these functions work towards dispelling the blues and keeping them at bay, at least for the time being.

The festive atmosphere of the dance floor is followed by a reprise of the opening strains of "Good Morning Blues" and the cycle is completed. The fact that the blues were dispelled by the end of yesterday does not mean that they won't be back the next morning. The blues always come back, because they represent a problem which has to be dealt with every day.

Second Lining, Third Liners— and the Fourth Line
Notes on a Jazz Tradition

Murray worked on this note in 2003 and 2004, at the same time he was working on "Jazz: Notes toward a Definition." This was in response to white critics who seized on and misinterpreted his photo caption on page 197 of Stomping the Blues. *This caption is among the most controversial items in Murray's career and among the most willfully misunderstood by those who would say that Murray underrates or downplays the talent or authenticity of white musicians. He wrote this piece to correct such misunderstandings.*

In Murray's caption to Art Kane's famous photograph A Great Day in Harlem *he identifies the local Harlem children (sitting on the curb with Count Basie) as belonging to the "second line" and identifies white musicians in the photograph as belonging to the "third line." This has created misunderstandings and drawn criticism over time, some of it disingenuous. John Gennari, in his near-definitive history of jazz criticism,* Blowin' Hot and Cool: Jazz and Its Critics *(2006), defends Murray on the charge of not sufficiently appreciating white musicians. Gennari writes: "critics of the Lincoln Center jazz program who condemn Albert Murray's* Stomping the Blues *do so for Murray's exclusive focus on black musicians, pinpointing for special opprobrium" the caption to Kane's photograph. "This opportunistic reading of Murray," Gennari explains, "narrows the focus entirely to the matter of identity politics, completely avoiding the substance of Murray's argument about the culture of blues and jazz—its ritualistic elements, its spirit of celebration, its dynamic link between the Saturday night secular dance and the Sunday morning church service. These critics evidently have not read enough of Murray to know that he has celebrated certain white jazz players for evincing a feeling for*

black culture that often eludes white writers" (364). As Murray wrote
in a late notebook entry, "I don't write about race—I write about
idiom."

*   In 2000, a historian who was acquainted with Murray wrote him*
a letter (to use "next time somebody tries to give you trouble about the
celebrated 'second line' caption in Stomping the Blues*"), pointing out*
that in 1977, one year after Stomping the Blues *was published, Chad-*
wick Hansen made an almost identical claim, distinguishing between
the use of "the second line" for parade followers and white musicians
who came along later, and, added the historian, "nobody said a mum-
bling word." This is in Selections from the Gutter: Portraits from the
"Jazz Record," edited by Art Hodes and Chadwick Hansen (1977).
It is interesting that Murray did not use this to his advantage. But it
was not like him to say, "See, look what this person said." He would
back up his own statement with his own authority, as he does here. I
am mentioning this for historical, scholarly, and contextual purposes.

In the context of the history of jazz music in the United States, the
second line refers to that element of the traditional New Orleans
street parade which consists of groups of admirers and protégés who
march and prance and dance along the curb and sidewalk beside their
favorite bands, sometimes for the length of the street in their neigh-
borhoods and sometimes as far as escorting traffic policemen permit,
with other enthusiasts joining in all along the route of the procession
to the ceremonial destination.

    Eventually, second lining came to be applied to followers or
protégés of non-marching musicians such as piano players, string
bass players, and so on. After all, following in someone's footsteps
was a very pragmatic survival technique long before the evolution of
ceremonial parades!

    Not that it should be assumed that all or even the majority of pa-
rade route second liners were aspiring musicians. A significant number but perhaps not even a majority. Some came along with friends
because the parade was something going on through their neighbor-
hoods or one nearby. Others from elsewhere joined in because they
just happened to be there. In any case, to the second liner, the parade
has a local stylization dimension, whether the feast day happens to

be sacred or secular such as Easter on the one hand or the Fourth of July or Labor Day on the other. As a matter of fact, over the years the second line was to become an attraction in itself.

A very well-known and widely celebrated historical example (if not prototype) of what I sometimes refer to as a third line (and hence third liners) were members of a group of apprentice musicians in Chicago known as the Austin High School Gang, back in the 1920s, who used to leave their ever-so-conventional section of town to spend as much time as they could get away with to hang around and out with and around and out in the segregated section of town known as the South Side in order to study and play along with Southern "black" and creole musicians whose musical idiom they admired and identified with above all others. Thus, whereas the old New Orleans second line may usually include more non-musicians than protégés, the third line was always made up mainly of musicians, with perhaps a few taste masters along to testify as to how hip it all was.

Speaking of lines, back during the years when black dance and stage show bands became nationally famous because of their recordings and radio broadcasts, when their schedules took them into the then widely and strictly segregated South, there was in effect a practice that amounted to a fourth line: a small number of white musicians and fans would arrange with the local legal authorities to have the venue owners and operators provide a special roped-off area from which there was a good view of the bandstand and within which they could dance with the dates whom some of them sometimes brought along, especially if they wanted to try out some of the new movements that the regular clientele were playing around with at the time.

In a sense the third line stretches all the way back to Thomas "Jim Crow" Rice and Dan Emmett and the invention of blackface minstrelsy in the 1830s, an American pop culture show business tradition that was very much alive in the persons of Al Jolson and Eddie Cantor during my childhood, before whom there had also been what was then called a light-skinned colored comedian named Bert Williams who had achieved superstar status, who also performed in blackface and spoke in what was assumed to be black dialect, which was no less contrived than that of Rice and Emmett, but was widely imitated by other "black, brown, and beige" comedians, especially those who performed in the olio sections of burlesque theater circuit shows.

"Basie's a special guy"
Interview with Billy Eckstine

Billy Eckstine was one of the most popular singers in the world from the 1940s through the 1960s and enormously important to the history of jazz. He was a trumpeter, a bandleader, and a major figure in the development of bebop. He was critically important in Count Basie's comeback in the early 1950s.

After World War II, the big bands that flourished before the war were not as economically viable and quickly began to disappear. The Count Basie Orchestra, which had had a miraculous run from 1936 to 1948, was affected by this change. Some of the most popular orchestras were able to barely hang on during this lull, such as Duke Ellington's (whose resurgence occurred after a performance at the Newport Jazz Festival in 1956, for which he made the cover of Time*). Some prominent leaders such as Basie were able to form new groups after disbanding. At the height of Eckstine's popularity he took Basie on the road with him. After that, Basie's spectacular residence at Birdland in New York set the stage for his permanent reestablishment.*

Eckstine and Murray did not really know each other well before this interview, which took place in 1983. The tape is labeled "Dangerfield's" in Murray's handwriting. Dangerfield's was a comedy club on the Upper East Side of Manhattan. Eckstine invites Murray to interview him again some weeks laters in Philadelphia, but if that interview took place, a tape is not known to exist.

Murray and Eckstine had a close mutual friend in General Daniel "Chappie" James, the first African American four-star general. Five years prior to this interview, James died of a heart attack at age fifty-six. I do not know how Eckstine met James or how Murray and Eckstine got on the topic of James, as the tape cuts out and starts again just prior to that section. James was one of Murray's closest friends, and

Dorothy Watkins James was one of Mozelle Murray's closest friends. Albert Murray often spoke fondly of General James. They had known each other since the late 1930s at Tuskegee. James, Murray told me, wanted to fly planes ever since he was a child growing up near an airstrip in Florida. A large man, James was too tall and too big to fit in a cockpit until fighter planes became larger after World War II. This discussion of James does not relate to music explicitly but it certainly reveals something about Eckstine and is a tribute to Murray's dear friend.

The end of this interview is of particular interest as it relates to the preservation of jazz. Eckstine's claim that "whitey is gonna run our legends down" offers a stark take on a sentiment I have encountered when discussing the early days of jazz repertory with figures who were involved in it. There really was a sense, in the 1980s, that classic jazz, particularly the music of black artists, was on the verge of disappearing. I've asked many people with a stake in various jazz institutions and a role in forming those institutions if this was the case in the 1980s. Without hesitation, the answer always was yes. This is the uneasy feeling about the future of the past that helped prompt the massive efforts to create the American Jazz Orchestra, the Carnegie Hall Jazz Band, and Jazz at Lincoln Center. The way Eckstine expressed it might not be the way that others would have chosen to express it, but it reflects a feeling that was in the air. And Murray's reply on the tape is immediate and unambiguous: "I know that."

BILLY ECKSTINE: Basie's a special guy. There's very few of them in this business. You get a bunch of assholes. But Basie? There ain't nobody like him as far as I'm concerned. He's one of the most beautiful people I've ever met. I know two people in this world that I met that never have I heard them say a bad thing about anybody: Joe Louis and Basie. If you say to him, "Aw man, that guy ain't worth shit," Basie will say, "Huh." That's all. He'll never offer an opinion about it! Joe Louis was the same way.

ALBERT MURRAY: Another guy who was a close third in there was Duke.

BE: Oh, Duke, yeah! Duke. Duke was another one. But Basie especially.

AM: I've been working with him for years on this book and he'll tell a joke on himself all the time.

BE: That's all he does!

AM: When it comes to somebody else, if something happened in 1923 on 127th Street and Seventh Avenue, he's not gonna tell it—he says the grandchildren might be alive!

BE: He ain't gonna tell nothing on nobody. Base used to tell me all the time, even before we went on them tours, when I was with Earl and with my own band—because I was always getting into fights. On the road, something would happen and he'd say "Don't tell that mother-fucker nothing!" [laughter]

AM: "He'll raise hell!" [laughter] Saturday—that's when you're leaving?

BE: I go to Philly on March first with Sammy. I'll be there for five days. It'll be much easier [to talk then].

AM: What Basie is screwed up on is in the last chapter. He credits you with being the real *moral support* that gave him the courage to go back into the big band business. It's all his words but he needs a backup on it. I've found all I could in the microfilm and newspapers. He needs the sequence of where you said certain things to him be-cause he wants to imitate you in the book. "Come on, Base, I need you out here with me, man, put this shit down." From about 1950 when he had the combo . . .

BE: I'll tell you how it came about. I took Basie out on the first tour with the big band. I made him get another big band. I did some touring. It was George Shearing, myself, and Basie had a seven-piece combo. So I went to Base and I said, hey man, I've got about 130 one-nighters—concerts—between the North and the South. Come on, go out with me. Basie said, "I ain't gonna go out with no band." I said, "I've got 130 days! That's enough to establish you. You ain't supposed to be in no fuckin' little band, man. You look funny up there with a little band." He said, "Man, shit man, I'm in the hole," and this and that. I said. "Man, this'll get you out!" And so, finally, I talked him into it. We went out, and then after that northern tour, then we had about a month off, in which I went south with Ruth Brown, the Clovers, and Basie. We did about sixty days down there. It was about four, four and a half months, back and forth.

AM: Was there any connection with Birdland or the Birdland tours? Was this separate? This is what I'm trying to understand.

BE: That's separate. That came after. That was after Basie established his [new] band and was recording with Roulette with the big band.

AM: Roulette. This was before Norman Granz?

BE: Oh, way before Norman! Basie went out with me for the first time in '51. '52 we went out again and '53 we went out again. We went out three years.

AM: At this time he had Paul Quinichette in the band—

BE: And the arranger—

AM: Ernie?

BE: Ernie Wilkins.

AM: Ah, so Clark was in there?

BE: No. It was Joe Newman, Paul Campbell. Who was the third trumpet player? The trombones were Henry Coker, Benny Powell, and Ernie Wilkins's brother Jimmy. He just had three at that time. The reed section was Marshal Royal—

AM: Poopsie [Charles Fowlkes] was in that band?

BE: Poopsie was there, playing baritone.

AM: At one time Joe Newman and Eddie "Lockjaw" were out on another tour with you, were they not?

BE: Yeah, that was the jazz group. 1950.

AM: Basie was not on that? You had seen Basie out in Chicago.

BE: Capitol Lounge!

[tape cuts out, and starts again with them talking about their mutual friend, General Daniel "Chappie" James]

AM: We used to fly up to where those guys were playing. National Records. Remember those?

BE: Yeah, sure!

AM: Many a guy had a party or a barbeque with those records.

[tape cuts out]

BE: I was over in Bangkok. Chap was wing commander over there. He found out I was over there. He said, "I'm leaving here Friday, I'm going to Lakeland, Florida." No, he wasn't a wing commander. This was going to be his first time as being a wing commander—in Lakeland, Florida. He was at a little base called NKP, "non-kom-pur" or something like that, up there in northern Thailand, right there in the Mekong Delta. He was the only black—all these white guys were under him. I get a call in Bangkok—they knew I was off that day. These son'bitches flew me up to NKP in one of them fuckin' 104s.

AM: Ohhh boy!

BE: These crazy cocksuckers flying me up there! I get up there and I walked in on Chap—and that son'bitch liked-to-died, boy!

AM: They surprised him?

BE: They surprised him! Brought me up there to him! Boy, we had a hell of a time. Chappie had on the side of his plane—he liked to tell everybody—"This was before the Black Panther Party." On the side of Chap's plane he had this *big black panther*!

AM: Right!

BE: And he was a colonel. It said "Colonel Chappie James" and underneath it in letters it said "*H.N.I.C.*"

AM: YEAH! [uproarious laughter] AND HE WAS! But you know what Chappie did after the war? See, he was too big [physically], he wasn't even supposed to be in the fighter plane—and he lived to become the number one expert *in* fighters!

BE: We sat with these pilots and the way they thought about Chappie, man, you wouldn't believe. They loved him like a brother.

AM: But you know what he did? He couldn't get over there in World War II. But when he got in fighters, he challenged *every ace*—and ran him out!

BE: That's right! We were sitting around, and John Glenn had just done some shit, I don't know, before he went up there [into outer space]. And they were speaking about him and they said that asshole, he ain't shit. They said Chappie would eat his lunch!

AM: [laughter] That's right, boy!

BE: They spoke so *glowingly* of him, these guys. They were sitting around the officers' club, there was about eight of 'em, just running it back and forth with us. Chap wasn't even there, man. I told Chap after, I said, "Man, goddam," I said "you'll never find no more loyal"—he said, "That's why I hate to leave here." He said, "These are the best bunch of guys I've ever seen in my life."

AM: And ol' General Olds he was working for over there—he swore by him.

BE: Oh, yeah. Chap would get in that goddam F104—that son'bitch looked like he took up the whole fuckin' plane! That big son of a bitch! [laughter]

AM: [laughter] He could fly!

BE: That he could, boy.

AM: Did you see him when he was at Colorado Springs?

BE: Hell, yeah! And I played golf with him! I went out there and played golf with him. And Sammy Davis's tournament up in Hartford—Chap would always come in for that and we'd play golf together. Chap was a dear old buddy of mine. How is his son?

AM: I haven't seen him. Chappie's wife and my wife were classmates and very, very close—

BE: I met his son—

AM: He's a pilot! And Denise, his daughter, was a nurse.

BE: Yeah. I met his son at some base and he introduced himself to me. Chappie was a hell of a guy.

AM: Speaking of Chappie tales—Chappie's daughters, Denise, and my daughter, Michele, are one day apart exactly nine months after a party at my house! [laughter]

BE: [laughter]

AM: I was going into the service. He was doing that CPT at Tuskegee—Civilian Pilot Training. Then, when they opened up multiengine flying to us, he could get in. At first he couldn't get in, because he was too big for a fighter. Then they desegregated, then he got into fighters—*and tore 'em up!*

BE: Tore 'em up, man!

AM: Chappie was terrific. What I really want to do is get the sequencing of those tours.

BE: By the time you come to Philly, I'll have it all. I'll run back in my mind.

AM: I can plot it from the notices in the paper. Then we can run it that way.

BE: I'm glad that Basie told you to ask me because I'd never tell it.

AM: I know!

BE: They weren't giving him shit. They were giving him—for the band—$600 a night or something. The fuck y'all doing? Give that man at least $1,000 a night. For about two weeks he did the thousand. I said, "Motherfucker, give him twelve!" The first tour I went south with we sold most of all the dates to a fella called Howard Lewis. Black guy out of Dallas. The northern tour was done by Norman Granz. It was my tour—I just let Norman book it. That great-white-father shit of his don't go with me.

AM: Basie was saying he had another job another time and you said "Get to me." He said, "How the fuck I'm gonna get this band all the way out there?" You said, "I don't know, but if you get here, you got a job."

BE: You got thirty-one days, I told him! Then I took him into, right here in New York, the place next to Birdland, it was called the Bandbox. And, rightfully so, because I mean . . . *whitey is gonna run our legends down.*

AM: I know that.

BE: If we don't try to keep 'em up? Whitey hoodwinks a lot of niggers—and won't let 'em stay up! Speaking in proof of that—I have a thing I used to do, Al—I used to tell people, these black disc jockeys—"Y'all hollerin' and screamin' on the air—you've got these young kids thinking that music started with James Brown."

AM: [laughter]

BE: I said, "Why in the fuck don't you take one time out of that and say 'moments in black history in music'?" Count Basie and Duke Ellington and Ella Fitzgerald. I said, "Y'all don't play none of these people. Case in point is this: I'll take you to Beverly Hills and you ask any Jewish kid who Al Jolson was, he'll tell you. Talk to the same age out in Watts, ask him who Duke Ellington is—he ain't gonna know! And I said whose fault is that? *It's y'alls fault!*"

AM: I'm gonna bring you a copy of my book *Stomping the Blues* when I see you in Philadelphia. I went through all that stuff.

BE: I know! I know, baby!

"It's not bad being Huck"

Interview with Janis Herbert and Foreword to *The World Don't Owe Me Nothing: The Life and Times of Delta Bluesman "Honeyboy" Edwards*, by David "Honeyboy" Edwards

This combination of interview and Foreword provides insight into Murray's thought process and the relationship of his speech to writing, thanks to a taped interview with Edwards's collaborator, Janis Herbert. The interview took place at Murray's apartment on March 28, 1993. (Edwards was there as well but didn't have much to say.) It is interesting to compare Murray's statements in the interview (such as "this may be the gimmick for the introduction") with the statement of his Foreword. Below is an excerpt from his interview, followed by his Foreword.

Interview with Janis Herbert

ALBERT MURRAY: What we mostly have in this big interest in creating wider markets and so forth for folk blues musicians, is [critics] talk as if that's the only . . . it's just the folk level of the traditional twelve-bar, eight-bar form, played as it was handed down. So, in a sense, within the context of music, it's classic in a sense, it's a conservative music, it's passed down, it's sung a certain way, just as spirituals are. They don't need any improvisation and whatnot and all that, variations and new-style, they want to get that true feel, just like hymns in church. It's a secular form, but they have the respect for the tradition that was there. It has certain limitations but it's something that people can be initiated into and if a taste can be created for it, then they can appreciate it for what it is. Just like folklore or folk cuisine, you see? It's not haute cuisine but you can't have haute cuisine without folk cuisine and nothing respects folk cuisine more than haute cuisine. You hear what I'm saying?

JANIS HERBERT: Yeah.

AM: And what we have in this phenomenon of interest, we've got a series of what I call *Tom Sawyer's history of the blues*. And it would be better if we had *Jim's history* or *Huck and Jim's history*.

JH: Yeah, yeah, I know what you mean. This is Honey's story. In his words. That's real important.

AM: Huck believed in Jim's humanity. You gettin' this? This is going to make you Huck.

JH: I love that.

AM: It's not bad being Huck. If Jim had a choice, he would've been. This may be the gimmick for the introduction, you see. Huck and Jim. You've got to explain to him about *Huckleberry Finn* and how this was, how it's one of the great American novels because, Mark Twain in telling about how Huck helps Jim to steal his freedom, comes to terms with his humanity, and that's the moral center of what should be the ethos, the center, of American identity. If we define ourselves in terms of this, of the social contract upon which the nation is based . . . In other words, it has to do with everything being predicated on the fact that all men are created equal. We want to proceed as if all men are created equal. Got that? And that the laws, everybody's got an equal chance in the pursuit of happiness; life, liberty, the pursuit of happiness. Equal protection under the law. Do unto others as you'd have him do unto you. You see, that's what the Constitution, what the United States, is about. Now, it has to have checks and balances because of human nature, people are greedy and selfish, people are that, but this is a social structure which is predicated on [the previously stated ideals] and the best people find themselves in terms of that you see. So what makes *Huck Finn* a great American novel is that at the core of it, it cuts through the things that divide people and recognizes their common humanity, you see? So, when Huck decides that he's going to help Jim, this is the way he puts it: "steal" his

freedom, then he becomes fully a man. He achieves his manhood doing this. So he says at one point, "I must be a pretty bad fellow. Here I
am helping this slave run away and that's Miss So-and-so's property.
She's always been good to me yet here I am helping Jim run away. I
must be a pretty bad fellow, maybe I'm goin' to hell. Guess I'm gonna
have to go to hell 'cause I have to help Jim steal his freedom." That's
the spiritual basis of heroic action in American life. And that's what
Twain has said. So, you want to see how he contrasts it. You remember this very well, don't you?

JH: Oh, yes.

AM: You get Tom Sawyer and what you got is a white liberal. So, when
he finds out that these guys have been up and down the Mississippi,
in the storm, he says, "What y'all doin?" "I'm helpin' Jim steal his
freedom." He said, "Yeah, that's a good idea, I read about that. You
know he's supposed to be in a dungeon, with vermin." So they go
through that. It's got to be Marxist, it's got to be this, got to be that.
No, it doesn't! It's got to be the Constitution. Don't need Marxism.
There's nothing more revolutionary than the Declaration of Indepen-
dence, the Preamble to the Constitution. The Constitution is like a
blues arrangement. How many chords you going to play, how many
amendments? You put this administration in, they'll run it this way,
play it this way. Put another administration in, they play it that way.
With this structure it can be changed, it can be improvised on. It has
room for personal creativity, personal identity, and all that, and it has
room for interrelationships.

Foreword

ALBERT MURRAY

All too often books about and supposedly by folk blues musicians
come across as products that are essentially undergraduate social-
science field-trip term papers about people who seem to be regarded
as being somewhat pathetic and somewhat provincially exotic and
titillating at the same time.

More often than not, such books strike me as having been
thought up and executed by some ivy-league-type throwback to the
likes of the ever so ideological or, in any case, bookish Tom Sawyer,

rather than some updated extension of a Huck Finn, whose insights and representations of the idiomatic textures of his friend Jim's world are as unspoiled and reliable as those of old Mark Twain himself.

Obviously, if somebody who is not native to the down-home conventions that the blues idiom stylizes into aesthetic statement is going to collaborate with someone who has remained as close to his regional roots as "Honeyboy" Edwards has, that person must achieve a rapport that is as close to family membership or, in any case, neighborhood membership, as possible, so that personal complexities can be seen in proper perspective.

My impression of Janis Martinson [Herbert] is such that I feel "Honeyboy" Edwards is, if anything, even luckier to have her along with him on this voyage of a book than Jim was to have old Huck on that raft on the river and during that encounter with the Royal Nonesuch. After all, besides being more state-of-the-art than old Huck, she's also even more profoundly converted to "Honeyboy"'s conception of his music than Huck was to Jim's conception of himself as a free human being.

In all events, what seems to have counted first and most to her in this undertaking are the nuances of the idiom that have made "Honeyboy" Edwards the musician he has become.

Three Omni-American Artists

Foreword to *Mitchell & Ruff: An American Profile in Jazz,* by William Zinsser

William Zinsser was a renowned journalist and author of numerous books, including the revered On Writing Well. *He and Murray were friends in New York for decades. Murray deeply admired his book* Mitchell & Ruff *(Paul Dry Books, 2000; originally published as* Willie and Dwike *by Harper and Row, 1984) and encouraged me to read it. I read it several times and thought about the lessons from Murray's Foreword before I began working on* Rifftide.

Foreword

ALBERT MURRAY

To my delight, this book is remarkably free of social-science findings and studies and speculations about race relations. Its fundamental concern is with the development of an American aesthetic sensibility. The author, William Zinsser, wants to find out how that sensibility was formed, and that leads him to approach Dwike Mitchell and Willie Ruff as artists. He isn't thrown off by issues of politics and justice and injustice. What he's after is how an American personality develops. There's something about these two musicians that attracted him to them. He wants to know: Where did they come from and how did they get to be where they were when I encountered them? What enables them to play the music that I admire so much?

John A. Kouwenhoven, in his book *Made in America,* talks about what's particularly American about American culture. He suggests that it's a mixture of learned traditions imported by emigrants from Europe with native or frontier forms, which together create the vernacular. That combination in turn gets refined, beyond folk, beyond pop, into the most comprehensive forms of fine art. You can find the twelve-bar blues stanza of a Mississippi delta guitarist, for example, elaborated into an American sonata form known as the jazz instrumental in Duke Ellington's "Harlem Air Shaft." The process has nothing to do with social status. It's a matter of how artists develop a growing mastery of their medium.

In *Mitchell & Ruff,* Zinsser never loses sight of that process. He focuses on why Dwike Mitchell plays the piano as he does, and why Willie Ruff plays the bass and the French horn as he does. He discovers that their music is a fusion of what was imported to this country and what evolved here. Everything he learns about the life of the two musicians reaffirms that dynamic. Mitchell realizes as a young man that the piano is his destiny. The more he learns about it, the more he wants to learn about it. He wants to know what a piano is, and what has been done with it, and therefore what he can do with it—what he can say with the piano about his experience. He can say more if he knows what other people have done with piano keys, so there's everything possible to be learned. His whole life becomes a search for what will make him a better artist. The same is true for Willie Ruff. He goes wherever he needs to go to learn what he wants to know next: to Yale to study with Paul Hindemith, to Africa to study the drum language of the Pygmies, to St. Mark's church in Venice to listen for "a distant sound."

Zinsser stays focused on that double search. He goes down to Florida and Alabama, where Mitchell and Ruff grew up—which is a long way from his own hometown of New York. But he doesn't confuse what he finds with exotica. He never forgets that he's dealing with American character and how it gets shaped into art. Being a down-home boy myself, from Alabama, I feel a connection between Mitchell and Ruff's early years and my own early years as I describe them in my novel *Train Whistle Guitar.* The novel is about a little boy growing up on the outskirts of Mobile, listening to the guitar players and juke joint piano players and becoming a serious schoolboy. I was that schoolboy, developing literary and intellectual interests at an early age and going on to win scholarships, right through college. Mitchell and Ruff did it a different way. I did it through literature and they did it through music, but they achieved the same level of sophistication in their chosen métier. Their way was more improvisational—their first conservatory was an Air Force base in Ohio—but for all three of us it was the same picaresque fairy tale.

The similarity really hit me when Dwike Mitchell talks about how he was made to play the piano in the Baptist church when he was a small boy in Florida and how the minister would preach about how everyone would be damned and go to Hell. What he says is very close to what I say about Sunday mornings in *Train Whistle Guitar*: "The sermons used to be so full not only of ugly prophecies and warnings but also outright threats of divine vengeance on hypocrites that when people all around you began stomping and clapping and shouting you couldn't tell whether they were doing so because they were being visited by the Holy Ghost or because being grown folks and therefore accountable for their trespasses they were even more terrified of the dreadful wrath of God than you were (whose sins after all were still being charged against your parents)."

The point is that I feel a close personal identification with Zinsser's portrayal of Mitchell and Ruff, not just because I'm from the South, but because his book is an excellent natural history of the development of our sensibility as indigenous American artists. The book has nothing to do with race relations as such. Zinsser has an omni-American sensibility—it's neither white nor black. That sensibility is also at the heart of my work. I never think of myself as an "African-American." As Willie Ruff says to the old monsignor in St. Mark's church, it's a word I don't use.

Mitchell & Ruff is the literary equivalent of a jazz piece. It's composed, it has themes, and it develops those themes. Zinsser's prose tries to get as close as possible to the rhythms these two men use in their music. To me the ur-father of jazz in prose is Ernest Hemingway. Hemingway swings; his prose is as precise as it is lyrical. What he did is exactly what Count Basie thought you should do when you're playing music: Don't use frills or curlicues; get a good solid rhythm, make it swing. That's what Zinsser does. He tells his story with a directness and a simplicity that add up to the kind of elegance that the higher physicists admire.

Zinsser sees Mitchell and Ruff just about as I would see them. That impressed me, because he's a Yankee, working in a context he's not as intimate with as I am. Ordinarily when people enter an unfamiliar situation there are two common reactions. One is insecurity, which results in xenophobia: fear, or hostility, or condescension. The other is to see the situation as exotic, or weird, or dangerous, and to find it fascinating—as all those people did who used to go slumming in Harlem. But here's a man who identifies with Mitchell and Ruff because their story is universal and he's sensitive to the local conventions that an outsider needs to penetrate in order to tell that story. He doesn't allow anything to get in the way of the relationship—the kinship—of these two men from the South.

So what you've got in *Mitchell & Ruff* is not only a profile of two people but, in effect, a profile of three people: Dwike Mitchell and Willie Ruff and William Zinsser. I'm completely comfortable with Zinsser's take on the down-home neighborhood he visited. He never got deflected from what he wrote this book to find out: how these two men forged their American identity as artists. It pleases me that he chose to move into this context and that he wrote about it so well.

"I know the *world* that these sounds come out of!"

Interview with Paul Devlin

On August 17, 2006, Albert Murray and I recorded the following conversation. This was around the time I had finished listening to all of the tapes of his interviews with Jo Jones and had begun transcribing them into what became Rifftide. *I was to enter the PhD program in English at Stony Brook University in two weeks, and I wanted to get a start on what would become* Rifftide *prior to the start of the semester.*

By this time Murray could not walk on his own. He spent his days in a hospital bed in his living room, though his outstanding regular nurses, Judy Lafitte and Neville Jones, would often lift him into a wheelchair so that he could sit at the kitchen table for meals and newspaper reading. This had been the situation since the previous year, after a variety of severe health problems caused him to spend most of July and August 2005 in the hospital. Murray's physical activity was curtailed but his mind was still sharp, but at age ninety, time was taking its toll. His speech was generally at a low volume and the bewildering speed of his discourse had slowed to a more conventional pace. Sometimes, after a long warm-up period, he would be talking as fast as his old rapid-fire self and at a standard volume, but at ninety he was understandably not as spry as he had been at eighty-eight, as he was in constant pain and was deprived of his previously busy social and intellectual life. It didn't help that his hearing was almost gone, and a visitor virtually had to shout to communicate. That made transcribing this interview a bit tricky, as I was constantly adjusting the volume to hear Murray and then to not hear myself shout.

Sometimes it took a long time to build into a conversation. It would annoy me when someone would tell me they had just visited

Murray and he was "out of it" or "nonresponsive." I wondered if the person actually tried to talk to him or just popped in for five minutes and made certain assumptions. Those who visited regularly knew that he needed time to adjust to company. He often did not seem like his old self at first, but it did not take long before it seemed as if nothing had changed. What bothered me most was when someone would say "I hear Murray is out of it" when I had just visited him and had a great conversation. During that summer of 2006 I made several evening visits with Michael James (discussed elsewhere in this volume). Mike passed away suddenly the following year. Mike felt that we needed to call and talk to Murray as much as we could in order to keep his mind active. Mike was a conscientious visitor and caller.

A day or so after Barack Obama was elected in 2008, I visited Murray along with the writer Sidney Offit (one of Murray's oldest friends—we would visit together several times a year). Earlier that morning David Remnick, editor of the New Yorker, *had called Murray to try to get his take on the magnitude of what had happened in the election, for possible inclusion in an article (so the nurse told us). Remnick and Murray had been friendly in the 1990s. Between Murray's hearing and whatever else, the conversation with Remnick didn't amount to anything. An hour or two later Murray was presciently telling me and Mr. Offit that "although they're going to try to paint Obama as very liberal, he's really not that liberal." I wish that insight had made it into the* New Yorker.

Now that my visits with Murray did not include errands anymore, it was logistically easier to bring visitors. I brought various professors (none from institutions where I was a student or teacher), along with personal friends and family, over the years. One of the last new visitors I brought, in 2012, was the writer and professor Aryeh Tepper.

Often Murray would be thinking about a topic before you got there and then would want to talk to you about it. This seems to have been the case with his riff below on the composer and music critic Virgil Thomson. You never knew what he'd want to talk about. I recall that he gave me and Michael James an unexpected lesson on Walt Whitman. On another occasion he told me all about Sigrid Undset, a Norwegian writer who won the Nobel Prize for Literature in 1928.

Often his discourses in this period would include riffs on the

earliest days of humanity. He was often thinking about the technolo-
gies and procedures of hunter-gatherers. His explanation below about
how fishing and trapping are forms of play is representative of this
direction of his thinking. I recall that Sidney Offit and I were dazzled,
on a 2010 visit, by Murray's impromptu yet scholarly history of the
bow and arrow and its various iterations in different societies. In his
precarious physical state, his mind turned to survival technology. On
another occasion Murray gave me the fascinating volume Firearms,
Traps, and Tools of the Mountain Men *by Carl P. Russell (1967).*
From his insights into the origins of play—and thus the origins of
humanity—he would make huge leaps of extrapolation and observa-
tion, such as that the rise in popularity of American football correlates
to the growth of the power of the United States (as he notes below).
But more often, his discourse on the fundamentals of play would set
up a discussion of jazz.

ALBERT MURRAY: There's a very good book I have somewhere. Look up
there where you see the theater books. Three shelves down from the
top. Do you see books on "play"? What are they?

PAUL DEVLIN: *Man, Play, and Games. The Seven Lively Arts. Lore and*
Language of School Children. Children's Games in Street and Play-
ground. Myth and Ritual in Dance, Game, and Rhyme. Free Play.
Homo Ludens.

AM: *Homo Ludens*! Yeah! Man the player. Pull that down. These are
anthropological insights into how culture is made. I can drop Jo into
the middle of all this. You can always do that when you're dealing
with the fundamentals of something in an anthropological context.
All those books in that section of my collection are on games: for-
malization of survival techniques. When you start playing with those
ideas like that, then you'll know why Negroes swing! You see what
I'm saying?

PD: Yeah. And specifically in the context of Jo—

AM: We try to deal with him in very broad, philosophical terms. Jo,
with all that talk and so forth, is really onto something. There was
another guy—we became friends—he could go back and show you

philosophically, that play is always work. Work-and-play. Play-for-food—like fishing, trapping, all that. When you go fishing and trapping you find that these are stylized games. *Homo Ludens*—this is probably the most popular of this kind of study. When you think of man the player, you see the element of play in all human being. In the element of play you also find the aesthetic element. In some of the art forms it's still there—you play music, you play a ballgame. But it's also play when you're hunting. You're getting it in chasing. The chase! Those are some expensive guns out there. These are types of equipment for consciousness. Basic anthropological technology for survival. In the end, it's all got an aesthetic quality. It makes it enjoyable. See, you still have this shit in football. You've got to take this precious thing and put it in the other end between those poles down there. It's interesting that Americans came up with the game and they called it football—you've got to run it, throw it, whatnot. As you see football getting bigger and bigger, Americans feel more natural because of their conception of exerting power or creating order. You learn it as a kid. It's never really hidden. These are all lessons about life. Gotta get that thing across that line! Do you remember Caillois's four types of play? What are they?

PD: Competition, chance, mimicry, and vertigo?

AM: Vertigo—that's gettin' high or dizzy, like a seesaw.

PD: Then there's Alfred Hitchcock's *Vertigo.*

AM: Oh, yeah. It's Christmas? No, *Vertigo,* that's out west. There's that tree in Northern California?

PD: In one scene they go out to the Redwood forest. Jimmy Stewart and Kim Novak.

AM: That's right. Anyway, there was a guy—a composer. Composer/scholar. He was from Kansas.

PD: Samuel Barber?

AM: No, no. He was a great critic.

PD: Virgil Thomson?

AM: Yeah! Virgil Thomson. He lived down in the Village. There's that

hotel down there [the Chelsea Hotel]. That stuff used to be heavy
on that side. Real cultural depth over on that side. You'd go down
the street and see the jazz clubs. If you look over to your right they
have the hotels and so forth going back to the turn of the century.
The Village as an art community—it developed, and you got characters and actresses and a lot of pop art. When I was in college it was
still thought of in terms of Edna St. Vincent Millay—modern poetry.
Dancers and composers, in that area about a block from the Village
Vanguard. But Thomson did some good writing. You'll want to look
at it sometime.

PD: I will.

AM: I met all these guys. I met them around time I was hanging out
with, you know, the composers society. I've been down to Virgil
Thomson's apartment. Maurice Grosser—he was an Alabama guy.
He used to live with Virgil Thomson. He was a painter. I guess I was
a board member of the [American] Composers Orchestra.[1] Some of
my friends, they're still around, they're older Park Avenue people
who were financing serious types of American music—out of a European background—and using American material. But then they got
prejudiced against jazz! And the place of jazz. Some of them are still
around. Some of the younger composers, they like jazz. But they also
take it as a challenge that some of the other modern composers didn't.
The syncopation and the swing and so forth—they're not very good
at it. But a lot of the stuff that jazz musicians do comes from the spirituals, comes from the blues, stuff like that. But this stuff that Jo and
these guys were doing—that's still a puzzle to them. It's like abstract
art of any kind. It's a challenge of improvisation. You want a certain
evolution of the perception of the music by other Americans, because
it never was just a folk music. Anywhere they went people liked it, no
matter what their own music was. The French made it sacred *immediately*. The British didn't fight it as not being British.

PD: Did Jo play tennis with the king of Denmark or somebody? Mike
told me something like that.

AM: The king of Denmark? Well, Jo would play with anybody. But
jazz really got to sophisticated Europeans. There really is a lot of fuel
for elegance in America. Yeah, Jo and these guys, you know—they

had ambition and imagination derived from what they learned in school, which was impressive once a guy went over and saw all that shit, they were ready to celebrate it.

PD: I was thinking about a way to arrange the Jo Jones material. I was thinking of arranging it with subject headings, in a way similar to *Music Is My Mistress* [Duke Ellington's memoir].

AM: Duke? I don't know. I didn't get moved by the *composition* and so forth. He had more stuff than he could handle.[2]

PD: I mean, we can take various topics from various tapes and put them together. Jo jumps from one topic to another. One section could be Jo Jones on literature. Another could be Jo Jones on drummers—Louie Bellson, for instance. Then, Jo on Basie, Jo on Ellington. There isn't one coherent narrative.

AM: That sounds OK to me. Subject matter. One day he'd feel like talking about this, the next he'd feel like talking about that. In some of your favorite books, you're not thinking about the narrative. You're thinking about certain passages. Then you can go into how it's related to other parts of the book if you want to. But you can fit it into a context that's autobiographical or historical.

PD: Do you have any other ideas on how to arrange the material?

AM: I experienced his career once it hit the headlines. And that was in Kansas City with Count Basie. You could then go back the other way and look for where he came from. Birmingham and whatnot.

PD: Omaha.

AM: Yeah, he mentioned he went out there. He was always on the freight trains. Going outside, carrying his drums with him—putting them in a tree! [laughter]

PD: Jo loved *Gem of the Prairie* [book by Herbert Asbury].

AM: Chicago. Yeah. I have that up there. In the world of entertainment, they got to know a lot of outlaws, gangsters, people like that. Especially in the Prohibition Era, especially out in Chicago—they'd bring the stuff in from Canada and so forth. When you get into a product of that such as the music, then you can understand it better when you get the whole thing that surrounded it. It'll tell you something about the public personality. It was a part of that milieu. This is background stuff. Once you've read that kind of stuff and you see Jo coming into it—the skyscrapers and stuff are here—and [you can see how] they're responding to it, they know it's here. It's influencing what they're doing and how they feel about the type of range their audience might include. So, you end up talking like Jo Jones! [imitates Jo Jones's voice] "I'm not just a natural artist, I'm giving some thought to this! Some *thought* and some *research*. I know the *world* that these sounds come out of!" That kind of thing. There's an element of play in art, but there's an element of play in everything. He had a feeling for it.

PD: He understood this anthropological dimension.

AM: Oh, no question about it! I think all successful artists do that. They don't have to be able to objectively define what they do, it's just that certain things make them emphasize certain aspects of their experience. Some people get status relating it to something else. If something relates to the opera or something like that. Sonny Greer used to say "I'll be right out, I gotta finish putting on my opera clothes." Sonny Greer and Jo—they were very humorous guys. And *tough* guys. You knew they knew the gangsters and so forth. And yet there's all that delicate stuff they did with those sticks, you know. And all the subtle stuff they did with the cymbals and various things. The jazz musician is a very interesting vehicle for studying Americana.

PD: Like a prism.

AM: Right. You put it in these larger contexts.

PD: And Sonny Greer brought Duke to New York.

AM: He brought Duke to New York?

PD: That's what I read, because he was from New Jersey—

AM: I'd have to think about it. Baltimore and New York stride players—that's what Duke knew about. In Baltimore and New York were the great piano players.

PD: Eubie Blake in Baltimore.

AM: Yeah! They were just loaded with stride piano players. They were all over New York, before jazz. It was Baltimore, New York, and New Jersey.

PD: Willie "The Lion" from Newark.

AM: They had all those German teachers and so forth. When you came into New York—those guys were all around the wall, man. Pittsburgh was another one. Earl Hines. Billy Strayhorn! Mary Lou Williams. The Baltimore guys hauled off and claimed it, but Pittsburgh and New York, boy. It depends on where these borderline and Southern Negroes went. If you were from Mobile you went to Pittsburgh, maybe Philadelphia, and Detroit was straight up the L&N [Louisville and Nashville Railroad]. Chicago—straight up the L&N. Georgia and Florida—they went up the Atlantic seaboard. From Alabama and whatnot they took the Pan-American down. You find many Negroes from Mobile in California. Maybe some in Texas, but they mostly went out to the coast.

PD: To change topics for a minute, and because this relates to Jo, you told me once when you were on summer vacations from Tuskegee that you'd pick cotton to earn extra money.[3]

AM: No. I didn't pick cotton every summer.

PD: Or was it between high school and college? That one summer?

AM: Yeah. That was down the Bay—an area of Mobile called "Down the Bay." Bay-side.

PD: Your theory behind it was not just that it was a summer job but a reenactment of a heroic experience.

AM: Yeah, it was like that. But I needed some money! I had scholarships, but I needed carfare.

PD: You told me one time it was something the slaves had done, so you wanted to do it.

AM: Oh, yeah, I was thinking romantically of the Negro past. By this time we were reenacting the whole business—what great-grandpa did. You didn't reject it or feel sad. I thought it was heroic!

PD: How did it feel as work? Was it hard labor?

AM: No. Hell, I was Clark Gable by that time! Shit. I wasn't Gary Cooper—but he was all right. I might be George Raft from time to time—*'cause he walked like us!* Clark Gable didn't walk like us. He had his own walk, but that was a white walk we could do, just like some of the military walks. But George Raft walked like us.

PD: I wonder how that ever came about.

AM: He liked to dance! He'd go to dance in Harlem—that's where you were gonna dance. If you're gonna be there with everybody else dancin', you've got to dance like the kids in Harlem. They always conceded that.

PD: Who were some of your favorite actors of the thirties?

AM: Clark Gable was the man. He was the one I most identified with. Name some others.

PD: Cary Grant?

AM: Yeah, I liked him. He was sophisticated. A city boy, see. Gable was anything—he could be the sharpest guy on the boulevard.

PD: How about Errol Flynn?

AM: Errol Flynn was OK, but he was a lighter-weight. I mean, I could see through him. I didn't like Franchot Tone. The other guys you didn't want to be all the way, you could still be them. Like—William Powell! People liked him!

PD: When did you first meet Jo?

AM: I don't know.

PD: It had to be by the fifties, because of that letter in *Trading Twelves*. You must've known him pretty well by '54 or '55.

AM: Oh, yeah!

PD: Do you recall when you first became acquainted with him?

AM: At Tuskegee. Some of the Tuskegee aristocrats—he knew them. The Drivers, a family at Tuskegee, he knew them. He was showing the young guys in the band what Booker Washington did, what George Washington Carver did. [imitates Jo Jones voice] "Hey, hey, boy—go

Count Basie (center) *and Jimmy Rushing*
(right) *hanging out at Newport, circa 1962.*

Charles Mingus at Newport.

Duke Ellington voicing Sam Woodyard's drums.

John Lewis
at piano and
Percy Heath
of the Modern
Jazz Quartet,
Hollywood,
California,
circa 1960.

Milt Jackson
on vibes and
Connie Kay,
Modern Jazz
Quartet,
Hollywood.

Ellington and Strayhorn strike up the band.

Billy Strayhorn works on a score.

Count and Catherine Basie share a laugh, late 1970s.

Ray Nance, trumpeter, vocalist, and violinist with Ellington.

Juan Tizol, longtime Ellington trombonist.

Three of Ellington's great saxophonists, left to right: Johnny Hodges, Russell Procope, and Harry Carney.

Ellington and Strayhorn look over a score in the control room.

Duke Ellington talking with his son Mercer
(a trumpeter, arranger, and composer).

Frank Foster (left) and Jo Jones (right), in foreground, in conversation at Newport. Sweets Edison, Duke Ellington, and Jimmy Rushing, left to right in background.

Ellington in the studio.

down there and look at that. Dr. Carver was a genius!" It was during the days of Sugar Ray Robinson. Sugar Ray was traveling with a band, and I was taking Sugar Ray around Tuskegee [circa 1950].

PD: What was Jo doing at Tuskegee?
AM: He was traveling with a band!

PD: And they played a gig at Tuskegee?
AM: Or, they stopped for the hotel! You're traveling in the South—which was mostly segregated—and you stop on a campus, you'd get first-rate service, first-rate universal taste in food. And Negro colleges love jazz! They may have those choirs and so forth, but they're very serious about jazz. They'd have some type of jazz band but they usually couldn't make it. I never heard nobody talk about a Morehouse jazz band, or a Fisk—welllllll . . .

PD and **AM** simultaneously: Jimmie Lunceford! [laughter]
AM: Jimmie Lunceford! He cleaned them up.

PD: Was he the only one who did that on that level?
AM: There were one or two others.

PD: Wasn't Erskine Hawkins the leader of a college band?
AM: OH, YEAH! BAMA STATE! Bama State was *strictly big league.*

PD: So, when you first met Jo, he was with Basie, and they were stopping at Tuskegee?
AM: No, he was with Sugar Ray Robinson and another band.

PD: Who was the leader?
AM: I can't remember. So many bands came through. Cootie Williams came through a number of times. And the other guy, the singer.

PD: Billy Eckstine?
AM: Yeah, he came, but another guy.

PD: Jimmy Rushing?
AM: "Straighten Up and Fly Right."

PD: Oh, Nat King Cole.

AM: Nobody was hotter than he was. He was carrying *another band* with him. They stayed at our house. Mozelle cooked breakfast— hot Alabama biscuits. Alabama Sunday morning biscuits. Nat King Cole—he was an Alabama boy. I saw him briefly among the Holly- wood and Los Angeles musicians. By this time he was so big I didn't get a chance to get near. But then I knew a bunch of key Los Angeles musicians, like Buddy Collette. You know that name? He was my closest friend.

PD: He was your closest friend when you were in LA?

AM: My closest *local* friend. He and some of the Ellington guys did a [version of] "Perdido." That long "Perdido"? [scats opening of that version of "Perdido"]

PD: Like the late-fifties arrangement of "Perdido" that was played in the Paris concert?

AM: Yeah. I had just come from Morocco. Of course, all those records were being flown to me. When I got to Hollywood, Long Beach, and so forth, for my next station from Casablanca, I had all this stuff. I had seen Mingus at the Village Vanguard. I had gotten "Fables of Faubus." Guys were flying them over—French jazz buffs, radio peo- ple, and so forth came by the consulate. The embassy is in the capi- tal, but Casablanca was the biggest city. The embassy was in Rabat, which was the capital. They invited me to give talk at the consulate. This was in Casablanca, which was *the* city.

PD: The American consulate in Casablanca? And you gave a lecture on jazz?

AM: I gave a series! Because they're French! They had write-ups in the paper. A French guy found his way to my house—on the base! [Re- cords] that were hard to get elsewhere—you could find them at our house. I used to have parties. Somebody would call up, bring around the wine. And we used to play records. "Ah, Cap-i-taine Murr-ay, est- ce que vous avez le dernier disque de Sarah Vaug-han?" You heard the latest from Sarah Vaughan? It was almost like *The Albert Murray Jazz Club*! We had a lot of wine and the latest records from the United

States. The first thing I did when I got back to New York was see Mingus at the Vanguard. I knew some Arabs too.

PD: Were these westernized Arab intellectuals? Like, French-speaking jazz fans?

AM: A few. I don't remember why the Arabs came to visit. But I was invited to the home of rich French Moroccans who had more jazz records than any Negro I ever saw. Then, some local Arab sheiks invited me to their house!

PD: What was that like?

AM: Well, he'd invite you into the living room, and you'd sit down and talk. He could speak English. You'd see his wives passing by.

PD: Like, a harem?

AM: Well, it was a family. He was some type of high official. He wanted me to visit, so I brought some records.

Notes

1. Murray was on the board of directors of the American Composers Orchestra from 1986 to 1989. He was friends with the orchestra's cofounder, Francis Thorne. Surviving letters suggest that Murray was an active board member and worked closely with Thorne on certain projects. It is unclear when the major donors to the ACO might have turned "against jazz," but the ACO performed at Jazz at Lincoln Center's fall fund-raising gala in 2006.

2. Murray's review of Ellington's *Music Is My Mistress* originally appeared in the *Village Voice* in 1976. It is included in his essay collection *The Blue Devils of Nada*.

3. Murray addresses this topic in detail in his Smithsonian Jazz Oral History Interview Project with Robert G. O'Meally, but not in the excerpt of that interview included in this book.

"Flexibility, the art of adapting, and the necessity of continuous creation"

A Talk on Jazz, Delivered in Morocco

From 1955 to 1958, Captain Murray was stationed at Nouasseur Air Base in Morocco by the U.S. Air Force. He was invited by the U.S. Information Service to give talks on jazz in 1956 and 1958, with the goal of improving relations between the U.S. military and local intellectuals. Murray gave several presentations, in French, at the U.S. embassy in Rabat, the Maison d'Amérique in Casablanca, and elsewhere. Notices for these talks were printed in French and Arabic. One of his presentations attracted more than one hundred people. There was more to these talks than what survives here, such as his commentary on various records after he played them. These talks were his first extended public statements on jazz and were met with critical enthusiasm. He received several good reviews in the local French-language press. He received glowing letters of commendation from U.S. diplomats and high-ranking military officers who believed the talks achieved their objective. This piece, all that survives of the talks, reflects the clarity and consistency also revealed in his letters to Ralph Ellison from these years, published in Trading Twelves: The Selected Letters of Ralph Ellison and Albert Murray *(2000). At the end of the preceding interview, Murray discusses his time in Morocco and his relationship with its community of jazz listeners.*

A Talk on Jazz

Translated from the French by Lauren Walsh

During our previous meeting, I spoke of some features of the form of expression of black Americans, of their sermons, prayers, spirituals, and gospel and blues songs. These are the fundamental elements of music that interest us.

Jazz is the ancestral form of expression of the black American. It is intimately linked to his religious sentiments and includes his folk-loric expression as well as his modern development. In point of fact, jazz is, without doubt, the richest and most significant form of artistic expression of the black American sensibility that we have in the United States.

Much has been written on African antecedents of jazz, a most interesting question, but it is important to note that jazz is the creation of the <u>black American</u> only, that is to say, *l'Américain d'Afrique.*[1] Africans in Europe do not play jazz, nor do Africans in Latin America; and jazz in Africa does not exist, with the exception of Lionel or Armstrong, when they come to Tangier, Casablanca, or Marrakesh.

Tonight I am going to play records that represent, in my opinion, the most eminent and remarkable accomplishments that jazz music has ever achieved.

After hearing each disc, I'd like your respective opinions on what you just heard. All questions or discussions will be welcome and could only be beneficial.

In particular, there are three aspects of this music that I would like to stress:

1. It represents the principal form of artistic expression of the black American. As such, it personifies almost all aspects of black life in the United States. (At the same time, we must add that this music exists not only as the intimate and personal expression of black life, but that it is meaningful and accessible to any individual in the world.) It is, moreover, the distinctive feature of all art to be meaningful at any time and any place.
2. In addition, this music represents life in the United States in our time. It is also a product of American society. It provides us a picture of the fundamental conditions of life in America. In this music, you will not find the "happy endings" of Hollywood films or the artificial sentiments displayed in best-selling novels. You will only find simple feelings, deeply real, such as: sadness, melancholy (the blues), despair, or exuberant happiness, which is nothing more than a reaction against this despair. In a word, you

have the portrait of the standard life of the average American.

3. The freedom of expression of black musicians and their improvisations are a lesson they offer to human beings, in order to help them adapt to the exigencies of modern life.

The principles of morality that can be drawn from this music are, in short: flexibility, the art of adapting, and the necessity of continuous creation in a perpetually oppressive and unstable world.

That is why this music helps us to free ourselves from conformity, which is just a form of stagnation and snobbery, thus always guiding us toward the future.

A Note on This Translation

I endeavored to produce a closely literal translation from the French but also to render this talk in graceful, contemporary English. Murray seemed comfortable writing in French, and even editing his own writing. In fact, the document from which this translation was performed contains Murray's handwritten changes, neatly inserted alongside the typed text of this talk. Each of those changes is reflected in this translation. Likewise, the phrase underlined here (black American) is also underlined in the original French.

—Lauren Walsh, New York University

Note

1. In keeping with the rest of Murray's oeuvre, this term appears in the French in order to obviate any association with the English-language term "African American," not current in the 1950s and, later, an expression that Murray often criticized (for instance, in this book, see pp. 136, 171).—Ed.

"We really integrated Fifty-second Street"
Interview with John Hammond

John Hammond is one of the most important figures in the history of American music. He is credited with launching the careers of Count Basie, Benny Goodman, Billie Holiday, Bob Dylan, Aretha Franklin, and Bruce Springsteen among others. In addition to being a talent scout extraordinaire, Hammond was a record company executive and was instrumental in desegregating the music industry. Hammond and Murray were friends and members of the same midtown club, where they often had lunch together. Here Murray interviews Hammond for Good Morning Blues. *The venue of the interview is unknown.*

In 1936 Hammond heard Basie broadcasting from Kansas City and wanted to promote the band nationally. That fall he brought the band from Kansas City to New York. After making some records in Chicago and a shaky performance in New York in December 1936, the band went on tour, during and after which numerous improvements were made that set the band on its way to stratospheric success from 1937 through the mid-1940s. One of the first stops, in February 1937, was the Chatterbox Club in the William Penn Hotel, a high-end hotel in Pittsburgh. Jo Jones recounts this in Rifftide *and also discusses Hammond elsewhere in that book.*

In this interview Hammond tells Murray about some trouble Jones had. In Pittsburgh, during the band's residency at the Chatterbox, Jones assaulted a police officer and was committed to the Mayview Asylum for the Criminally Insane. Hammond, a great-great-grandson of Cornelius Vanderbilt, was born at the top of high society, but in his own right he was a shrewd businessman and a savvy impresario. Somehow he secured Jones's release from Mayview and arranged for his care by Dr. Abraham Clinko in New York. Whether or not Jones had psychiatric problems has been a subject of debate.

Many who knew him say it was obvious that he did, but he garnered an outstanding record in the U.S. Army from 1944 to 1946. The army accepted him in spite of any preexisting medical record and Jones did well there. (Jones, who had a remarkable sense of humor, insisted to Murray that the real reason he was committed to Mayview was because he claimed a black band was playing in the segregated William Penn Hotel.)

This could not have been the only conversation between Murray and Hammond about Basie et al., but it seems to have been the only one that Murray taped. Other topics of interest here include the desegregation of Fifty-second Street jazz clubs, Gene Krupa, and the aftermath of the Basie–Benny Goodman battle, which resulted in Goodman (later, Hammond's brother-in-law) hiring Mary Lou Williams. N.B.—for the story of how Murray came by the fact that Claude "Fiddler" Williams was still with the Basie band in Pittsburgh, see the Foreword to this book by Gary Giddins.

ALBERT MURRAY: What sort of led up to you and Willard—

JOHN HAMMOND: Well, Willard Alexander had, of course, put Basie into a couple of spots, like the William Penn Hotel, which was almost as great a disaster for Basie as the Roosevelt Grill was for Benny Goodman—they were used to Lombardo-type bands in both places. I can remember, of course, the opening night at the William Penn Hotel. I was sitting next to Harold Cohen of the *Pittsburgh Post-Gazette*. He was also the *Variety* correspondent for Pittsburgh. Harold looked at me when he heard Basie's first set and Harold said, "John, this is never going to go in Pittsburgh!" [laughter]

AM: [laughter]

JH: Like all downtown spots in Pittsburgh, it was strictly segregated. It was an all-white and *very* square audience. The band was playing beautifully. And in that place you could tell all the faults of the band. There was Joe Keyes, playing first trumpet; drunk most of the time and flat all the time. There was Caughey Roberts, who looked very disagreeable. At the William Penn Hotel three terribly important changes were made in the band. In the first place, Ed Lewis came back as first trumpet. Ed I'd heard when he was with Harlan

Leonard's band out in Kansas City. A young, very good-looking saxophone player from Ohio came in to replace Caughey Roberts, and that of course was Earle Warren. And who was the other? Harry Edison came into the band.

AM: Harry came later. The other new guy at this time was Freddie Green. He played a little bit with them there, right?

JH: No, he had joined the band in [the] Roseland [Ballroom in New York City].

AM: But don't you remember, John, that "Fiddler" was still with the band in Pittsburgh?

JH: I didn't realize that!

AM: In the broadcasts he's got a couple of solos.

JH: I didn't remember that!

AM: In the air shots. Freddie said he went with the band but was up in his room half the time and he'd come down and play around with them. "Fiddler"—they must have made the final change, he must have left when you went back to New York.

JH: I had to leave Pittsburgh after the opening night. I drove to Pittsburgh. I was working for the William Esty advertising agency at the time. I didn't go back to Pittsburgh for about two weeks, I guess, and that was when I heard that Jo Jones was put in Mayview.

AM: Would you remember who the substitute for Jo was when Jo was in the hospital?

JH: I think it was Harold Austin.

AM: He hadn't been a guy who had been with Fats?

JH: Harold was a journeyman drummer. He'd been a great friend of Bobby Moore's.

AM: Ah, so that would get him in there.

JH: We were on the subject of the Famous Door. I'll never forget Willard came to me and said, "You know, John, we have a chance to put—it's a crazy idea!—we have a chance to put Basie into a room which has got a wire." As a matter of fact it has two wires: it has CBS and WOR. WOR was not a network but it was so powerful it was as a good as a network. It was heard all over the country: it was a clear-channel fifty-thousand-watt station. But he said, "There's only one problem: we don't have air conditioning." The summer was coming on and it was gonna be murder in this tiny, smoky room with no air conditioning. I remember putting up dough, but I got it back. I remember striking a deal with Al Felchen and Jerry Brooks, who were the two guys that owned the club. I said to them that I would do this but I wanted to be sure that black people would be welcomed as customers at the Famous Door—which they had not been! Not in any of the clubs on Fifty-second Street. So, Jerry Brooks was resisting this. However, Al Felchen, who was a great big guy, said, "You know, John, my brother is the business manager of the *Daily Worker*." I don't think I put that in my book. I said, "I'm glad I have a sympathetic ear here!" We really broke—we really integrated Fifty-second Street. The band by this time did have Sweets [Harry Edison]. It had both Herschel and Lester and it had Earle Warren. As I recall, Helen Humes was singing with the band too.

AM: Right! She'd come in that spring, before they went on that long swing back out to Oklahoma City and down into Texas.

JH: The band was just really wonderful. I have a lot of air checks of the band from the Famous Door.

AM: I heard a few of those that were issued. But you have more than that?

JH: Oh, I have more than that!

AM: Oh, Jesus!

JH: I sold them all to Bob Altshuler at CBS [CBS Records]. He's got my whole record collection. You can hear any of those that you want to.

AM: I wish Basie could hear them again.

JH: He would love it! Basie was playing a lot of piano. There was a good piano at the Famous Door—we got a Steinway in there.

AM: He said when they went out of there the next year, they let him buy that piano.

JH: I didn't know that. That's wonderful.

AM: Do you have any pictures of the Famous Door?
JH: No. Frank Driggs has them all.

AM: There's a nice one where Lester is snapping his fingers and Herschel is playing.
JH: Yeah, that's right. That was the greatest band that had ever been! Because the rhythm section was *cooking at all times*. This was before Walter Page had fallen off the bandstand in front of Eleanor Roosevelt in Washington. That's why he left the band.

AM: Oh yeah?
JH: The stage of the Lincoln Theater.

AM: Do you remember any other little stories or anecdotes or things Basie should remember about things that happened in the Famous Door?
JH: Well, Basie was there two times.

AM: He was there from the tenth of July through the middle of November [1938] for the first time.
JH: He didn't leave for a week or anything?

AM: He might have done a date. There was that Martin Block thing at Randall's Island.
JH: Oh, yes. I don't think I went.

AM: A jazz festival, swing festival?
JH: The problem about Randall's Island was a terrible echo. You know what it's like in Yankee Stadium or Shea Stadium—off the concrete the sound would bounce about three times. You couldn't really hear a band—the speaker systems defeated a band.

AM: They went out and did that one afternoon but they were solid in the Famous Door until November. That's when they did the recordings of "Shorty George," "Panassie Stomp," and Helen did the thing. When they came out, that Sunday, they went up to the Savoy and played a Sunday dance. Then they went over to the Paramount in

Newark. Then the following week they had the Paramount in Times Square.

JH: I went to both of those. It was a wonderful band. They looked great! Jo Jones was a wonderful drummer and the most swinging drummer in the business. I was always so pleased, you know, that we got Jo out of Mayview there. He was back in the band, you know, within two weeks!

AM: He was swinging like hell! Basie was talking how Jo was swinging at the Apollo and you were shocked—

JH: It was incredible! I was flabbergasted! Dr. Cheshire and Dr. Arthur Clinko were the two psychiatrists that took care of Jo. Clinko became the biggest psychiatrist in Hollywood later. But he was a musician! And he knew all about musicians' neuroses. Cheshire didn't know. But Clinko was so impressed that Gene Krupa would come up and practice on the drum pads with Jo *every day*. Gene was a saint. And Gene really respected Jo too. *Really did.*

AM: He did a critical and appreciative article in *Metronome* [in 1938] on Jo Jones's drumming. He said *this is a master.* He said I was fortunate enough to catch this band at the Reno [club in Kansas City, before they were famous]. I predicted that it would go far, but so much for my business as an oracle, because what I was predicting wasn't anything as great as what this really is!

JH: That's wonderful. That's typical of Gene. He was such a lovely guy.

AM: He said I want all you guys to go up there and take lessons, because I'm at the Famous Door every time I get a chance.

JH: Gene left Benny's band right after the Carnegie Hall concert. He was fired at the Earle Theater in Philadelphia.

AM: That would be January of 1938.

JH: January or early February.

AM: But the concert was in January because that was the time of the Chick Webb battle.

JH: Exactly, yeah.

AM: They were running the feuds in the magazines about him, which I read all through. After the Apollo, Basie went down into Baltimore and Washington. Then they advertised a battle of bands with Benny Goodman in Newark.

JH: I don't remember where it was in Newark.

AM: At the Armory.

JH: I'm sure I was there.

AM: I'm sure you were. Because Willard was managing them both and you were involved with them both. It really wasn't a gloves-off battle I don't think because Benny was helping to promote—

JH: Basie, no question about it.

AM: What was the nature of the night of music? They were not deliberately pulling punches, but it wasn't tooth and nail?

JH: It was very competitive. Much more so than Basie thought. But at the same time, I know Basie took charge. Benny would have a kind of showmanship that Basie's band didn't have at that time.

AM: Basie would say that was rough; after all, Benny had Teddy [Wilson], he had Lionel. Who else did he have?

JH: He had Krupa. Harry James.

AM: Charlie Christian?

JH: Charlie Christian didn't come until 1939. He had Ziggy Elman, he had Harry James. He had Gordon Griffin, who was the best of all the three trumpet players, I thought. He had Red Ballard. After Basie, in Newark, Benny decided he needed some new charts and he got Mary Lou Williams to write for the band.

AM: Ah, some Kansas City–oriented stuff.

JH: And Mary Lou was on the record Benny made, too. On Benny's record of "One O'Clock Jump" it was Lionel Hampton on drums. Lionel Hampton, he really replaced Gene a lot on drums after Gene left, because Benny could never find a drummer that really satisfied him. Dave Tough came in briefly but Dave and Benny didn't get along very well. That's all you need as far as personnel is concerned. Benny was, of course, a monster star—the trio started in '35, the quartet started in '36. That lasted until Charlie Christian came into the band in October of '39. When Charlie Christian came in he did "Flying Home." It was Charlie's licks despite the fact that Lionel and Benny put their names on it. These were really Charlie's.

AM: He would just toss them off.

JH: I was there when they got "Flying Home" together for an Old Gold radio show. That was in '39. That's how we got Charlie in the band. Benny was allowed a couple of hundred bucks a week for a guest on the show, and that was Charlie!

AM: Wouldn't let him go after that!

JH: No, no!

"No better example of the ungaudy"
Biographical Sketch of Count Basie

This was possibly written for an encyclopedia in the early 1990s, but Murray asserted copyright over it in 2004 and included it in a Jazz at Lincoln Center Playbill. *Murray is one of the foremost authorities on Basie's life. What he created for Basie in* Good Morning Blues *is one of the most historically accurate and reliable jazz autobiographies. Murray researched it, according to Basie's wishes, as if it were more biography than autobiography. This plain sketch is far from one of Murray's most important or memorable works, but it is undoubtedly a solid outline of Basie's life. For a literary portrait of Basie, see Murray's poem "KC4/4(I)" in his volume of poetry,* Conjugations and Reiterations.

Count Basie, né William James Basie (August 21, 1904–April 26, 1984), pianist and jazz orchestra leader, was born in Red Bank, New Jersey. He was the second son of Harvey Lee Basie, a coachman and resort estate caretaker, and Lilly Ann Childs Basie, a part-time domestic worker and laundress. Both parents were natives of Chase, Virginia. Their first son, Leroy, several years older than William, died in childhood.

"I didn't start out to be a piano player," Basie states in his autobiography. "The first thing I really wanted to be was a drummer." But his earliest formal musical training was the piano lessons his mother required him to take. He turned to the keyboard only after he measured his best efforts on the drum against the casual expertise of Sonny Greer, another youngster from nearby Long Branch, New Jersey. Greer later became famous as a charter member of the incomparable Duke Ellington Orchestra.

Basie dropped out of school before finishing the ninth grade. Although he did not regard himself as having any special musical talent, he, along with Elmer Williams, a saxophone-playing pal, set out to seek his fortune in the world of entertainment. By that time, however, he had already become a journeyman stride (Eastern ragtime) piano player, having had several years of semiprofessional experience with pickup groups playing in dance halls and nightspots in the vicinity of Red Bank.

His first stop was Asbury Park, just beyond commuting distance. He and Williams then moved on to New York where they were hired by Katie Crippen, whose group was the olio in *Hippity Hop,* a big show on the Columbia burlesque wheel. As part of that group, he made two tours that took him as far west as Omaha and as far north as Montreal on a circuit that also included Philadelphia, Pittsburgh, Chicago, Detroit, St. Louis, and Omaha. He then returned to the Palace and Hurtig and Seaman's Apollo in New York.

At the end of his second tour on the Columbia circuit, Basie became a catch-as-catch-can piano player making the rounds in Harlem during the era of such stride-style keyboard masters as James P. Johnson, Luckey Roberts, Willie "The Lion" Smith, Willie Gant, and Fats Waller. It was from Fats that Basie wheedled free organ lessons in the Lincoln Theater on 135th Street where Waller was playing incidental music for the silent movies. Basie did not achieve any public reputation or show any exceptional promise during this time. However, he was competent enough to work with groups playing in Leroy's, a very exclusive club on Fifth Avenue and 135th Street. From time to time he also sat in at Small's Sugar Cane Club as a substitute pianist with a group led by trumpet man June Clark and the legendary Jimmy Harrison, an all-time great trombone player.

In late 1926 Basie again left New York, touring on the Theater Owners Booking Association (TOBA) circuit with Gonzelle White's Big Jazz Jamboree. This tour led to the crucial turning point in his career. One morning in Tulsa, during the summer of 1927, he heard Walter Page's Oklahoma City Blue Devils, a regional or territory dance band. He was so impressed that after sitting in with them, he decided to become a jazz musician. So, when Gonzelle White disbanded in Kansas City not long afterward, he stayed in town and became an organist at the Eblon Movie Theater. At the same time, he applied to and was accepted by the Blue Devils.

Basie toured with the Blue Devils for a number of months, but scarce bookings led to his return to the organ at the Eblon. By mid-1929 he had maneuvered his way into the prestigious Bennie Moten Orchestra as an assistant to staff arranger Eddie Durham (a guitar and trombone player and also an ex-member of the Blue Devils). Within weeks he was sitting in on piano for Moten, who began using him as a pianist on all subsequent records. Basie and Durham not only worked up arrangements that were strongly influenced by the Blue Devils, they also convinced Moten to hire such key Blue Devils as Hot Lips Page, Jimmy Rushing, and finally Walter Page, himself. Their most famous collaboration was "Moten Swing" (falsely attributed to Moten), the veritable anthem of high times in Kansas City.

After the death of Moten in April 1935, Basie became leader of a small group at the Reno Club in Kansas City. By January 1936, he was being featured in a radio program that so impressed a talent booster named John Hammond that Hammond encouraged Music Corporation of America, the highly prestigious New York booking agency, to take them on. By autumn, the group had expanded to a thirteen-piece all-purpose jazz band and was on its way to New York.

Between then and the end of 1938, tours on major entertainment circuits, nightly radio broadcasts during extended stands at the Famous Door (a club on Fifty-second Street), and such recordings as "One O'Clock Jump," "Good Morning Blues," "Sent for You Yesterday," "Swingin' the Blues," "Doggin' Around," "Blue and Sentimental," "Jumpin' at the Woodside," and "Do You Wanna Jump Children" brought Basie into the front rank of outstanding band leaders. He maintained this position for the remaining forty-six years of his life.

The key Basie sidemen for varying tenures between 1935 and 1949 were Jo Jones, drums; Walter Page, bass; Freddie Green, guitar; Herschel Evans, Lester Young, Buddy Tate, Don Byas, Illinois Jacquet, tenor saxophone; Earle Warren, Tab Smith, alto saxophone; Jack Washington, baritone saxophone; Buck Clayton, Harry Edison, trumpet; Eddie Durham, arranger, guitar, trombone; Dan Minor, Benny Morton, Dicky Wells, trombone, and Jimmy Rushing and Helen Humes, vocals.

Despite the temporary loss of such key sidemen as Jo Jones, Buck Clayton, Lester Young, and Jack Washington to Selective Service, the band maintained its high standing during World War II. It not only continued to play to sellout audiences in major showcase theaters across the country, it enjoyed extended and repeated engagements at the Blue Room in the Hotel Lincoln off Times Square and Café Society Uptown. It was also a great favorite at War Bond rallies, troop morale shows, broadcasts, and dances. It also made special recordings called V-Discs that were distributed to all theaters of operation.

When Lester Young was called to active military service, the list of his replacements on tenor saxophone included Don Byas, Lucky Thompson, and Illinois Jacquet. The key arrangers during that period included Buck Clayton, Jimmy Mundy, and Buster Harding. When Jo Jones was called into the service, his replacement on the drums was Shadow Wilson. Significant recordings from that period include "Avenue C," "Tippin' on the Q.T.," "San Jose," "B-Flat Blues," "Queer Street," "Rambo," and "The King."

Declining bookings forced Basie to disband in 1950. But after leading a sextet (occasionally expanded for theater dates) for a year, he assembled a second full band, which he kept going for thirty-three years. With this band he not only earned a future from concerts, festivals, dances, and recordings, he also came to be booked for tours of Europe and the Far East on a regular basis. He also played a command performance for the Queen of England and an inaugural ball for President John F. Kennedy.

Recordings most characteristic of this band include "Blee Blop Blues," "Basie English," "Sixteen Men Swinging," "Softly with Feeling," "Every Day I Have the Blues," "The Blues Backstage," "Corner Pocket," "Shiny Stockings, Li'l Darlin'," "The Comeback," and "April in Paris." The most distinctive sidemen over the years were Gus Johnson and Sonny Payne, drums; Eddie Jones, bass; Freddie Green, guitar; Joe Newman, Snooky Young, Wendell Culley, Reunald Jones, Thad Jones, Sonny Cohn, trumpet; Eddie "Lockjaw" Davis, Paul Quinichette, Frank Wess, Frank Foster, Eric Dixon, Marshal Royal, Ernie Wilkins, reeds; Henry Coker, Benny Powell, Al Grey, Booty Wood, Bill Hughes, Richard Boone, trombone; and Joe Williams, vocals.

Count Basie received the Kennedy Center Honors (for outstanding achievement in the performing arts) in 1981. His accolades also include many popularity poll trophies as well as honorary degrees in music and the humanities from numerous institutions across the nation, including the University of Missouri at Kansas City. He did not attain his prominent position in the pantheon of contemporary American musicians through his extension and elaboration of the basics of the blues and popular songs, as is the case with Louis Armstrong and Duke Ellington.

His claim to fame, as an orchestra leader and piano stylist, is based on his distillation and elegant refinement of the fundamentals that make the blues and pop music swing. For all its up-to-date reflection of ongoing stylistic and technical innovations, trends, and fads, the music he played in concert was never any less dance-beat-oriented than that which he played in the ballroom.

In 1942, Basie married Catherine Morgan, a dancer from Cleveland, and their daughter Diane was born in 1944. Basie died of cancer on April 26, 1984, one year after Catherine. Funeral services were held at Abyssinian Baptist Church in Harlem, followed by cremation.

The two most comprehensive sources of information on Count Basie are *Good Morning Blues: The Autobiography of Count Basie* as told to Albert Murray (1985) and Chris Sheridan's *Count Basie: A Biodiscography* (1986). Other useful information about his band and his sidemen can be found in *The World of Count Basie* by Stanley Dance (1980) and *Count Basie and His Orchestra* by Raymond Horricks (1957).

The Basie hallmark was always simplicity, but it is a simplicity that is the result of a distillation that produced music that was as refined, subtle, and elegant as it was earthy and robust. There is no better example of the ungaudy in the work of any other American artist in any medium. Count Basie's music is not about protest. It is about celebration, and celebration is about achievement, whether material or better still existential (intrinsically personal) and what it generates is a sense of well-being that even becomes exhilaration!

"It's a mistake to think of any art form in terms of progress"

Interview with Susan Page

On May 6, 1997, Murray was a guest on The Diane Rehm Show *on National Public Radio at American University in Washington, D.C., to promote his third novel,* The Seven League Boots, *which had just been published in paperback after first appearing in hardcover at the end of 1995. Susan Page of* USA Today *was guest-hosting for Diane Rehm. This is the second half of the conversation, in which Murray responds to the show's callers. The first half of the interview is mostly about the novel and not so much about music. In talking to the callers, he ends up talking about music a lot and saying some things that he says nowhere else. In this interview Murray addresses hip-hop more directly than he addresses it anywhere else. He also theorizes an unusual definition of heroism, where, instead of slaying a monster and then receiving rewards, one has to do heroic deeds in order to justify previously attained but unearned good fortune—and he applies that idea to his own life. He also addresses the alleged fallout between himself and Ralph Ellison.*

SUSAN PAGE: Mr. Murray, during the Depression you were a schoolmate of Ralph Ellison, the author of *Invisible Man,* when you were at Tuskegee Institute. Tell us about your friendship over the years. You helped shape one another's thinking.

ALBERT MURRAY: We shared interests in things. We could deal with the idiomatic particulars in terms of the whole world of literature that we knew about. We saw ourselves as operating in that particular context. And we didn't think that other writers had exploited all the universal possibilities in our idiom, what I call the blues idiom. They simply were interested in civil rights and justice and injustice and so forth. If I were that interested in that I would have been a lawyer. But I was trying to make images out of this experience which shows what our take on human life is. Now, that's what the musicians did. That's why we dominate the world of music—not because the music fights a battle of civil rights—it simply seduces people into wanting to move and sound like us—like the idiom that we grew up in. And I've already described it as the most adequate and most comprehensive expression of the American attitude toward experience.

SP: There was a time, I read, when you and Ralph Ellison were estranged from one another and at his eightieth birthday party there was a reconciliation. Is that right?

AM: No. That's not right. That was because a guy writing an article went around asking various people, "Tell me something embarrassing about Murray, tell me something weird about him, what kind of trouble has he been in?" And you're always gonna find people who will oblige that. That's ridiculous. Ralph was a loner. He bragged about being a loner. He would not discuss me with anybody. I certainly never discussed him with anybody. So where could this come from? Somebody was interviewed. And I know who some of these people are. They just made it up. But they never were in our presence. They were never in my presence at the times Ralph and I were together—so we can forget that.

SP: Let's go to some callers. Let's go to Dave in Dallas, Texas. Dave, you're on the air.

DAVE IN DALLAS: Good morning. Mr. Murray you're an incredibly eloquent person, the way you talked about riffing on the break—completely from a musician's perspective.

AM: Well, I want that to be the basis for more and more American conduct. When the country works, that's really the way it works.

DAVE IN DALLAS: Were you a musician?

AM: Not really. I mean, I played bass. I was interested in music. But I don't hire out as a musician. [laughter] People can write murder stories without committing murders! [laughter]

DAVE IN DALLAS: I know that's what the real great writers do. They don't have to commit the act.

AM: No, they listen. I was very close to Duke, and that put me close to Count. When I was introduced to Count as a candidate to do his memoirs, and he found out I was one of Duke's boys, that made me OK with him. You see? They liked my ear. I could hear everything. I listened like a composer. I remembered all the parts. I probably have absolute pitch.

DAVE IN DALLAS: I'm a jazz musician and it's that constant not knowing what's coming but knowing you're prepared for what's coming, and like the rabbit, scoot around.

AM: That's what I'm trying to get Americans to see, that we're all rabbits in a briar patch. So once something happens, you don't say, "Look at all the briars out there." That's what you call protest fiction. I want to know what you're gonna do about it. I spelled out what was wrong with the country in *The Omni-Americans* and what was stupid about it—it's mainly stupid! So, what do you do about stupidity? You try to educate!

DAVE IN DALLAS: Did you always have this fresh outlook?

AM: What can I tell ya? At least I got eighty-one choruses almost. I've been riffing for eighty-one choruses, how's that?

SP: Let's go to another caller. Jonah in D.C., you're on the air.

JONAH IN D.C.: Mr. Murray, it's a pleasure to speak to you. I wanted to ask you, what is your perception of progress in the art form of jazz music? How would you define progress and where do you think the music is going in the future?

AM: I think it's a mistake to think of any art form in terms of progress. I think the word *progress* when you're talking about aesthetics can only be applied practically to a given effort at stylization—some special approach might start out of as something new and develop to a certain point. But then it joins the ongoing process of the music—which is not necessarily a progression. Any time you say progression you ought to be thinking *regression*. Any time you're talking about extension, elaboration, and refinement—that can lead you to decadence and degeneration. There's a certain optimum point where you get masterpieces. But it can lead to attenuation. It can degenerate into nothingness. I agree with André Malraux, who talks about the tradition of art. Each aesthetic effort is an attempt to join an ongoing dialogue with the form. Each time you succeed, you alter the existing emotional scale of the form. But that doesn't mean progress. It just means that the form that you're in continues. But it doesn't necessarily get better. How many contemporary writers are better than Shakespeare, or Goethe? How many young writers are better than Thomas Mann or Hemingway? Fiction hasn't improved, it just changes to keep up with the sensibility of the time.

SP: Let's go to another caller in Houston, Texas. Jocelyn, you're on the air.

JOCELYN IN HOUSTON: Albert.

AM: Yes?

JOCELYN IN HOUSTON: You and I meet up in the oddest places.

AM: We're not meeting here! Are we meeting? Oh, we're having a meeting of minds!

JOCELYN IN HOUSTON: You know who I am, right?

AM: Of course I know who you are. I met you in Washington!

JOCELYN IN HOUSTON: Yes!

SP: Well, I don't think we know who you are, Jocelyn.

JOCELYN IN HOUSTON: I'm actually one of Albert's colleagues from the Dallas Institute of Humanities and Culture and Albert's been helping me with a new book I'm working on about the divas of the Harlem Renaissance. I'm very proud to know you.

AM: Speaking of your book—the divas—you remember how they started out? They started out as *red—hot—mamas*. They were not *sob sisters*—let's get that straight. We don't want to get people confused.

JOCELYN IN HOUSTON: There's no way that we're gonna confuse them.

AM: People get the blues confused with torch songs. A torch song is where you wear your heart on your sleeve. But the blues divas come out of the red hot mamas. They were not the most glamorous-*looking* women around, but they *were* the most glamorous women around. How about that?!

SP: Jocelyn, thanks for your call. Let's go to Frazier in Baltimore. Frazier, you're on the air.

FRAZIER IN BALTIMORE: It's wonderful to be talking with you, Mr. Murray. I don't know if you remember me, but you gave me a seminar similar to the one you're giving the country right now across the desk at Bedford Air Force Base in Massachusetts thirty years ago.

AM: I'll be darned. Yeah, that's right, it was thirty-two or -three years ago, I'd imagine.

FRAZIER IN BALTIMORE: I feel like I'm back on that island of civility again with you. Just talking to you in those days really sort of got me through that. It was wonderful, talking about Mann and Faulkner and Ellison and everything you've been talking about this morning. I just hope the rest of the country reads your work.

SP: How did you happen to be doing this in the Air Force?

FRAZIER IN BALTIMORE: Well, Captain Murray and I were in the Air Force together. I was a second lieutenant. We were both in the base supply operation on this base, Bedford Air Force Base, just outside of Boston.

AM: Right off 128. Hanscom. Hanscom is the name of the base.

FRAZIER IN BALTIMORE: Oh, you're absolutely right. Hanscom, in Bedford.

SP: Thank you for your call.
AM: *Thank you.*

SP: Albert Murray, you were in the Air Force for quite some time.
AM: I'm a retired Air Force major.

SP: You didn't publish your first book until you were fifty-four years old.

AM: That didn't mean I wasn't writing!

SP: Do you have any regrets that you served in the Air Force and your writing became preeminent only when you were a little older?

AM: No. I was doing what I was doing. You know, when we play around with these fairy tales—when you're a jazz musician, you invert—you go this way, you go that way, you go the other way. If I look at my life in terms of a fairy tale, it was not a matter of pursuing or killing the dragon or finding the Golden Fleece and that sort of thing and then getting it. I started out with the most beautiful girl, the most beautiful fairy-tale princess you could get. On the 31st of May I shall have been married *fifty-six years*. So I had to *justify* all those things. I had to justify being healthy, being nice-looking, and all that, and having many admirers. I had to justify that! It's not a matter of trying to get people to like you. Why are these people liking me? That keeps you going more than anything else. I'm glad I didn't publish stuff back before I was ready. But some of the stuff was published much earlier. The train-hopping episode from *Train Whistle Guitar* was published back in the fifties. When I got around to it, I just went back to what I was doing. Meanwhile, the civil-rights movement had come in and people were misdefining themselves and misdefining the aims of the country and so forth. I tried to get that in focus for myself and that's why I wrote *The Omni-Americans*. It's a mulatto culture. It's all related, culturally, and *physiologically*! We don't know who's white and who's black. They're all mixed in. It's unrealistic to pretend that you're not. I never thought of myself as an African American. I'm a quintessential American. If you want to put something ahead of American, say quintessential American. Nobody is more American than I am. I don't want to be hyphenated or whatnot. And I want to write something people will identify with the way they identify with jazz and the blues. Look at what is happening at Lincoln Center. We're trying to synthesize *all* of jazz. We want young people coming up to be aware of the whole tradition of jazz. It's like T. S. Eliot's essay "Tradition and the Individual Talent." If you have four bars to play, it should be informed by the whole history of jazz. Your individuality consists of that which you like—and say, and also and also—or that which you don't like or which you question and you say, "But on the other hand, what about?" That particular combination is

what your originality and your individuality is made up of. There's
so little of you in there that somebody put in there. It's the interaction
of your sensibility with life.

SP: Let's go to another caller. John in D.C., you're on the air.

JOHN IN D.C.: Mr. Murray, you made some comments this morning about
protest in music and I'm wondering how you feel about modern rap
music. A lot of it is, whether indirectly or directly, music of protest. Is
there, for you, room for protest in music?

AM: Yeah. There's a little. But I'd rather creativity than protest. I'd
rather action. I'd rather combat rather than propaganda. I'd rather
sling fists rather than woofing and jiving. And I think that you find in
much of the music now—if you studied marketing or something like
that, then you'd get to what that's about. I don't know whether the
motive is self-expression or a matter of career building and becoming famous or rich. Anything that will sell, some people will produce.
But I don't think that's the same as people who are really dedicated.
When you're talking about Louis Armstrong, you're talking about
the greatest of all American musicians. When you're talking about
Duke Ellington, you're talking about the most comprehensive of all
American composers and probably *the* quintessential contemporary
composer. Here's a man who was very serious about expressing life
and his conception of life through his form. The other people are
looking for something that will sell. That's a different thing. I don't
take that seriously, except to try to find something to counterstate it.
I'd rather for you to be listening to Lester Young or Charlie Parker
or Roy Eldridge—they've got all those records in the store, too. Just
like they have the junk in a bookstore, they also have the classics in a
bookstore. And I think you shouldn't waste your time on junk *except*
for a little recreation here and there. And I'd go to the beach for that,
and read a very sophisticated detective story.

SP: John, does that answer your question?

JOHN IN D.C.: I have one follow-up. I'm wondering if he listens to any
contemporary musicians, and if so, who?

SP: John, thanks for your call. Who do you listen to?

AM: Well, our program at Lincoln Center. Wynton Marsalis is one of my closest friends. We commission works. We've got a thing coming up by Wayne Shorter. I listen to all of it that's good. Most of the young musicians are sort of falling in line behind Wynton. I think that's sort of the way we're going. I want it to remain as comprehensive as possible.

SP: Thank you for joining us, Albert Murray, on *The Diane Rehm Show*. I'm Susan Page of *USA Today* sitting in for Diane Rehm. This is NPR, National Public Radio.

"There was no gap: educational gap, cultural gap, between music education and what Negroes were doing in music"

Interview with Robert G. O'Meally

Robert G. O'Meally is the Zora Neale Hurston Professor of English and Comparative Literature and founding director of the Center for Jazz Studies at Columbia University. He met Murray in the 1970s and was among his most devoted acolytes. He wrote the preface to a 1989 edition of Train Whistle Guitar *from Northeastern University Press. In 1994 he interviewed Murray for the Smithsonian's Jazz Oral History Project. The entire transcript is more than one hundred pages, but the excerpt that follows is the most important in relation to music. I made minor edits and some corrections to the original, flawed transcription (done for hire). Professor O'Meally approved my changes and abridgement.*

ALBERT MURRAY: You've seen this before, haven't you? You haven't? You've read Ellison's handwriting, so you ought to be able to read it.

ROBERT G. O'MEALLY: This is a copy of *Invisible Man*, first edition, inscribed "For Albert Murray, my friend who was schooled in the same briar patch, to confound the squares, bears, and fools thereabouts. Passion is his and with it consciousness, but best of all, self-acceptance and self-respect. In his ear, my voice becomes richer for the love and knowledge of the experience we both . . .

AM: share—

RO: . . . we both share. For the love and knowledge of the experience we both share, Sincerely, Ralph Ellison." And then it says "Tuskegee 1954, two years late but deeply felt."

AM: But that's because he sent me a copy of the first—the book when it came out, an advance copy of the book when it came out. But it was always in Tuskegee. Then when he came down to Tuskegee, he went to the shelf and got the book and wrote that. Because I didn't bring the book to New York, to get an autograph from him. [laughs] But when he came down there, he took the book and wrote that in it.

RO: Wow! And how would it [Ellison's reading of drafts of scenes of *Invisible Man* to Murray] work? Would you meet at his office or his home or yours, and—

AM: He would like to read. When I was going to graduate school [at NYU, 1947–48], if I didn't have any special reason to be down on Fifty-second Street, if it was a night when Dizzy Gillespie and Charlie Parker and those people, or Duke was not in town, then I'd go by and probably have dinner with him and Fanny. And he always had the opportunity to read and test out of the stuff and we'd see where I laughed and what comment I would make about it, because we played with things. And so he'd say, "I've got this man, I've got this crazy guy that's got the so-and-so and he's from so-and-so and did so-and-so." And then he might read it if he had it worked out, he might read a little bit, you see? Well, it goes like this, you know? So, he's got to be walking around in the world because he invented it. It's like in a playhouse, see? And then I was the other guy in the playhouse. That was the way it worked with him because he enjoyed that. And I had my reservations about how some of the stuff in *Invisible Man* worked and whatnot. And I never wished I had written *Invisible Man*. I thought, "That was his book." That was not the way I write. You know? It was fine. You know, we'd laugh about it and say, "Man, these guys really were taken in by that big lie you made about so-and-so. Boy, they couldn't see it at all!" And then he'd tell me stuff like, "All these guys," he says, "man, all these white guys, they come up and they keep saying they can't answer Ras the Exhorter." And I said, "Man, the answer to that son of a bitch is right there in the book!" And they keep saying, "Man, he's got a strong case." You know, that's why they have all these newspaper articles about

Farrakhan and all these guys. A guy comes over and says, "Well, I guess that does make sense." Man, that doesn't make any sense!

RO: But it must have been a great thing for both of you, to have somebody else who had this sensibility, who had read Malraux and Burke and—but also knew how to make pig feet just right and who knew . . .
AM: Yeah.

RO: . . . all about this other dimension—
AM: Well, it gave him a kind of freedom to play with it, because he could test it. And I would even say, "What is that?" and all—those idiomatic particulars would ring a bell. And not only that, but since we had read the same books, I would know how it could be played with. How—if you're doing Joyce on that. Because we knew what we were trying to do, what I expect Joyce would do with it [idiomatic particulars]—Joyce was writing about a bunch of Irishmen! I mean, every time you hear Joyce or you want to read Joyce, try to sound like Barry Fitzgerald, and it'll be Joyce! You see? But then we had our individual differences. [Ellison was] deep into Dostoevsky. But that's his stuff. If not for Dostoevsky, no *Invisible Man*. And he likes the discursory type, where you discuss what's going on, and he's got a lot of opinions about what is happening. That is, the narrator's got all this stuff and he's philosophizing and doing all that kind of thing. My guy is just as discursory, except it's got to go through the Hemingway test. But there are places where what they'll say on the amount of lyricism—you can get to Mann's discursive dimension. And a little bit of the Jamesian stuff. But then you got Joyce, Mann, James, and then you got Faulkner. But, you see, Faulkner is like—almost like a competitor. You had to be careful with Faulkner that you don't fall into the trap of sounding like him. And that's what I was talking about in *South to a Very Old Place* when Walker Percy and I were talking. And then, of course, there's Cormac McCarthy getting away with it. And, of course, he writes like a guy who was born reading *As I Lay Dying* [laughs]. I mean, he knows more to do with rednecks, poor white trash—he takes it a step beyond Faulkner's Snopes. See, he can deal with that stuff. He takes 'em back to pre-Gothic [laughs] Europe, when people were still living in poverty and caves. Before you could get to Dracula. [laughs] You know what I mean?

He got that type of thing. So, we had that thing and Ralph found a voice. The whole idea is to find your own voice. And yet we know what they're filtered through and what they're earned from. But it's got to be your arrangement and your voicing and your instrumentation and things like that. I don't think that our writing is similar at all.

RO: Another difference, don't you think, is that Ellison was always more deeply committed to European classical music?

AM: Right.

RO: And that's really where he lived and what you never did.

AM: Right. I did all that stuff, because I wanted to know. I had to fill in the sound track. Since I was interested in drama, you see? So I got into this. That's a good ways to start out to be a novelist. Because you're thinking of scenes, you're thinking of dialogue, and that's a way of writing fiction, too. You see? So I wanted to know all these things. I would say, "How would you put the costume on this?" You know, it's like making movies. "Why do these guys put their hands up like this, and why does he pose, I mean, hold his saber as he does this?" I want all of that. So it's like choreography, and you've got to know all the stage business. I was wanting to know what they heard. You see? I was reading George Bernard Shaw, and he'd start talking about "Well, this is *Don Giovanni.*" Then you've got to go running over there to [William L.] Dawson's place, over to the music school, and say, "Do you have *Don Giovanni?*" You know? I mean, you do this and that, then if [Alexander] Pope was listening to it, then you've got to go over there, you know? "This is *The Marriage of Figaro.*" So it's all filling in, in that sense. So I had no prejudice against it. It's a matter of just—because you love costume drama! So you have to have the proper sound for it, and the movies had as much to do with that as much as anything else. Because you were used to that. We were used to having a sound track. So now I've come to the point where I write fiction just like you make a movie. I mean, I hear it. When you see a movie or television, you hear it. Right? You know Clark Gable is coming, you're going to see the skyscrapers and so forth, and Clark Gable will be there. You've got all kinds of little songs that you associate with the vision of the thing. And when I zoomed in on idiomatic particulars, all that had to be that. It wouldn't be like Alvin Ailey or Balanchine. But if the steps were consistent with the music, then you could make a ballet on it. It would be a matter of finding the music that was saying what you were saying. So, if it's "Cottontail," that's what it is. It's the briar patch, it's the rabbit in the briar patch. In many of the letters to me [Ralph is] going to be quoting me. Not like it's the same briar patch—that's me. That's acknowledging me. That's not his thing; he was not into Uncle Remus in the same way I was. He knew it all, but he wasn't into it in the same way.

RO: There's a—

AM: And yet, he comes in there and he sneaks Uncle Remus in with the thing. "Ah ha! So the satchel [briefcase] is the tar baby, huh?" Couldn't get rid of that satchel, [laughing] you remember?

RO: Oh, yeah.

AM: Kept turning up. That's why I was completely disgusted when the novel *Tar Baby* came out, because the person wasn't engaged in the mythology or mythological dimension which you could appropriate in ways of putting it on another level.[1] Take it out of the folk level, you see, and put it up there. There was another great story like that. It's in *The King and the Corpse* (1948) and it's called "Abu Kasem's Slippers"—where the guy keeps throwing his slippers away and they keep coming back to him. You see, he made a lot of money, and so he finally decides to go into the public bath and have a bath and all. So, he leaves his old slippers, but he doesn't get rid of his slippers—you know, those Arab slippers? So he comes out of the bath and his old slippers are gone, and some new ones are there. He just figures that's his good luck. So he steps into the slippers. But these old slippers keep coming up. So it's another thing of where the thing sticks. Like the briefcase in *Invisible Man,* right?

RO: Right.

AM: It keeps coming back.

RO: What can the writer as artist do that the trumpet player or piano player just can't do?

AM: Well, I said that in the opening part of *The Hero and the Blues.*

He can articulate things. See, [musicians] deal with the ineffable and make us aware of its existence and give us the experience. They can stylize the feeling of the ineffable and make that an experience in itself. But there are certain things that need precise articulation. And you try to get articulation as close to the ineffable as you can. You bring them right—bring consciousness to that level. And then you know that beyond that, you destroy the aesthetic experience, or you impinge upon the aesthetic experience, if you start explaining it with an expository technique. As much as we like jazz and as much as I use it, I never forget what Thomas Mann had one of his characters say in *The Magic Mountain*: music is politically suspect; it can be just as good for something bad as it is for something good. See? A piece of music can be just as beautiful celebrating dope as getting off dope. You can have just as good musicians playing for the Nazis as playing for freedom. You didn't have anybody over here no better than Furtwängler or whoever that guy was, see? You might've had Toscanini, but they had Furtwängler. Von Karajan was big. We didn't have better musicians [laughs] than the Germans; we beat 'em out on the battlefield, but we didn't have better musicians. Except the jazz musicians, of course, but that's ours, you see? They invented the saxophone, and they haven't figured out what to do with it yet, whereas it's a major instrument because of jazz, right? No symphonic composer has figured out what to do with the saxophone yet.

RO: Didn't you say you played the bass a bit?

AM: This was in the 1950s. J. J. Johnson, who was in the Special Services Office at the Veterans Hospital at Tuskegee, recruited a bunch of guys and had a band gigging around. Johnson got me a bass. I had an ear. I had as good an ear as anybody. I mean, I knew everybody's part. And we started playing little gigs around there. We were playing frat dances over at Auburn, you know, which is about twenty-eight miles from Tuskegee, but was all white at that time. We played dances, you know, all around. We played over at the Veterans Hospital for recreation, things like that. But I never bought the bass. I went down to Cuba in 1953 and came back with conga drums and bongo drums. When I was down there practicing on this test thing, the drums, the Cubans were looking at the thing, and everything I played, that would say "jazz." [laughs] I mean, I thought I was playing Cuban. [laughs]

I could play note for note some of the simpler stuff by Chano Pozo, Candido Camero, Jack Costanzo. I could sit down and imitate them.

RO: We were talking about modernism and music before, but one thing that all the writers that you've mentioned have in common—correct me if I'm wrong—including Ellison, is that you were all concerned with what you call the vernacular imperative, using the materials around you. Joyce was concerned with the blarney, and even Eliot uses the materials around him. But then this is what Kouwenhoven says you must do. You want to see that in terms of the larger picture, too.

AM: Right. Because you're trying to impress us. You're trying to reach the level of fine art. You take the vernacular, but the product—that is, the aesthetic statement—should achieve the level of sophistication. The control is what enables you to do it—that qualifies as the fine art. And it's the control that the artist has over the medium which enables him to do that. See, he can play it in more keys; he's got better control—mastery of the instrument itself; he's got a greater range, and he's got a greater precision. So many of our so-called black writers, they get the folk level, and they get stuck there. And at one time—I have a letter from Ralph in which he's warning me. Okay, so he says, "Well, you have to watch out for those folk rhythms at such and such a point. I know how strong a pull they can have, and they can make you want to write." But in effect you have to realize you're writing a book. And a book has a language that's got to be to a certain extent like other books.[2] You see . . . you get over that. You can't take what some Negroes are saying on the street and just write it down— but that's the kind of stuff that Langston Hughes would do. You say some smart remark and then you chop it up like it's a poem and put it down. When you read Dylan Thomas or something, you heard that on the street. But a genius worked it into a poem. Or Yeats: nobody could be more vernacular than Yeats if he wanted to be. But he's a guy who's writing the best poetry he can possibly write. You see? And Langston would not accept that particular challenge. He thought that he could put that aside. And you can see that the work—the control, the depth, the range, the precision, the subtlety, is not there. See, you can't get on the bus and say "Just be simple." I mean, Hemingway had to earn that simplicity. It is harder to write that type of simplicity than it is to be garrulous.

RO: Yet, to bring it back to music, one thing that you admired in Louis and in Duke is that they can come right out of the pot of chitlins, but they can also—in other words, they can be very local in their reference, but they've got it scored for full orchestra, so to speak.

AM: Right. Well, listen to all those country songs. You can't get more country than the sounds in "Happy Go Lucky Local." You know, [imitates a train whistle]. All these country sounds, you can hear it. You can smell the doggone piney woods with the sound going through 'em and resonating on the ponds. But the control that he [Ellington] has is what enables him to do that. You see, that's what happens in *Finnegans Wake*. [Joyce is] playing a tune. He's not just saying that's the way people gossip when they're washing clothes. "You know about Anna Livia? I'll tell you about Anna Livia. Oh, gee, well—" But he's writing a poem. And he's using these rhythms so they will sound natural, but he's controlling them. You see?

RO: One thing you share with Ellison in a sort of disappointment in African American writers. And that's really—if you look at Sterling Brown and Zora Neale Hurston and Langston Hughes—to your mind, they just don't put enough spin on—they don't see it in the experience—

AM: In the larger literary sense. That's the problem. They stay at the folk level. They think it's—well, and you read it to those people, they have never seen anything stylized, so they think that's what literature is. But they don't know Joyce. See, they don't read—they haven't read Mann; dealing with the German burghers and so forth. They haven't read these things and said, "What can be done with that?" You see? That's where they're so different. See, we're not pulling them down. They don't measure up to Armstrong or Ellington. Our challenges as artists are not among—as we saw it—were not among black writers of any kind: [the challenges] were among the greatest artists, and those were Louis and Duke. But whether you knew it or not, you see? Duke clobbered Honegger. All we have to do is put the record on right now. And for locomotive onomatopoeia, Honegger is not as sophisticated, not as profound, doing *Pacific 231* Honegger is the one who's closer to genre than Ellington. Because Ellington's guys are having a ball playing—they're still playing "Daybreak Express" or "Happy Go Lucky Local," and the guy's still doing all this other aesthetic stuff. So, we didn't find any of our literary people accepting that type of challenge, as Ellington could do, and he's acting like he's kidding. "Oh, yes, we love you madly . . ." And he's out there doing the most abstruse stuff you ever saw. Stravinsky would look and say, "Well . . . how does he do that?" If you're a composer, you want to jump out of the window! [laughs] But they didn't get that message, because most of those writers thought that Louis and Duke were pop musicians. They would get the thing, "Mood Indigo" or something like that, and they'd say, "Yeah, he came pretty close with that." But [Alain] Locke and none of these guys, they never knew.

RO: Can I put some pressure on that? I remember Ellison gave a reading at the Y here in town, and somebody at the reading said, "I'm a young black writer. What do you suggest I read to prepare to do the best work I can do?" And Ellison was walking out of the room and he said, "I don't have time to tell you, but go read the Russians."
AM: Yeah.

RO: [laughs] And this guy was just so dumbfounded by that advice. And that is—that's a part of your message, that you need to have this wider frame to see it. And yet with Louis—if you were meeting young Louis, you wouldn't say, "Go listen to Mozart. Go get Beethoven."
AM: No.

RO: What's the difference?
AM: Well, the difference is that they knew the literature of the trumpet, because they knew about John Philip Sousa and all these people. They knew what that was, but [Armstrong] grew up in a thing where something was actually being created. You see what I'm saying? Something was being created which he latched onto. And besides, they knew it. You would talk to Louis, you know, [an interviewer] would say, you know, "Well, what did you hear?" [imitating Louis Armstrong]: "We heard it all. We heard all the stuff they playing, we had the radio, we had the phonograph records, we like music!" And

the interviewer says, "Yeah, but did you listen to people, you know, like . . . you know, Brahms or Mahler?" He'd say, "Yeah. We're into Brahms. Yeah, all that stuff, and we heard Gustav Mahler! And don't forget Fats Waller!" You see, he was always together with those things [laughs]. It was just music to him. He makes much of when Erskine Tate and those guys were playing classical music. He'd say, "Yeah, they're playing those overtures, man, tell you to turn back five pages. You have to be able to read that stuff. I picked up on reading quite a bit in the pit band." It's Erskine Tate and who was the other one? In the Vendome Orchestra in Chicago—Dave Peyton!

RO: Oh, Dave Peyton.

AM: Dave Peyton and Erskine Tate. Well, you see, you've got to remember that Chicago was a capital for music education. Especially among Negroes. N. Clark Smith was there teaching. Ray Nance studied under him. You realize that? Ray Nance. Same guy that had been at Tuskegee, wrote "The Tuskegee Song" and all that? Ray Nance studied under him in Chicago. Then Smith went from Chicago to Oklahoma and Walter Page studied with him. William L. Dawson, that's where his education comes from—his formal music education. And then he played with Doc Cook's 14 Doctors of Syncopation, that was in Chicago. And all these guys had degrees in music. These guys were hand in glove with Oberlin graduates. And that's where Negro musicians—that was the conservatory at the time. Nobody heard of Juilliard, stuff like that. Lucy Ariel Williams in Mobile, came out of Mobile County Training School and went to Oberlin. You know? So there was never any—there was no gap: educational gap, cultural gap, between music education and what Negroes were doing in music.

All these guys took the best music lessons they could get, and had the exercise books and talked to each other about what system they were using on these things. But the way we celebrate them, and where you—what you're trying to deal with, with me, is how do you know all that stuff and still be a jazz musician? He was trying to make another kind of literature based on that. But they should not forget the quality. Let's call it the academic quality of the music instruction that you're always competing with. Some people wore it a little more obviously on their sleeves than others, and you could tell.

But other guys would never say anything about it. They could cut the same dots. You know? And it was just a natural thing for those New York piano players, for example. They would wipe you out. You see, with Teddy Wilson, from Tuskegee—everybody said, "Well, you know, he went to a conservatory, he did this and that." Well, these guys were waiting for that stuff. And they're taking all the lessons they could get too, like, James P. Johnson and these guys. They knew what it was! If you're messing with Harry T. Burleigh or Will Marion Cook? They had that stuff down. They knew exactly what the technology of music was about. And when they came across a guy that was ahead of them, finally they would catch up. Like Duke went right over ahead of them. So a guy said, "I can't figure this out." This was Rex Stewart. He thought he knew so much music. You know? Then he couldn't get, what—"Rugged Romeo" or something like that? He thought Duke was violating too many things. Of all people, Jelly Roll Morton said, "Keep listening. You'll get it." [laughter] Two or three years later, Rex was one of the big stars of Ellington's band! [laughs] But by the time he got there he knew how to listen.

RO: One thing people often misunderstand about that band—isn't this true?—is that there was all of this exchanging within the band. You got Ellington's band, you got guys from all over the country, some who could read as well as anybody in a conservatory; others who could barely read. You know, Hodges never read very well. But there are people bringing all this, New Orleans, Chicago—and Duke—it's an ongoing seminar, in which Duke is soaking it all in.

AM: Right. Synthesizer, boy, you talk about a synthesizer—he was a synthesizer.

Notes

1. Murray made some remarks when receiving an award in the 1990s that may shed light on his comment about *Tar Baby:* "And now, one more bit of signifying about Scooter [the protagonist of Murray's novels] as Brer Rabbit in the complexities of the American briar patch. What do you think my first book, *The Omni-Americans,* was written to warn you about? *The one thing that faked Brer Rabbit out was a phony imagine of 'his people'!* What I see when I look at social-science surveys of 'my people' (which is to say my idiomatic American relatives) is a bunch of social-science fiction tar babies. . . . My rabbit, it turns out, is not

literally the same as the one old Uncle Remus used [to] tell the white boy . . . about. My rabbit is the Alabama jackrabbit version of the one that Duke Ellington had in mind when he orchestrated the concerto for tenor saxophone entitled 'Cottontail.'"

2. Ellison writes in the letter: "The only other thing that I would watch and I had plenty to watch in this thing that I finished *[Invisible Man]*, are those [folk] rhythms from which you derived part of your style. I know how powerful they can be, indeed they can move a man to write, make him will to endure the agony of learning to think and see and feel under their spell—even before he learns what he must say if he is to achieve his own identity. Well, you have an identity and what you're saying no one but you could say. So watch the trailing umbilicus of rhythm" (*Trading Twelves*, 29).

The Achievement of Duke Ellington
A Discussion with Loren Schoenberg and Stanley Crouch

Loren Schoenberg is the founding director and senior scholar at the National Jazz Museum in Harlem and was a good friend and protégé of Murray. Stanley Crouch is the author of seven books, a prominent columnist and cultural commentator, cofounder of Jazz at Lincoln Center, and for the last several years, president of the Louis Armstrong Educational Foundation. He was one of Murray's most prominent acolytes in the 1980s and 1990s. In 1989, Schoenberg, a saxophonist, historian, theorist, raconteur, and author of The NPR Curious Listener's Guide to Jazz *(2002), had a radio show on WKCR in New York. He had the inspired idea to bring Murray and Crouch on the show together and to ask both of them to bring rare Ellington records to play and discuss. The richly informative discussion that resulted, presented here in print for the first time, will become an important source in the realm of Ellingtonia. It offers a strong corrective to recent misinformation. Although Schoenberg was only thirty years old at the time of this interview, he was able to swing along with Crouch (who was forty-four) and Murray (who was seventy-three).*

LOREN SCHOENBERG: Loren Schoenberg with you on a Tuesday afternoon's *Out to Lunch,* and right now it's my pleasure to open up the microphones for three hours' worth of conversation with Albert Murray and Stanley Crouch. Now, the way that this show came about was that I was fortunate enough to run into both of these gentlemen the other day at a concert at Carnegie Hall. I've been wanting to do a show with them for a long time. Stanley has been up here before but I hadn't been able to snag Albert yet. Just seeing them together made me think it's now or never, so we actually have them here together in the studio. The concert we were at was a re-creation of a famous Carnegie Hall concert of 1912—that of the Clef Club and James Reese Europe. And hearing that concert certainly helped place Ellington's innovations in many different contexts. And I think we're gonna be concerned this afternoon with placing Ellington in musical, sociological, and aesthetic contexts. And that's going to be very important so we know exactly what we're talking about. Any thoughts about the concert, gentlemen? Albert? Stanley?

STANLEY CROUCH: Well, I think the thing that was most clear about the concert was that the music that they were working on, Europe and those guys, was much closer to ragtime music, actually, than it was to jazz. The rhythm that they used and the way that the songs were written that they were playing showed what the music was like before Louis Armstrong really changed the rhythm in the way that he did. But you could easily say also that it was phrasing that predated Sidney Bechet too.

ALBERT MURRAY: Mmm hmm.

SC: Because, as Duke Ellington said, he considered Bechet the great originator when he first heard him play "I'm Coming Virginia." I think it was in the late teens or the early twenties in Washington. And that was the beginning for him, of hearing how swing would sound. But the thing I found most interesting—I was talking to Maurice Peress, the guy who conducted and organized it and did a great thing—the thing I found most fascinating about it in terms of the orchestration was the use of the mandolins and the banjos in the orchestra. Because I was saying to Peress that it seems to me that one of the distinctive things about jazz is the statement of the harmony with a percussive inflection. Hearing those banjos and those mandolins strumming out the harmonies in that band gave the band a different sound, just the way tubas were later used in jazz bands, and finally, that kind of percussive carrying of the chords by the bass. And I think that one of the things that is most distinctive in Duke Ellington's music is the way that he utilizes that combination of percussion and harmony together in so many different ways throughout his career.

LS: Yeah. Albert?

AM: Well, from a historical point of view it [the concert] was very relevant to Ellington. What you saw is the context into which Ellington came, and you had people who had a direct effect on him. You had material there by Will Marion Cook, and he was Duke's mentor. That was a direct line to what was going to happen in terms of the Afro-American use of European devices and so forth in this American music. In effect, you have Duke, a number of years later, coming into Carnegie Hall and really being the apotheosis of that in purely vernacular terms—*bringing the blues in.* Duke comes out of the ragtime context just like everybody else of his generation. He's very much ragtime and his first pieces were ragtime. Well, stride, which was eastern ragtime. But that was the thing that got me. I happened to grow up on that particular music too. Duke was about the age of my father. But all this was in school and this is what we heard—like, "Swing Along" and all this Jim Europe stuff. As a matter of fact, I heard some things in there which I could identify as phrases in "The Tuskegee Song," the Tuskegee Institute song, which was written within the first decade, and they were still using some of these phrases. Many of these people knew each other. Now, of course, Jim Europe was from Mobile originally, where I'm from, and where Cootie Williams was from, along with a number of other people. But it provided a historical context which a number of people missed. Stanley, you know, when this guy Collier was talking about Ellington's background, he wanted to go to Washington to pick out something that he could snoot at, and he didn't get the serious input that the assimilation of devices and so forth from Europe was already taking place. By the time Ellington came to maturity and began to use them, these things had already become part of the vernacular.

LS: Yeah. It's also fascinating in that context what Bubber Miley brought into the band and the kind of music the Ellington band was playing in the early days, which I guess what back then was called "dicty" or society kind of music, when you listen to the records of the band and contrast Miley's contribution with what Ellington was doing, it seems as though Ellington was a lot closer to people like Will Vodery and Will Marion Cook.

AM: Oh, he was personally close to Will Vodery. Will Vodery was the musical director of the Cotton Club in addition to being the musical director of the Ziegfeld Follies. Then you had Will Marion Cook, who was around there all the time. And he was from Washington. You had a context there that was perfectly natural. When you look at Ellington against this background, his evolution just makes all the sense in the world.

LS: One strange thing about the concert—you had all these composers, some of them integrating choral devices and different kinds of *blues kind of effects* into the European concept of writing for strings and the whole kind of symphonic music of the late nineteenth century. But what I'm curious about to bring it to Duke Ellington is—what would Ellington have been in the twenties—it's a hypothetical question—if Bubber Miley hadn't joined the band? And if that blues strain hadn't come in? And that improvisatory element? I mean, granted, that he heard Bechet, and he *hired* Bubber Miley—so, you have to give him credit for that. Could Ellington have done it without people like Bubber Miley?

SC: The thing I think that we always have to realize about Duke Ellington—which is something that Earl Hines said about him—he never forgot anything he heard. Had he not heard Bubber Miley, the development of his band might have been different. What we always have to recognize when you're dealing with a genius of this proportion as a fundamental issue is the sensibility of the man. Obviously, blues would have struck him. One time when I was interviewing him about twenty years ago I asked him about that and he said when he first heard Bubber Miley growling he said he realized he would never really play sweet music again. Just because that happened to be Bubber Miley—I mean, it could have been another guy. I think the thing was that that caused him to hear an arena of music that he wanted to address. I think when you look at his evolution—that's the way he evolved throughout his career. He would hear things that he liked and he found ways to put them inside the ensemble that he was working with. But also I think what's really important about him too is that here you have a guy who was able to completely remake all of those musical directions that we heard in the James Reese Europe concert and elevate them to a much higher position and emotionally give them a much grander breadth. But see, the thing too—he maintained, and Albert and I were talking about it that night—part of what I think the appeal of that music is that there's a real sense of joy to it that's not contrived. And I think in some way, if we understand what that joy is, I think we understand something about swing.

LS: Did you see those little gestures that Jester Hairston made while he was conducting the choral group? I think that was one of the cruxes of the whole matter right there. And there's a man who goes back to the 1920s. And while he was conducting a very beautiful choral arrangement, at one point he brought just a little bit of humor to it, a little sardonic quality, when he put his elbow out like this or when he was conducting: he went like this with his hands. I think that's something about the joy and the humor and the nonseriousness, not in a negative sense, of enjoying that kind of concert music that other people miss. In terms of jazz repertory, people seem to be missing that too.

AM: One of the things that people miss, also, is the direct connection that Ellington had with a general interest in creating a serious music, an art music, as the saying goes, which was truly American. And that's why they brought Dvořák over here in 1893. Harry T. Burleigh studied with him. Will Marion Cook worked and studied with him and had met him in Europe. There was a big interest in creating a native—heh—American music, assimilating the various aspects. So, that was really there in Will Marion Cook. Duke told me one night about how mad Will Marion Cook got when he came back from studying with Joseph Joachim and he gave this concert and somebody said he was "perhaps the greatest black violinist in the country." Duke says he [Cook] found out where this guy, the critic, was working, and went down and broke his violin over the man's desk, and said he wouldn't pick it up anymore. Then he began to deal with vernacular forms. He did *Clorindy; or, The Origin of the Cakewalk,* and so forth, and then he started working with Williams and Walker and these people. All this, Ellington came into—not just as a general heir of it but as a *specific protégé* of both Will Marion Cook and Will Vodery. And that sort of set him into *doing larger things,* not out of the pretentiousness of some of these people but out of a very natural evolution of how far will and can this stuff go.

LS: That leads us into the next record. It just seems so perfect to hear this recording right now. This is one of the very early Ellington recordings, from 1926—we're going to hear Ellington just a little over a decade after the Clef Club concert and before his own stamp had really made itself heard. I think we'll be able to hear him halfway between what came later and what came before. Let's hear "Parlor Social Stomp." This is a rare Ellington record from March 1926. Bubber Miley was out of the band at this particular moment—he had been there. Interestingly enough, in the band for the record session: Don Redman. That's a whole other avenue. "Parlor Social Stomp."

[Plays "Parlor Social Stomp"]

LS: Well, I guess the first striking similarity to the music we heard, as Stanley mentioned as the record was playing, would be just that banjo sound—something that was still a holdover from Clef Club days and before.

SC: Yeah, well, the important part about it is the relation of percussion—of percussive attack—the way people used woodblocks, the way they used cymbals, the way, of course, they used little drums. I think the percussive attack is what's important. But what we were saying earlier about Ellington—an observation that should be made about him is this, it seems to me: when you have someone of that degree of genius, what a person like that is capable of doing is really perceiving the essences of idioms more clearly than most people. Whether it's an Ellington, or a Picasso, or a Goya, it doesn't really make any difference. When they see other things or they hear something, they really understand what it is. They understand something beyond the technique that's being exhibited at the time—they understand the *conception.* And it seems to me that where a lot of people make mistakes in terms of how they develop as artists is they confuse the technique with the conception. So, they'll imitate the way somebody *does* something rather than understand what the idea is. And what Duke Ellington is constantly dealing with throughout his career is a basic set of ideas that—it seems to me—that he addressed over and over in various transmutations throughout his career. He understood . . . the value of vocalized approaches to instruments—whether people used half-valve effects like Rex Stewart or whether they used plungers like Bubber Miley.

AM: Right.

SC: He *really heard* Sidney Bechet and understood what that was. And Bechet is a constant influence in his band throughout the career of the band, in the way that Johnny Hodges appropriated Bechet and expanded that into his own conception. He understood all the things that he heard from the trombone players—the many ways that the trombone could be used, as personified by the three guys that he had in his band—you had the so-called straight approach, then you had Lawrence Brown's approach, then you had "Tricky Sam" Nanton's approach. He understood many different ways to use percussion. Long before other guys started using a lot of other auxiliary percussion instruments he had Sonny Greer using those different things. See, my theory about his orchestration: it seems to me that his orchestration is *grounded* in the polyphony of the New Orleans front line. Oftentimes, rather than just the trumpet, the clarinet, and the trombone, he'll turn his whole band into, like, this *gigantic version* of the trumpet, the clarinet, and the trombone with all of the originality that he was able to bring to it throughout his career. And the thing that's most fascinating, finally, is that here's a guy that evolved without ever losing sight of the fundamental things that he heard. And we always must remember too that however many recordings we have of Duke Ellington or Count Basie or whomever—these guys heard many, many, many more performances and many, many more notes than were recorded by even the most enthusiastic Jerry Newman or whoever the person was following guys around. When he was jamming with Don Byas or any of those guys, or listening to Art Tatum or Fats Waller or whoever it was: he didn't forget what that was. Sonny Greer told me once that Ellington would say to him often, when he would hear something that was interesting to him—his nickname for Sonny Greer was Nasty—he'd say, "Nasty, you know, this is very interesting to me and I have to figure out how we can use that kind of an idea in our band." It didn't matter if they were listening to a jazz band or a symphony orchestra.

LS: I'd like to ask Albert Murray, who heard the band a lot dating back to—I believe I've heard him say he heard the band in the late twenties on the radio as a young kid—

AM: Oh, yeah!

LS: —who has a long history of hearing the Ellington band and knowing Duke and being around Duke Ellington. Where would you place the Ellington band in the contexts of the other bands of the era? Unfortunately, Ellington's band is usually lumped with as being the best of but still in the same category as the other great bands of the era: the Basie band or the Goodman band or the Thornhill band or the Mills Blue Ribbon band. What sets Ellington apart, or should he be considered part of that?

AM: When they started the business of, you know, the band-of-the-year type thing, and newspapers got into the act during the so-called swing period, they would have people talking about favorite bands. After a couple of years, they decided that Ellington didn't belong in that balloting at all. *Down Beat* came along and they started doing it too. But in the *Pittsburgh Courier* and the *Chicago Defender* and papers like that [black newspapers], they would ask people not to include Ellington in the balloting of the band of the year, but then he would still get enough votes to win even though he was not supposed to be in it. Most people somehow or other had the feeling that what he was doing was always totally different from what other people were doing. It was the *apotheosis* of what they were doing. Because *he was a composer.* They could see it, they could feel it—whether they articulated it in that way or not. These other people had arrangers, they did things, you had these other bands that were very popular in hotels and so forth. Their music was popular music derived from more serious aspects of this music. And Ellington was not just providing that type of entertainment. *He was stylizing his own life.* In fact, I remember very well a definition that he gave of jazz. Someone said, "What is your definition of jazz?" And he said, "It is *Negro American feeling expressed in rhythm and tune.*" Now, there's a direct connection between that and what people were trying to get from Dvořák, what Will Marion Cook never let him forget, what Will Vodery could do. And Will Vodery was some technician. This is where Duke picked up the business or writing arrangements upside down or correcting them upside down. The band would be rehearsing and he would come by and just look down on the paper and reach down and make the correction. He told me Will Vodery would do that and say "Five dollars for every note I get wrong." But he really was always considered separate, separate from everybody else. Or, as he said of Ella Fitzgerald, you know: *beyond category,* in terms of popular music. He was like Shakespeare, in a sense, in that he could go into the Globe Theatre and provide as much entertainment as the hacks would provide, and at the same time he was meeting the highest requirements of the finest of stylizations, the finest of fine art. There never was a time when people were not aware of that during my lifetime. When we would stay up listening to the bands when I was in college, we would listen to the bands from Harlem, all the way up to Les Hite in California. And it was always a different matter when they'd start with the Cotton Club. Everybody was aware of it. He *always* knew he was different. Irving Mills knew he was different and showcased him as something which was different. And they all had that particular feeling about it. That's my impression of how it went.

LS: It's 12:34, you're listening to Tuesday afternoon's *Out to Lunch* on WKCR-FM here in New York. That was Albert Murray who was talking, and before that it was Stanley Crouch. Right now, Albert and I agree; let's hear some music. Right now we're going to hear something from the Stanley Crouch collection. Stanley, can you introduce it?

SC: This is a piece from 1937 called "Chatterbox." And I think again we hear this, well, I don't want to say obsession but perhaps it's right word for somebody dealing with jazz—it's another attitude toward the use of percussive devices from instruments that aren't necessarily percussion instruments. The way the brass functions on this piece, "Chatterbox," and how you can hear . . . Now, I wouldn't say necessarily that Thelonious Monk studied this piece for a piece of his like "Evidence," but I think that there are ways that the accents move inside the arrangement that set up certain kinds of things that Thelonious Monk was very interested in.

LS: Right. And, of course, it also wasn't the first time that a composer had dealt with the various melodic, rhythmic, and harmonic implications of offbeat accents. So, we don't want to—you're not saying this was the first time this problem was addressed?

SC: No, I'm not saying that at all.

LS: But was it the first time it was addressed in jazz, or?

SC: Well, no, I'm just saying in this particular piece—in terms of some of Monk's music—this is a piece that shows, perhaps, some of the things that Monk heard in Duke Ellington that were very interesting to him. I think also that the overall sound and rhythm of the piece, and the way that the piece moves as much on the basis of the accents themselves as of the notes and how he gets this perfect fusion of percussion, melody, and harmony. Going back to what Albert was saying about him being a composer—one of the things that stands out the most, it seems to me, about Duke Ellington is that his selection of who the players would be on a given piece were real *compositional decisions*. A lot of people just want guys who are, like, good soloists, so-called, to stand up. Duke Ellington really knew that you get a particular development of a theme if you pointed to Johnny Hodges. You get another kind if you pointed to Cootie Williams. You get another kind if you pointed to Lawrence Brown.

AM: Stanley wanted to avoid the use of the word *obsession*. Percussion is definitive—it's the *definitive* element in the blues idiom statement. That emphasis on percussive statement is definitive. It's not just an obsession. To tie this in with a thing I was addressing on another level before—most of the bands were playing within the convention—which is popular at the time. Ellington was playing in terms of the *essences of the idiom* he was working with. He might satisfy the current convention on one level, but his deeper interest was in the basis of the thing. So, when you get into the so-called swing era and he's doing variations on percussive statements, and they're just getting to swing and he's already beyond that and into other dimensions of it. Let's hear "Chatterbox."

LS: Rex Stewart on the cornet.

[Plays "Chatterbox"]

LS: I've just gotta say just two quick things before I turn it back to our guests. One is the old *canard,* the *oft-repeated canard* that many old musicians are still bound by—that "Oh, well, the Ellington band, they didn't really play what was on the paper anyway. And when a new guy came he made up a new part." Well, that might have been true a very small percentage of the time. But recently, with the Ellington scores that have surfaced at the Smithsonian, when you compare—and I've seen them with my own eyes—Ellington's sketches for "Never No Lament" and things like this, and "Braggin' in Brass"—I mean, that band played *precisely* what Ellington wrote. I think sometimes that undermines Ellington's stature as a composer. People will unconsciously undermine him and say, "Well, the guys were making up parts half the time." First of all, that wasn't true—they played exactly what Duke wrote. And second of all, what a *fascinating recording* to hear Ellington write something for Rex Stewart knowing Rex was going to play it, writing for the trumpets as if Rex was playing all the time, and then to hear Rex improvising on top of what Duke already wrote knowing what he was going to play on it—I guess there's really no precedent for this in Western music.

SC: Well, you know, there's another thing too about that garbage about "the guys made up their own parts" and all that business. See, if those guys had been responsible for those voicings, right, why is it when Lawrence Brown and Johnny Hodges and those guys made their own records they used traditional kinds of harmonies?

LS: Rather stock things.

SC: Yeah. I mean, *Inspired Abandon* and all those records—those records don't reflect the kinds of things that were distinctive about the Ellington orchestration for brass and reeds. But what I think happens is—when somebody is as great as Duke Ellington: *that's often hard to believe!* Some people have a very difficult time addressing something as big as this.

LS: Like Mr. Collier.

SC: Well, Collier, I mean—that's a horse that needn't be pulverized anymore, I imagine.

AM: [laughter]

SC: James Lincoln Collier's biography of Duke Ellington, so called, is *a fraud.* We needn't say any more about it. It's fraud, badly researched, and it picks a lot of material out in a very specious way to avoid dealing with Duke, with the grandeur of Ellington. So much for James Collier.

LS: Just when you said that a lot of people are afraid to deal with Ellington in the magnitude of his creation—

SC: As Albert knows and I'm sure you know, there have been people since I was a little boy who've been trying to say that Shakespeare didn't write all those plays and write all those poems!

AM: [laughter]

SC: They say there were a group of people who did 'em, some even say that Christopher Marlowe did 'em, the Queen of England did 'em, Bacon did 'em. "There was not one guy who could've written that much stuff that was good."

LS: Of course, I know Stanley knows and I know—Albert Murray's books, *The Omni-Americans,* and specifically for me, *Stomping the Blues,* and a whole bunch of other things that he's written have laid the groundwork for so much of what we're saying today and so much of what we understand to be the truth about this music, but one point that I made to Albert on the phone the other day—and I didn't even realize that I had probably read it in something you had written and was spitting it back to you—was about the thing about Shakespeare writing his plays for specific actors at the Globe Theatre. And I'd like to ask both of you about one specific problem facing jazz repertory. What do you say to the folks who say "I don't care who plays it, if Cootie Williams doesn't play 'Riding on a Bluenote' or Johnny Hodges doesn't play 'Sultry Serenade,' it's never gonna be the same. Duke wrote it for them and no matter who plays it after, it's never going to be as good. Only they could play it because he wrote it for them."[1] Albert first. How do you answer that?

AM: I think you have two things there. The first thing you have to know—many times that statement that that particular performer makes becomes part of the piece and is in the public domain, as any jazz riff is. Any statement that you make in jazz can be answered, can be counterstated, can be extended. If they give you something—say, a Ben Webster piece—you're going to take your bow to Ben Webster, then see if you have something else to say to it. I think that's about what you could get from that particular situation. We'd have had the same problem if we had Mozart's recordings of his own stuff. Since we don't have that, we have a different problem for jazz because we know how the arranger or how the leader wanted it to sound. When you play "Airmail Special" . . . well, certain things you play the solo on. You play Illinois Jacquet, you play Arnett Cobb. If you're gonna play . . .

LS: Charlie Christian.

AM: Charlie Christian. It becomes part of the basic thing. A final word on that—Cootie was great! Cootie was, we thought, you know, *definitive in his area.* When he came back [into the Ellington band after leading his own band], when he could do "Take the A Train," he could play Ray Nance's solo on "A Train" and play with a different tone and so forth. But Ray Nance's solo had become an indispensable part of "A Train."

SC: I wanted to say also—there's another problem to that too, though, which is that when we study Ellington over the years, *he didn't use the same people even when they were sitting in the band every time he recorded something.* That's something that the private collection of those CDs shows. He'd say, "Oh, 'Serenade to Sweden,' let me see, I'll take Ray Nance and Paul Gonsalves and see what that makes." Or you take the long version of "Take the A Train" with Betty Roché on it where you get that fantastic long tenor saxophone improvisation from Paul Gonsalves. That's an "A Train" that's a completely different way—it's got two tempos. What I mean is that when you're dealing with somebody like that, sometimes you have to say, "Well, this is the version most people like, maybe including me more than others"—and I don't think that television show they did on PBS was very informative about that, just in the different versions of "Mood Indigo." There wasn't a set "Mood Indigo" either.

LS: And the one that's shown up in the last few years where they do the whole "Mood Indigo" double time, with double meter. Imagine if someone else had come out with the record and some reviewer writes "Oh, it's sacrilegious, how could they do a version of 'Mood Indigo' and speed it up? It's such a beautiful ballad."

AM: Two different conceptions of music, of this music. One is trying to make it European music and the other makes it the vernacular music that it is.

LS: What's the crux of the difference between what you're calling European music and what it is? What are the dangers of trying to make one the other?

AM: It seems to me in jazz you have the composer having the piece voiced as he wants it voiced, as closely as possible. You have that. And if it's successful, then people remember it. They respond to it on that level. They just have the score in European music. Or they might have some favorite recording of it by some orchestra or some conductor.

LS: Or some composer—playing his own work. There might be a recording of a composer playing his own work.

AM: Yeah, but they get into peculiar things on that, it seems to me, because any number of people would prefer somebody else to conduct Stravinsky.

LS: Right, right. Of course.

AM: They don't prefer Stravinsky's—well, of course, it wasn't his band either [laughter].

LS: In the bottom line, can there ever be a performance of the *Harlem* suite or any Ellington piece that can exist on the same shelf as Ellington's recorded interpretations?

AM: What do you say, Stanley?

SC: I don't think that's the point.

LS: Well, it's my question.

SC: What I mean is, the problem is a different one. I've heard two or three different versions of the *Harlem* suite by Duke Ellington and each of them were different. What I'm saying is, say someone saw Olivier do an extraordinary Hamlet onstage. Are they to stop going to see *Hamlet* because they're not going to see Olivier do it every time? See, a first-class performance of *Harlem* will reveal two things: one, it's an exceptional composition, and two, if it's a first-class performance, then you're listening to a first-class band play *Harlem*. Now, if somebody says that a first-class band has to be the Duke Ellington band, then that's going to eradicate going to hear it. I was sitting next to Benny Golson when the American Jazz Orchestra played *Harlem* in the final evening of the performance when Maurice Peress conducted. It was an extraordinary experience of an extraordinary piece of music, but I wasn't sitting there going "That's not Paul Gonsalves."

LS: OK, so then, is our appreciation of Ellington as a composer—and it's another question to ask—was he—when he said that everybody was beyond category, he might have invented a new category of composer too.

AM: One hundred percent.

LS: Are we suffering right now because of our chronological closeness to the memories of emotions and sounds and the nearness of the Ellington band? And do you think that somebody when there is no one left on the planet Earth who ever saw the Ellington band and never heard it, that his reputation will change, or the perception of him will change?

AM: I don't know whether that follows. Since you don't get progress in the arts . . .

LS: That's right.

AM: Overall, you don't get progress in a given device of stylization. You might get that refined to a certain point, but it doesn't mean it's better than another way of stylizing it. You see? But I just can't imagine anybody coming up with a "Come Sunday" that would wipe out the Johnny Hodges "Come Sunday." Just like somebody writing a new New Testament or Old Testament or new group of Shakespeare's sonnets—it's a fait accompli, it's there, it's a part of our heritage. If somebody else can do it, make variations on it, bring something else to it—I don't think it has to change its definition. Because *Duke Ellington invented Johnny Hodges*—and everybody else! They would not have had that context. They would not have made the statement that they made without him. I don't see how you could change his standing any more than he could change Bach's.

LS: Oh, OK, so then Ellington stands in a new category, because part of the way we view him as a composer is inextricably bound with who played it and who he wrote it for—and I think that's something that never happened before.

SC: [objects, interjects]

AM: OK, well, we're gonna put on the next record. [laughter] The next record is "The Minor Goes Muggin'," which was not written by Ellington, but was recomposed by Ellington, you might say, just by him sitting in with the Tommy Dorsey band. It was written for Duke by Sy Oliver. I think Stanley will want to comment about the Monkish dimension of this particular record too. I had this record back in the forties. It just wiped out forever all those questions people used to have about Ellington's piano playing: "He was a good band piano player, but you know, as an individual soloist . . ." They were thinking about virtuoso soloists like Earl Hines and people like that. But Duke was doing something else. Since I was always listening to all of his music, I was listening to how his piano went with it. Here he is as a guest soloist with the Tommy Dorsey band. Look at the transformation that takes place in the band and in the piece.

[Plays "The Minor Goes Muggin'"]

AM: Justifies Buddy Rich right there! [laughter]

LS: Amen. It's fifteen seconds before one o'clock and we're here on a Tuesday afternoon's *Out to Lunch* with Albert Murray and Stanley Crouch. And we just heard "The Minor Goes Muggin'," which is a Sy Oliver original done by the Tommy Dorsey band with Duke Ellington on piano, with a lot of Ellington influence in there. The piano playing is totally abstract! And swinging, at the same time.

SC: Part of what has to be addressed with Duke Ellington and Thelonious Monk is that even in the finest jazz piano players you often hear the legacy of Chopin in terms of the digital idea of how the piano is to be played, even though people may be playing blues phrases and so on. But it seems to me that Duke Ellington, Count Basie, and Thelonious Monk—it seems to me that they form a triumvirate of attitude about the piano that really is not horn-derived, as in European music, or even an emulation of the speed of violin playing and that sort of thing. They really deal with the sound of the piano and the percussive possibilities of the piano. And they often are improvising an orchestration. When they say Earl Hines plays a trumpet-derived style of piano or Bud Powell plays a Charlie Parker-style piano—obviously, those are great ways to play the piano when you hear great people play it. But when you hear Duke Ellington play the piano or when you hear Thelonious Monk play the piano, you're really hearing something, to me, far more derived from the Afro-American idea of harmony and percussion that Albert was talking about a bit earlier. It's a successful approach to that kind of percussive stuff that we were talking about even earlier with the banjos, *using the piano.* That doesn't mean that Duke or Monk or Basie won't play melodic phrases on the piano. For one thing, those guys really knew how to make the piano part of the rhythm section. That ongoing percussive harmonic structure that the rhythm section forms is something that has no precedent in Western music anyway.

AM: The other thing is, of course, the closeness of the apprenticeship which Ellington served to two ragtime pianists, two stride piano players—to James P. Johnson and Willie "The Lion" Smith. It's always operative in these statements. There was some kind of a funny thing between Ellington and Jelly Roll Morton. That's one of the guys he was not terribly complimentary to. But the influence of Jelly Roll on Duke is just about unmistakable. It had to be there because it preceded him by that many years. Jelly Roll was doing stomp by 19'4 [1904] or something like that. But he said something that was really significant and Duke would have to agree with it, because I talked to him about this stuff from time to time: anybody who really wants to play the piano as a jazz musician is always trying to make it sound like a band. That's Duke in a word! See? On that great *Paris Concert* album somebody makes a request for "Rose of the Rio Grande" and they don't have the arrangement there. So, Duke just remembers the arrangement and plays it.

SC: That's another thing too about him as a piano player. When you hear him working in the rhythm section, he often plays very differently from other piano players because he improvises when there's not a set arrangement. He often plays the piano from the standpoint of improvising an ongoing arrangement as the tune progresses.

LS: Well, I think he's into the point you made before about Ellington orchestrating his band as a glorified frontline New Orleans band. Basically, what it comes down to is an appreciation of counterpoint.

SC: Right.

LS: I mean, like the solo background on "Eastside-Westside" ["The Sidewalks of New York"]. John Lewis loves that because he says that's just plain old Bach counterpoint—of course, taken to a different realm. Whether it came from the bands in New Orleans or whether he heard the recordings of the Creole Jazz Band—

SC: I think too much emphasis is put upon guys listening to records. I'm not saying they didn't listen to records. You know this as a musician. There's an enormous amount of music that you learn listening to saxophone players play the saxophone. There may be something you pick up on a given night. And if somebody hears you play something later—and there's some obscure Dexter Gordon record that came out in Denmark, five hundred copies—and he uses the same approach on a certain bridge, and they'll say, "Well, Loren, I know you got that from . . ." [laughter] I'm not at all sure guys in that period listened to that many records.

LS: I want to address that. I think there's a real dualism or dichotomy or—*two things that don't meet, but they're both true*—I do think people overstate the importance of listening to records. I've heard it, I've read it in books. On the other hand, it is a fact that the records were seminally important to the players, especially back in the twenties. Lester Young did carry around Goldkette and Paul Whiteman records. Those specific solos do show up on some solos. "Singing the Blues" was a very influential solo. And all the trumpet players were listening to the Hot Fives, because Louis Armstrong after 1925 was *not* in New York City. I think that, yes, it's overstated, but back in those years I don't think it can be overstated. I don't know if Ellington went to Chicago in '23, '24, '25. If he didn't, he must've heard the Creole Jazz Band.

SC: Don't forget, there's one thing that is often overlooked too—Duke Ellington in his early bands had authentic New Orleans musicians *in his band*. If he wanted to ask about a particular practice in New

Orleans, I mean, he had people like Barney Bigard sitting right there!

AM: Wellman Braud!

LS: Wellman Braud, Rudy Jackson.

SC: That's what I'm saying. That's a very important thing. I think that that's a part of Ellington's development that really has not been discussed very well. He often had guys right in his band from whom he could get specific information . . .

LS: . . . who played with King Oliver, it's true. Right now I'd like to play a recording of the first extended piece by Duke Ellington, called the "Creole Rhapsody," from 1931. This is the second version, not the original Brunswick but the Victor version that was done several months later. And that features for one of the first times in Ellington's recorded work, tempo changes—within one work. There had been the Cotton Club—"A Night at the Cotton Club" 78 where they did different pieces in kind of a suite-like fashion. But this is the first time when one specific composition had tempo changes. And that was certainly a red-letter day for jazz. Albert Murray and Stanley Crouch are here. Stay tuned.

[Plays "Creole Rhapsody"]

LS: And now we're gonna go right from "Creole Rhapsody" into "How High the Moon."

[Plays "How High the Moon"(from Ellington's 1948 Cornell University concert, featuring Ben Webster)]

LS: Well! I've never heard that before! The only version I ever heard of that was a scratchy radio broadcast. This is a marvelous concert version or something.

AM: Yeah. I must've played that for Stanley about ten years ago or fifteen years ago.

LS: It's fascinating to me how Ben varies his melodies and everything and as he loses coherence, a certain kind of melodic thing as the tempo goes—but he has enough whatever to bring it back on the coda. That's weird!

AM: That's right.

LS: That's fascinating. What we heard were two recordings, the original "Creole Rhapsody" from 1931 and then kind of three different tempos on a feature for Ben Webster during his little-known third stint with the band for a short period in 1948, which not many people know about, but now we know about—thanks to that rare recording from our guest Albert Murray. What kind of statement do you think Ellington was making by recording the "Creole Rhapsody"? And where does it stand in relation to his shorter compositions? Do you like it is as much?

SC: I like it as much. In his long pieces, he uses a leitmotif, as he does in *The Tattooed Bride,* as he does in the first movement of *Black, Brown and Beige* [scats opening]. The whole piece is built on that, including "Come Sunday." In this he has this melody that recurs and he uses these different key changes and tempo changes. He also takes different pieces—that's the thing that fascinates me about him. He's got a core body of stuff—he's like a great chef—like those cooks who can take some leftovers and make them taste like two or three different kinds of things [laughter]. Duke Ellington would say, "OK, we got this line here." And he'd take those pieces out and those things become accompanying parts. This is one of the points—he really begins to expand upon the influences he got from King Oliver and Sidney Bechet and others. We're getting closer and closer to what became the Ellington sound of the *thirties.* There's a different Ellington for each decade—that's something else too. There is no definitive Ellington sound because that sound kept evolving. One piece that he brought, a long piece called "Portrait of Ella Fitzgerald," that I want to play later, is a piece from the fifties. We know it's Duke Ellington and all who are Duke Ellington listeners are aware that that's Duke Ellington, but if you were to play that after "Creole Rhapsody" or even after some of things in the famous 1939 to 1942 band [The Blanton–Webster Band], people wouldn't necessarily know immediately that that was the same band. This guy's stuff kept evolving. One of the arguments Albert and I have had with people for years is about this cliché about the 1939 to 1942 band [that it was the best], which seems to me to be such a terrible reading of what this man brought off.

AM: Which he wiped out simply by playing any piece from any period as well as it was originally played, with the current band that he had. I wanted to speak to something else you brought up earlier. I think it's terribly important, especially when you're talking about this type of music, and that is the matter of influence. It's not as simple as it is in some activities. You have, and this is derived from some of the notions of André Malraux about art, that is, art is derived from other art. My corollary, my extension, my attempt to extend that is to say that each *individuality* is comprised of what one *accepts* from the *given* and says "and also and also"; *yes*—and also and also—or *rejects* and says, "But, on the other hand, what about this?" It means, according to Malraux, that you're involved with an ongoing dialogue with the form. In jazz, it seems to me, that works very well. As soon as you play something, it's in the public domain. It can be answered, it can be extended, it can be re-formed, it can be repeated verbatim. When you move through those decades that Stanley was referring to, each time somebody comes up, he's gonna say something about that. When you get to the question of influence, it's not a matter of copying, but rather counterstating or extending, or elaborating or enriching. Or, rejecting! You can do it with satire, you can do it with parody, you can do it with a number of different things. But when you speak of influence, the study of jazz makes us aware of it in ways that other art forms don't make us quite as aware. When you deal with certain musicians—many are craftsmen, not artists—they've mastered the conventions of the time. They live in terms of the going convention. When you deal with a great artist or an artist of the genius of Ellington, he's always outside the convention—he sees it, he can operate in, but he's always above it. You gotta be careful with your modifiers when you say somebody influenced him, or he picked this up from this person. It's also not just where the phrase came from—it's what the person did with the phrase and the circumstances in which he used the phrase. It's terribly important. Otherwise you're gonna be unfair, inaccurate, and misleading about who influenced whom.

LS: It's true. And jazz has really suffered from so many authoritative statements about who influenced whom just purely by the fallacy of people thinking that all that existed back then was on records. There I was talking about how important records were—and they were—

but what was important, what was going on seven days a week in Harlem and Chicago and places in where jazz flourished, are things we'll never know.

AM: *Quotation* is, you know, the lifeblood of jazz. Just as it's the life-blood of the poetry of T. S. Eliot, in another form. When you take it over, you remake it. In art, you get the altered or the unaltered found object. You can take something as it exists, put into a new frame, give it a new highlighting, and it's a new composition. That is something you can also get a special insight into by studying jazz. There's that phrase that Duke played around with for a long time—and then he made a little piece called "Band Call." [LS and AM scat "Band Call"] Then, when somebody made an arrangement for Basie, of "A Train," they get to a certain point and the band shouts that [opening phrase of "Band Call"]. I was talking to Freddie Green about it—about pulling another dimension of Ellington into "A Train." He said, "Yeah, Willie Gant used to use that." Which is *way* back! We know that Duke knew all of the stride piano players and their phrases. He could go back into all kinds of territory and quote things for you on the piano. I'd be talking to him backstage or in his dressing room and he'd go out there on the stage and play something from the period that we were talking about. He liked to quote from the 1948 period. You know the piece "You Oughta"?

LS: I don't know it.

AM: I have it here.

LS: I'd like to hear it.

AM: [scats "You Oughta"]. We'd talk about it and he'd put it in a solo in the next set.

LS: There's a marvelous universe of Ellington and we're talking about it here with Albert Murray and Stanley Crouch. Any comments, Stanley?

SC: I wanted to talk a little bit about this next piece we're going to hear, *The Asphalt Jungle Suite,* which is from the late fifties. It's in three parts, but the opening section, "Wild Car," and the last section, "Cops," are both variations on the middle section. The main theme comes in in the second part.

LS: Yeah.

SC: There's an abstract version of it in the front. Then a blues variation of the main theme. I think it's another example of just how fertile this guy's imagination was and how he was constantly doing unusual kinds of things. This is something he did in the studio. It was unknown until André Hodeir found it. It was just one of the many, many things that Duke Ellington did on a given day. Near the end of the first section, "Wild Car," there's a phrase you'll hear him play on the piano. Near the end of the second part he'll play that phrase again and he'll use it under Johnny Hodges when Hodges is playing.

[*Plays* The Asphalt Jungle Suite]

LS: Alright. Some originally unissued Ellington from 1960. We heard *The Asphalt Jungle Suite.* Aaron Bell is heard to great advantage on this. Marvelous piece, yeah! That's a weird form. It's an odd form. But Ellington was always introducing forms. We were looking for a version of "Eastside-Westside" to make a transcription of it. So, of course, we have the famous Victor version, which everybody knows. And I said, "Wait a minute, I think they did it in Fargo." It's on that third album of stuff from Fargo that wasn't issued. So I went and I found it. And, wouldn't you know, like guys say he did—what Ellington does—if the section is A, B, C, and D, the record is D, B, A, and C—I mean, it's all backwards. And you know, it works! It works marvelously.

AM: That's one thing I remember most from Ellington rehearsals or recording sessions. "Letter A . . . will be . . . Letter C!" And he'd be reaching over and making a little note. In the last rehearsal before putting on their uniforms to play, these guys would make the note. And there I'd sit out in the audience and watch these guys play it as if they'd rehearsed it, just like that.

LS: Are there parallels to this kind of invention in other areas of art? Or is it unique to Ellington?

AM: You probably have it in painting in some ways, especially in contemporary painting. You print new colors around, you change values because of the way things relate. Because it's *highly* improvisational. Once they broke down the business of perspective and representation—illusion—and started dealing with equalized surface tensions and went back to, you know, the classic Oriental paintings and brought it back up to mosaics and Romanesque painting, they were free to deal with the intrinsic qualities of painting. They became more aware of the type of improvisation that was possible.

LS: As writers, I'm curious, because I know you're both not just Ellington fans and lovers of his music—I know it's something more deep than that to you. How does Ellington's playing with form or just Ellington period relate to when you sit down, pen in hand, to write something? Do the formal structures of Ellington's music in any way translate themselves to creating writing?

AM: That's how I learned to write. That's how I realized how I could deal with form—was how he did it. The vamps. The choruses. Just the classic form of what I call the indigenous American sonata. I try to make it as obvious as possible in *South to a Very Old Place,* which is an Ellington sonata! It begins with a verbal transcription of "A Train" [i.e., poetic prose riff inspired by "Take the A Train"] and goes out with "Cotton Tail." I wrote a whole book on it, that's derived in terms of context, called *The Hero and the Blues.* But it's very close to me. It's a matter of encompassing chaos, encompassing raw experience, and then bringing it under control for transmutation into aesthetic statement. It's indigenous, it's available, and it means something to me in particular.

LS and **AM:** Stanley?

SC: The thing I found most interesting about it from the standpoint of writing is what you can learn about narrative from Ellington. A conceptual idea about narrative. Like this piece we just listened to. The part the variations are made on is the second part. The thing too about how he develops pieces. The people that you pick to improvise on a given piece—they develop not only the musical texture of it but the psychological and emotional context of the music. You not only have a different musical sensibility with a Johnny Hodges playing but you have a different emotional orientation than you have with a Ben Webster or a Paul Gonsalves. And these guys have so many different *guises.* There are so many different things that they can do. In writing, if you really understand what narrative is, what dialogue is, what a monologue is, what an interior monologue is, what stream of consciousness is, what setting and scene is—if you can come to understand those things as well as Duke Ellington understood what 4/4 was, what blues was, what an improvisation was, what a song was, what a voicing was, how the different tensions that you get from using one section of the band one way at this point and then another—I think what he does is perfectly applicable to any kind of art that anybody does.

AM: Sources tend to come from your own métier, as it were. I got the idea of looking for a vernacular or indigenous source of music from Thomas Mann, whose works are based on German composers. He used devices including leitmotif, theme, variation, all kinds of things like that. I responded to it when I first started reading him, which was *fifty years ago*. [laughter] The summer after I finished college I really plunged into Thomas Mann. Then I started looking on my own— what was available to me. I could see it first in the Kansas City style. Because it's so clean-cut: the vamp, the chorus, the getaway, the first solo, the out chorus, the tag. Then you could see that that stuff is really derived from Duke. The riffs are so smoothly integrated into it that you don't isolate them and say "Look at this riff here, look at this riff there." He had done it. Speaking of other forms, my friend, the late Romy Bearden, learned to paint by listening to music—or learned to apply the dynamics of music to painting. But he got it from somebody in his medium. He went down to talk to Stuart Davis about what Stuart Davis had learned from modernists, so-called modernists, in France, and Davis wanted to talk to him about Earl Hines's use of interval. Bearden realized that he already had a sensibility—his sense of form that he was responding to every day could be applied to the medium he was working in. He became a purely improvisational painter. He'd put something down to see how it relates to another form. Just like playing around on a keyboard.

LS: They say Ellington could have had a great career as a painter. He was given a scholarship to Pratt Institute but he decided to play the piano anyway. Of course, he did have a great career as a painter—a painter with notes and harmonies. What do we know about Ellington's actual work with a brush? Did he talk about feelings about putting things on canvas, ever? Did the topic ever come up?

AM: He was always interested in it. I never talked to him to a great extent about it. Ruth [Ellington, Duke's sister] could tell you about some of his involvements. Somebody else who liked to sketch and could sketch very well was Paul Gonsalves. He had other people in the band like that. But Duke never lost his intense interest in the visual arts. Of course, you've got that *Degas Suite*!

LS: Oh, yes! [station identification]. Right now I'm going to hear another thing that I've never heard before. This is?

AM: "How You Sound." This is from the mid-forties, the height of the bop period, and so the Ellington staff decided to engage in a little conversation. This fits in with what I was talking about—influence or dialogue. You should be aware of the ongoing dialogue with the existing form. Questions arise in form as well as content and you work it over to see how much you want and it sort of settles down in a certain way. It's a sort of tongue-in-cheek Ellington bop takeoff: "How You Sound."

[Plays "How You Sound"]

AM: I thought you'd get a kick out of that.

LS: Yeah! It's funny, there are these broadcasts from the Spotlight Club in 1946 of Dizzy Gillespie's band, and when Dizzy introduces "Things to Come" he says we'd like to dedicate this to the master, Duke Ellington. And, you know, in one of those Bill Gottlieb photos Dizzy is wearing a Duke Ellington tie—a tie with a picture of Duke Ellington on it. And I guess Duke was returning the compliment with his own brand of humor. There's so much humor in "Boogie Bop Blues," too.

AM: Right!

LS: We're gonna switch from something called "How You Sound," which was obviously a broadcast air check, to something that Stanley Crouch has here that Don Cherry knew about—

SC: This is called "The Mystery Song." It's one of the first great features for Harry Carney. I think that one of the things that's fascinating about it besides the mood and color of the music is the sense that

Ellington had of the dramatic power that you could get out of the baritone saxophone. One of the things I've become fascinated with is the relationship of Ellington's devices to certain operatic devices, and how he uses the vocalized approaches to instruments and how he uses them often in this idiom for, like, operatic ends. People perform, like, arias, duets. The orchestra itself functions like a choir. You get these different developments of the pieces. You have a different, extended version of singing through instrumentalists. On "The Mystery Song" you get one thing. After that, we're going to listen to "Rude Interlude" in which he does something very fascinating. You get a French horn effect from the trombone early on. One of the things that Ellington was very good at, too, was getting the effects of instruments that he didn't have in his band. As you know, Loren, as a musician, and as you know, Albert, as an extraordinary listener and perhaps the best of all Ellington students, he does things sometimes where he'll, like, use two clarinets in a way where you hear an arrangement and you'll hear an oboe in there—it's not an oboe, he'll use two clarinets and get the effect of an oboe. The last thing we'll hear is a short piece from 1959 called "Hero to Zero," from *Anatomy of a Murder.* You'll hear him in two minutes and twenty seconds coming out with a fully rounded piece, which shows that at any time in his career, he could, as he did during the 78 rpm era, go back and fit it perfectly.

[Plays "The Mystery Song," "Rude Interlude," and "Something to Live For"]

LS: Alright. We heard "The Mystery Song" followed by "Rude Interlude" followed by "Something to Live For." Stanley?

SC: These are examples of how Ellington dealt with the same problems throughout his career. A lot of people who came up during the 78 era were often dismayed as jazz performances got longer, when the LP came in. He could always, at the drop of a hat, go in the studio and say, "Three minutes? Here we go. Here's three minutes for you." But I also I think we see in these pieces an extension of moods that he was introducing. One of the things Duke Ellington did that was as important as the technical devices he introduced, he also expanded the emotional range of jazz more than anyone. I think that before pieces like "Rude Interlude" that emotion wasn't expressed in jazz.

Or even a piece like "The Mystery Song." I mean, that's another kind of a mood. It's not blues.

LS: It's not "Chant of the Weed," either.

SC: It's none of those things: it's another mood. Even in this late version of "Something to Live For"—and here we have Ellington in the studio in 1960. Lawrence Brown was back in the band. Here we have Ray Nance singing the line out, and it's another piece, with him. Somebody could say, "Well, in the original one Jean Eldridge sang it and it was this, it was that." And it was great. But here is another "Something to Live For" that can stand up next to the other ones. I think the early Ellington music is classic music, without a doubt, and towers over other things being done in those periods. I contend that the later music is the greater music because all of the musicians were greater musicians. Duke Ellington at age fifty or sixty was a greater musician than Duke Ellington at thirty-five, however great a musician Duke Ellington at thirty-five was. Somebody like Johnny Hodges—as great as his sound was in the thirties and forties. I mean, *the sound that Johnny Hodges had on the alto saxophone in the middle fifties?!* Here's a guy who's been playing the instrument that many years longer. You know it as a saxophone player yourself.

LS: Mmm.

SC: I mean, each note, the more years you play it, the ramifications of expression you understand about that note become greater and great.

LS: As in life. I have a question for the two writers here. Could Duke Ellington write as good a novel as he could a short story, in music? Was he a better short-story writer than a novelist, in musical form?

AM: That brings up a whole thing where people get tangled up in the pieties associated with European music. If we start with art as the ultimate stylization of the basic attitude toward experience, that is, of our interaction with our environment, and our art form comes out of that—then you've gotta be responding to something. Now, when you had the need for longer pieces, or when there was a demand for these things, he was ready. He was the one who was ready. He never was just a short-story writer. They were recording short stories, but these were always condensations from actual performances. That's the basic fallacy to wipe out—that they were only playing for three minutes. They were up there playing more than three minutes! The pieties get in the way—you think it's gotta be this, it's gotta be developed that way. He knew it was developed in another way. The adaptations, or the borrowings, were purely functional. He would use the thing almost like a metaphor—a "tone parallel." He said *suite,* which is a functional word—combination of several dances at different tempos. If you'd really went back and studied European music and find out what adagio means, you'd find out that things develop from the environment in which they lived.

LS: Not the other way around.

AM: Not the other way around! If you put on any Ellington LP and you time how much music there is and you look at how the pieces go together, I mean, the man was writing five or six symphonies a year! The equivalent to an extended form. Now, the question of whether or not this was a novel—the interesting thing about the analogy is *I have yet* to find anybody who really knows what a novel *is* or who can define what a classic form for a novel *would be.* You have great masterpieces that you call novels, but they aren't anything alike! There's nothing similar about *War and Peace* and *Madame Bovary,* for example, or *Moby-Dick* and *The Sun Also Rises.* Even Henry James, who worked out a whole *theory* of the novel—you have different kinds of novels coming out of Henry James.

SC: Wynton Marsalis was saying something to me about the making of an album. Making an album is a very hard job—and being Duke Ellington didn't make it an easier job. To fill up both sides of an album with enough music, where you create an entire forty-minute experience—that's a hard job.

LS: So the LP became for him a form; his novel.

AM: Exactly. That is the form. He's making an LP. He was making an extended piece, but that was already present in the nightclub. You could extend it for how many choruses you need. It's like the thing we get in Kouwenhoven's book *Made in America: The Arts and Modern American Civilization.* These people came over from Europe and wanted to build European buildings. People who were really interacting with their environment—who happened to be the engineers instead of the architects—they built suspension bridges and cantilevered bridges, not Roman viaducts. When you get a person really operating out of the experience, he moves, he makes those steps towards a new form. When you had the skyscraper—and Kouwenhoven makes this point—now, the whole business of architecture changed with the I beam. You see, the older skyscrapers have capitals; they *end*. They have steeples or this or that. But then later on they found out: that really wasn't the form. It's just, how many choruses can you run? It's just, how much money to do they have for how many floors? How many étages? Then you stop and you put a television antenna or radio antenna or air conditioner up there. That's what the form is. Whether it's fifty stories, seventy stories, eighty stories—there's an American form. The jazz form is like that. You tell Ellington you want him to play longer, he can add that many more choruses.

LS: Or, as Lester Young said, necessity is a mother. [laughter all around] It's 2:25 and we're with Stanley Crouch and Albert Murray and right now I'd like to tell you folks out there in radio land about something that's very special coming up. If you like what you're hearing this afternoon, and you think that the insight is important, which it is: these gentlemen are putting something together with another very important person, Mr. Wynton Marsalis. Albert Murray, Wynton Marsalis, and Stanley Crouch provide new insight into the work and meaning of Duke Ellington—as artist, American, and symbol of the elegant-bawdy-witty-high-minded-Democratic-metaphor that is jazz. This is a lecture series, first of all, given by Albert Murray on Monday, July 31st and Wednesday, August 2d at 7:45. This is happening at the New School, those two lectures. Then, there's a meet-the-artist supper with Albert Murray, Wynton Marsalis, and Stanley Crouch at Lincoln Center on Wednesday, August 9th at 6 p.m. This is all part of the Classical Jazz happenings happening in August at Lincoln Center. Now, for information about the New School summer registration, you would call 212–741–5611. For seventy-five dollars it includes the two lectures by Albert Murray on Ellington and the meet-the-artists supper. I also am going to ask Stanley Crouch to tell us about this marvelous series you've put together. It's the third year at Lincoln Center. It's called Classical Jazz at Lincoln Center. Can you just tell us briefly about the concert series coming up?

SC: On Friday August 4th we'll have a Billie Holiday remembrance subtitled "Ladies and Tenors." Abby Lincoln and Jimmy Heath will be performing together. Etta Jones and Houston Pearson and Shirley Horne and Buck Hill. These aren't gonna be imitations of Billie Holiday performances, they are gonna be performances by three great individual singers who will sing songs that are associated with Billie Holiday. Then, on Saturday August 5th, we're gonna have a performance called "Bouncing with Bud: The Music of Bud Powell." There are gonna be original arrangements of Bud Powell pieces by Jimmy Heath, Slide Hampton, and Walter Davis Jr. in the second half. In the first part, there will be small-group performances and some of the performers will be Art Farmer, Jackie McClean, Barry Harris, John Clark, Earl Gardner, Bob Stewart, Ray Drummond, Kenny Washington, and the Tommy Flanagan Trio. Then, on Monday, August 7th, we're going to have something very special as well, we're gonna have "Mr. Jelly Lord: The Music of Jelly Roll Morton." We're gonna have real New Orleans guys under the direction of Dr. Michael White. We're gonna have the great Danny Barker—

LS: Ohhh!

SC: He's gonna be playing banjo. Danny is, I think now, eighty-one or eighty-two. He's performed with King Oliver, Jelly Roll, Louis Armstrong. We'll get the real New Orleans music. They're gonna perform all Jelly Roll's pieces. On Tuesday August 8th we're gonna have a night we call "Happy Birthday Benny Carter." Benny Carter will be celebrating his eighty-second birthday. Some of his guests will be Dizzy Gillespie, Ernestine Anderson, Hank Jones, Sylvia Sims, and Ray Brown. The last two nights, Wednesday August 9th and Thursday August 10th, will be Duke Ellington's suites and blues. We're gonna do *The Tattooed Bride, The Nutcracker Suite, The Queen's Suite,* and then there are gonna be a number of blues pieces that cross the decades: "The Mooche," "Diminuendo and Crescendo in Blues," a piece from the sixties called "Bonga," and "Frère Monk," his tribute to Thelonious Monk. All of those things will be at Alice Tully Hall. They'll all be at eight o'clock.

LS: I strongly recommend all of it, and, of course, especially the marvelous lectures on Ellington to be given at the New School by Albert Murray. It's 2:31. My special guests—Stanley Crouch and Albert Murray. We're listening to Duke Ellington's music and we have a rather extended suite.

SC: This is something that Albert and I have been talking about lately. This is another one of those Ellington gems that has been laying there and has been missed, as so much by Ellington has. This is from, I think, 1957. This was commissioned by Norman Granz, who I think when the smoke clears will easily be in the running with John Hammond for the championship belt of jazz producer given the enormous amount of material that Granz produced that was very fine. He commissioned this piece from Ellington and Strayhorn, and we get some wonderful monologues from both Ellington and Strayhorn. It's called "Portrait of Ella Fitzgerald." I think it shows very clearly how far the language of Duke Ellington had extended itself by the time this was recorded in 1957.

[Plays "Portrait of Ella Fitzgerald"]

LS: There it is, the "Portrait of Ella Fitzgerald."
SC: There it is. Duke Ellington.

LS: It's 2:49. That was Stanley Crouch. My other guest is Albert Murray. We have time for two more tracks from Albert Murray's collection.
AM: The first is "Rockabye River" and next is "Let the Zoomers Drool."

LS: I read in something that Ellington wrote or an interview with him where he actually explains what "Let the Zoomers Drool" means.
AM: It's on the record! It's on one of the versions.[2] Which one is first?

LS: "Rockabye River."
AM: This is a very personal piece for me. It's what I call a blue-steel lullaby. It really gets to the heart of how you're brought up as a down-home Afro-American kid. If you listen, at the very end, Johnny Hodges really puts the baby in his arms and coos the words "Go to sleep little baby." It's like a Paul Laurence Dunbar poem about, you know, the little brown baby with sparkling eyes. You can hear beneath it

one of the old down-home pieces he's playing with. You can hear "Swanee River" and a number of other things in there.

[Plays "Rockabye River" followed by "Let the Zoomers Drool"]

LS: We just heard "Let the Zoomers Drool" and "Rockabye River," which were brought to us courtesy of Albert Murray. Albert, why those pieces?

AM: I think that's an excellent example of the unique voicing of a band. It exists like a living, breathing organism. The beat of the band is incomparable. The imagination. It's a thing with a voice all its own, made up of all these living people. Nothing illustrates it better than "Rockabye River" and "Let the Zoomers Drool."

LS: I've heard a lot of great music today, and heard it in a different way. I'd like to thank Albert Murray and Stanley Crouch for coming up. It was an honor. And a pleasure. We're going out with "Informal Blues" by Duke Ellington.

Notes

1. Maurice Peress addresses this issue in his essential book *Dvořák to Duke Ellington: A Conductor Explores America's Music and Its African American Roots* (2004). While discussing his 1999 re-creation of Ellington's 1943 *Black, Brown, and Beige* concert at Carnegie Hall, Peress writes: "[Rex] Stewart was the undisputed master of the half-valve [trumpet technique]. He humanized his solos with 'ghost' notes that seemed to come from deep inside the instrument. Jon Faddis, best known for his pyrotechnical *altissimo* (piccolo range) trumpet playing, came down to earth and recreated Stewart's solo. It was obvious he had spent long hours studiously analyzing with which valve and at what depth, he would find a given sound" (178).

2. The announcer at the beginning of the record says, "Do you know what a zoomer is? Well, the Duke tells me a zoomer is a chronic moocher, you know, 'Got a cigarette, pops?' Here now is 'Let the Zoomers Drool.'"

Murray's Final Published Nonfiction Statement

Jazz: Notes toward a Definition

This is the final nonfiction piece that Murray saw through publication. He started it in January 2003 and published it in October 2004 and thought of it as his final statement. He originally intended this for the New York Times Magazine, *envisioning it as text to accompany photographs of the new home of Jazz at Lincoln Center in the recently constructed Time Warner Center at Columbus Circle. That didn't work out, and it ended up in the* New Republic. *Murray was friends with Leon Wieseltier, the* New Republic's *longtime literary editor. Wieseltier had published a long review essay by Murray on Louis Armstrong in 1999 and a poem by Murray on William Faulkner in 2000. I never asked Murray how he felt about Martin Peretz and the perceived racism of the* New Republic's *political section in the early 1990s, but I know he admired the arts section. He was also friendly with Jed Perl, the magazine's longtime art critic, and regularly read and discussed his work. The penultimate sentence in this essay was cut by the magazine and is restored here.*

I

Jazz music, as is also the case with the old down-home spirituals, gospel, and jubilee songs, jumps, shouts, and moans, is essentially an American vernacular or idiomatic modification of musical conventions imported from Europe, beginning back during the time of the early settlers of the original colonies.

Specifically, jazz as such began as a secular dance music that evolved from ragtime piano music, brass-band music, and the guitar, vocal, harmonica, barroom, honky-tonk, and juke-joint music called the blues, which generates an atmosphere of groovy delight and festive well-being in the very process of recounting a tale of woe. As any church member will testify, generating a Dionysian atmosphere is precisely what honky-tonks, juke joints, barrooms, and gin mills are all about.

In any case, the jazz musician's blues should not be confused with the torch singer's lament, which is a matter of wearing one's heart on one's sleeve because one has loved unwisely and not well and has become not the one and only, but the lonely, "ain't these tears in these eyes telling you." In this sense, Billie Holiday's famous recording "Strange Fruit" is not blues music. It is a political torch song, a lament about unrequited patriotic love. We have loved and fought and died for this country for all these many years, the song asserts, because it has been our official homeland for this many generations, and now just look at what some of these other folks think they have a right to do to somebody because they want to think that they are better than them.

Actually, "Strange Fruit" is not even written in any of the established blues stanzas. "The St. Louis Blues," by contrast, is also about unrequited love, but it is written in the most widely used blues form, the twelve-bar blues chorus. And what it inspires, whether in up-tempo or in slow drag, regardless of the words, is not regret and despair, but elegance and good-time movement. (For a jazz musician's inflection of a famous torch song, listen to Roy Eldridge's rendition of "After You've Gone" of 1937, and also the Jazz at the Philharmonic version of 1946, featuring Mel Powell, Charlie Parker, Howard Mc-Ghee, Lester Young, and others.)

Ironically, as little as it has been noticed, it is the pale-skinned or so-called white European, not the dark-skinned Africans, the brown-skinned inhabitants of the Middle East, the so-called yellow skinned Asians, or the so-called red-skinned people of the Americas, and so on, who describe their moods in terms of changes of the color of their skin (mainly of their faces!), which have traditionally been described as becoming red with embarrassment, green with envy, gray with concern, dullness, or "the blahs" of boredom, and blue with sorrow and self-pity. Hence, the blue devils of torment or torment by blue demons, as in the case of delirium tremens. (Blue skies are another matter altogether.)

There was a time between the 1890s and the early 1920s when ragging a tune and jazzing a tune added up to just about the same kind of musical statement. Did the word "jazz" win out because "jazzing" sounded more Dionysian than "ragging"? After all, legendary accounts of early jazz in New Orleans place great emphasis on its connection with the red-light district of Storyville. According to *Webster's Collegiate Dictionary*, jazz is "a Creole word meaning to speed up, applied to syncopated music, of American Negro, and probably of African origin; a type of American music, characterized by melodious themes, subtly syncopated rhythms, and varied orchestral coloring."

But neither the earthy ambivalence of the blues nor the elegant syncopation of ragtime is indigenous to New Orleans. It was in Memphis that W. C. Handy, who was from Alabama, codified and put the old down-home blues stanza (which he first heard in Mississippi) into the public domain of American popular music, as Scott Joplin from Texas had done for ragtime in Sedalia, Missouri, a few years earlier. Perhaps the most obvious—if not the most definitive—characteristic of early New Orleans jazz was its special emphasis on polyphony and improvisation, though it was Kansas City jazz that was to become known and celebrated for the subtle syncopation of its swinging 4/4 stomps, jumps, and shouts.

Even so, there was a small group in New Orleans in 1908 that was sometimes known as the original Creole Jass Band. Also King Oliver, after moving to Chicago following the closing of Storyville, once led a group called the Original Creole Jazz Band, and at another time he led one called the Dixie Syncopators. Most ballroom or dance-hall bands outside of New Orleans continued to bill themselves as "syncopated orchestras" until the early 1920s. By the mid-1930s, they were advertised as swing bands as well as jazz bands. But by then jazz had become the generic term for an American secular dance music with its own style, variations, and repertory.

II

A jazz tune, melody, or composition is usually based on either a traditional twelve-bar, eight-bar, or four-bar blues chorus or on the thirty-two-bar chorus of the American popular song. In either case, the overall structure is a series of choruses, which may be preceded by an improvised vamp instead of a conventional prelude or overture, and it is climaxed with an out chorus that may or may not be followed by a coda, the jazz term for which is a tag.

Duke Ellington's "Ko-Ko" is in effect a blues-obbligato minus the original twelve-bar melody. "Moten Swing" by Count Basie and Eddie Durham for Bennie Moten's Kansas City Orchestra is in effect an obbligato minus the thirty-two-bar chorus of the original melody of the pop song "You're Driving Me Crazy." Thelonious Monk's ob-bligato treatment of "Please Don't Talk about Me When I'm Gone" became "Four in One," his version of "Sweet Georgia Brown" became "Bright Mississippi," and "Straighten Up and Fly Right" became "Epistrophe." Thus did Charlie Parker's recording of "Ornithology" come from "How High the Moon," and Dizzy Gillespie's "Groovin' High" from "Whispering." And so on it goes, with the jazz musician treating even the most sophisticated popular standards as if they were folk ditties.

The improvisational nature of jazz musicianship is such that a truly competent performer must be prepared to function as an on-the-spot composer who is expected to contribute to the orchestration in progress, not simply to execute the score as it is written and rehearsed. In fact, the "score" or lead sheet may often turn out to be "dictated" verbally or instrumentally rather than written. There is much to sug-gest that it is this special aspect of jazz musicianship as it is exercised, developed, and refined in informal jam sessions that accounts for the rapid rate at which jazz (which was perhaps never really a folk art!) moved from the level of a popular art around the beginning of the twentieth century to the precision and the sophistication of a fine art by the mid-1930s. Nor should the matter of aesthetic refinement and existential depth be confused with social status: it is the innovating artist, regardless of his or her formal training and certification, who actually creates that which the so-called critical establishment evalu-ates and values after the fact.

III

The dance-oriented percussive emphasis of jazz was derived from West Africa along with the various tribal natives imported during the years of the North Atlantic slave trade, although very little African music as such continued to be performed by them in North America.

Not only were ancestral African rituals generally forbidden, but also, as a rule, the local slave population was almost always so diverse in language and in tribal culture that the erstwhile Africans could not communicate with one another in their native tongues anyway. Moreover, they were inevitably more preoccupied with practical techniques of coping and surviving on harsh local terms than with preserving procedures, relics, and talismans from their past environments, however sentimental they may have been.

In any case, there are grounds to believe that the definitive percussive emphasis in jazz is owed finally to trains—that it is more a matter of an aesthetic involvement with American railroad locomotive onomatopoeia than with transmitting tribal messages. Messages to whom? About what? After all, slave owners were always on the alert and were notoriously preemptive about Africans' talking drums. But it is the locomotive onomatopoeia that is so characteristic of down-home guitar, harmonica, and honky-tonk piano folk blues: its employment as an elementary local color or atmospheric device should be obvious as soon as you listen seriously to the music.

Trains, train whistles, and train bells came to suggest all kinds of possibilities and aspirations. There were the metaphysical trains in the sermons and songs of the Christian church, which incidentally the captive West Africans seem to have embraced with fervent enthusiasm largely on their own. There were the metaphorical trains of the underground railroad escape routes from bondage to freedom, the likes of which existed nowhere other than America. And there were also those actual north-to-freedom locomotives running on railroad tracks that captive West Africans had been used to help lay and maintain, inventing section-gang spike driving and track alignment rhythms and chants even as other slave workers invented field chants, woodsman's calls, swamp hollers, and so on. Moreover, it is not very likely that any creatures anywhere in West Africa were more impressive than these man-made, man-controlled mechanical creatures that also had voices, personalities, and even names and numbers.

Incidentally, in many instances, especially in down-home folk blues, the syncopating locomotive onomatopoeia is very literal, and the music (that is, the sonority) as such as well as the rhythm and the beat is in effect as programmatic as it is in Honegger's Pacific 231 or Duke Ellington's "Track 360," or as in such novelty popular features as "Alabama Bound," "California, Here I Come," and "Chattanooga Choo Choo," all of which employ programmatic devices in much the same way as, say, Prokofiev did in *Peter and the Wolf.*

But time passes, and over the years the refinement of locomotive onomatopoeia as a definitive device of jazz sonority as well as rhythm has been such that the locomotive elements now function in the way that dead metaphors function in conventional discourse. In Ellington's "Harlem Air Shaft," the blues locomotive sounds are still there, but now they represent a storyland panorama of people in a given area of a great metropolis. The locomotive onomatopoeia is also still there in Ellington's "Mainstem," but there it evokes the sights, the tempo, and the sounds of Broadway, including the special glitter of midtown Manhattan and Times Square. A very popular early "swing era" example of Ellington's programmatic use of locomotive ono-matopoeia is his rendition of the old ragtime showcase novelty tune "Tiger Rag" as "Daybreak Express."

Fletcher Henderson's arrangement of "Shanghai Shuffle," by contrast, and his orchestra's recording of Benny Carter's arrange-ment of "Limehouse Blues," are excellent examples of musical dead metaphors. The syncopation is definitive, but it is no longer about locomotives as such. It is about a dance tempo. But then there is El-lington's three-part *Uwis Suite,* written near the end of his life, as a tribute to the University of Wisconsin while the band was in res-idence on campus. The first part is an instrumental prom chant of deluxe-hotel-ballroom-type music that goes nicely with fraternity and sorority functions, groovy and up-tempo plus offbeat by turns. The second part is a tongue-in-cheek polka to charm the Midwesterners and the outsiders alike. And then comes the third part, which at first sounds for all the world like an old down-home juke-joint bump-and-grind stomp, but turns out to be "Loco Madi," a fine onomatopoeic account of the band's train trip—from, say, Chicago up to Madison and the University of Wisconsin. Incidentally, in this instance the lo-comotive onomatopoeia is somewhat less obviously programmatic than in its use in the "Happy Go Lucky Local" section of Ellington's *Deep South Suite,* where, as in "Daybreak Express," the train itself is the subject. Here it suggests how the composer feels about his desti-nation, the happiness with which he anticipates his arrival.

Whether it is a dead metaphor or a thematic program, the syn-

copating locomotive onomatopoeia is precisely what provides the velocity of celebration that drives the jubilee songs, shouts, jumps, and
ever so elegant stomps and grinds, shakes and shimmies and wobbles,
on festive occasions. There is also reason to believe that locomotive
onomatopoeia may be the most direct source of that definitive emphasis on syncopation that distinguishes jazz percussion from the
West African percussion from which it was derived, and also from
the Afro-Caribbean percussion to which it is so closely related.

The juke joint, the honky tonk, and the ballroom also represent
one more thing, anthropologically speaking: a ceremonial context for
the male-with-female-duet dance flirtation and embrace, upon which
the zoological survival of the human species has always been predicated. The Latin American influence on this aspect of jazz as dance
music is quite obvious. (The African dancing most familiar to Americans tends to be ensemble or choral dancing that suggests military
preparation for aggression or defense.)

Although jazz music for such dancing is generally regarded as
secular, neither the music nor the dance movements (which may be
ceremonial reenacts of primordial purification and fertility rituals) is totally forbidden at religious feast day celebrations. They are
excluded from church ceremonies as such, but not from such sacred
but extramural church-based celebrations as public Christmas and
Easter season dances and post-church wedding receptions. And the
relationship of male–female duet dances to rituals of season changes
and of planting, cultivation, harvesting, storing, and preserving
should not require elaboration.

Jazz music has come to be internationally recognized as something like the musical equivalent of Constance Rourke's idea of
American humor: an emblem for a pioneer people who require resilience as a prime trait. Jazz is also the musical equivalent of what
Kenneth Burke called representative anecdotes. By its very nature,
jazz typifies the national dynamics or natural history of exploration,
discovery, and improvisation; and the ever so tentative settlement of
what might become a great metropolis, a pit stop, or a ghost town of
lost chords. As the musical equivalent of representative anecdotes,
not only do jazz performances make people around the globe feel
that they know what the texture of life in the United States is like,
they also make a significant number of those people want to become

American. (I wonder how many immigrants to America the performances of Louis Armstrong were responsible for.)

How appropriate then that what amounts to a national shrine to exploration and improvisation is now being inaugurated as a world-class jazz performance venue at Columbus Circle by an institution bearing the name of Abraham Lincoln. So let the trail blaze on and on, and the riffs, too, those elegantly improvised tidbits that inevitably turn back into solo opportunities!

AFTERWORD

The Blues and Jazz as Aesthetic Statement

GREG THOMAS

> *We could say that art is a means by which you process*
> *raw experience into aesthetic statement . . . the aesthetic*
> *statement . . . feeds back into general human consciousness*
> *and raises their level of perception of their possibility in the*
> *face of adversity.*
>
> —Albert Murray to Wynton Marsalis

Murray Talks Music is a fascinating addition to the oeuvre of Albert
Murray. As of the writing of this Afterword, Murray hasn't been ac-
corded the scholarly consideration of his friend and fellow literary
colossus Ralph Ellison. Notwithstanding recognition by peers in elite
institutions such as the American Academy of Arts and Letters, the
lifetime achievement award from the National Book Critics Circle,
and other honors, the wider American and international intelligentsia
remains underinformed about the value and potential application of
Murray's ideas to contemporary intellectual discourse. Strange bar-
riers of politics, fear, ideology, American racial mysticism, and academic specialization have left Murray's work as a whole is in a kind
of no-man's-land. Thankfully, Murray is championed by professors
such as Henry Louis Gates Jr. and Robert G. O'Meally, but remains
conspicuously absent from conversations on civics, philosophy, and
aesthetics in which his work is central. Be that as it may, Murray's
corpus is chock-full of multidisciplinary wisdom addressing predic-
aments that continue to rip and rend the American and global body
politic since his first book, *The Omni-Americans,* was published in
1970.

Murray's ideas about music center on natural history and cultural dynamics, on how music as an art form develops through the
relationship between environmental conditions and the vernacular
materials musicians and other artists employ for freedom of expression and to fulfill a basic need to create form to make sense out of existence. Murray ingeniously illuminated the meanings of those forms,
especially the blues and jazz, as they correlated both to primordial ritual and to everyday ceremonial life in modern times. As an art form,
as Murray explained here and elsewhere, jazz has three fundamental
levels of sophistication in the processing of life's raw experience: folk,
pop, fine. In fine art we'll find the most comprehensive, elegant, and
eloquent means of "stomping the blues," of affirming life despite the
hysteria, histrionics, and confusion of the moment. Through fine art
we can feel and envision greater horizons of aspiration in the very
forms and implications of stylistic content. How such content com-
municates with us, moves and inspires us, is the psychocultural function of aesthetic statement. Once we add Murray's update of the hero
image to these insights, his paradigm becomes a wisdom portal for
application to social reality, to politics, to life generally. This collection is notable because by focusing primarily on Murray and music,
readers, whether lay or scholar, can perhaps better divine Murray's
figure in the carpet.

As you may have noticed in this volume, Murray's thought
contains active tensions. Control and resilience are among these. Of
course, such complementary polarities are resolved when seen from
a spiraling, developmental perspective: apprentice and journeyman
artists strive for mastery by developing control over their means and
methods of expression and reenactment. Achievement of mastery
gives maximum resilience and flexibility to improvise with the vernacular resources at hand. Such mastery of aesthetic statement is consistent with Murray's conception of fine art. You develop control to
have the freedom to flow and improvise with elegance. Phrases such
as "antagonistic cooperation" and "dynamic equilibrium" also give a
sense of a poised dance of thesis and antithesis generating into what
Murray called a "durable synthesis."

Murray's angle of vision, his depth of field and sharpness of focus, extended from the idiomatic to the national and global as well
as consciousness to culture to the cosmos. But as abstract as he could

be, never did he lose touch with the pragmatic connection of his ideas to everyday life, which he narrated time and time again in the space of his fiction, essays, and, indeed, in conversation. The very ideas he formulated about the blues and jazz as found in *Stomping the Blues, The Blue Devils of Nada, From the Briarpatch File,* and this collection derive primarily from the organic idiomatic and national cultural experience of blacks in the United States, not as a theory from outside imposed on the music or the culture. I have deeply studied his worldview—the blues idiom—for more than a quarter century. The way he bridged the profound and the quotidian, and complexity with fundamentals, all with an earthy sense of humor, was magnetic to me. He bristled with charisma and insight, which comes through in this book.

Although my love of jazz began about ten years before I became aware of his work, which occurred through reading essays by Stanley Crouch in the *Village Voice* and references to Murray by Wynton Marsalis (who inspired me in high school and college to always strive for excellence), once I began to study Murray's work I was awestruck by his breadth of knowledge and clear articulation of the power and grandeur of jazz. I had been immersed in jazz as a fan and apprentice alto saxophonist, marinating in the music's blisses, most especially the bebop period up to the renascence of acoustic, swinging jazz generationally pioneered by the Marsalis brothers. I had felt, in my gut and heart, that, indeed, jazz was great. But through Murray (and Ralph Ellison) not only did I gain emotional validation; my intellect was lifted to a horizon that clarified my very identity as a U.S.-born black male, with Southern roots, who had as much of a birthright to the national ideals and responsibilities of e pluribus unum, of equality, democracy, free speech and expression, and the pursuit of happiness as anyone.

I didn't quite understand the dynamics at play in my early years of musical enchantment, but Murray's words to Wynton in this book perfectly captured my experience:

Art is a secular companion to religious devotion. It's just as profound. It's basic equipment for living. So you listen for yourself and when you find yourself responding, it's because the musician is getting to you and you say "Oh yeah, this is

it!—oh Lord, am I born to die?! Why can't this happen over
and over? I'm gonna *buy* this record and play it!" Time and
time again, if the record is good enough, it will continue to
dispel the blues.

By the time Murray's work entered my awareness in the late 1980s,
around the time of the interview moderated by Loren Schoenberg
with Crouch and Murray on WKCR, I was primed.

Murray obliged me by visits to his Harlem abode, in the Lenox
Terrace apartments off 132d Street, which Murray insiders call "The
Spyglass Tree." He introduced me to Michael James, Duke Ellington's nephew, and Mike became a dear friend, mentor, and confidant.
Along with a graduate-school-level inquiry into the work and thought
of Ellison and Murray, Michael and I discussed literature, history,
philosophy, anthropology, politics, and so-called street knowledge
that rarely ends up in books. One of my more formal (yet freewheeling with brio) conversations with Murray is captured in this volume,
which I undertook in 1996 to frame my own work as a graduate student in American studies at NYU. In the twenty years hence, my respect and admiration for Murray's perspicacity, for his generosity as a
friend and teacher, and for his, yes, genius, have grown even stronger.
By the time of the conversation in this collection, I had committed
myself to lifelong study of culture and jazz, and to sharing my knowledge and feelings about these dynamic realms of human reality and
art as a professional writer. In fact, such a commitment derived from
what Ellison and Murray called an ancestral imperative.

They were both fond of saying that you can't choose your relatives but you for damn sure can choose your ancestors. Relatives
come by genetic and idiomatic inheritance; ancestors can too, but the
expansive conception of what I call the *Ellison–Murray Continuum*
allows for the incorporation of heroes from the past in one's métier
or even outside it. An artist can be inspired by a scientist and vice
versa. Ellison and Murray were more inspired by Armstrong and Ellington to be first-class writers than by their writerly cousins of the
Harlem Renaissance Langston Hughes, Sterling Brown, and Zora
Neale Hurston. But the main point is the imperative to make the
old folks, so to speak, those who have laid down blood, sweat, and
tears to make it possible for you to be alive, and, hopefully, to thrive,

proud of you. To fulfill the dreams of generations gone by so that their values will live on and be enacted by what you strive to achieve and actually accomplish. To do the level best you can so that your ancestors would say: Well done.

Murray's extensive interview with an honored and revered ancestor, Dizzy Gillespie, contained in these pages will certainly dispel the rubbish that he didn't appreciate bop, but, moreover, the conversation between Murray, a critic-scholar-native insider to the jazz idiom who literally grew up with the music as it manifested its variations on blues idiom themes, and Gillespie, cofounder (with alto sax grandmaster Charlie Parker) and the greatest teacher and promoter of bop (and one of its greatest composers), will provide historians and fans a thumbnail sketch of the cultural and musical scene which the two men shared. As they riffed back and forth, recalling names, songs, places, territory bands, the special role of the piano in jazz improvisation, the imperative of *style* in aesthetic endeavor, great teachers and moments from the past, giving representative anecdotes about how bop was received, and acknowledging their own place as honored elders, a picture of shared meaning, values, and internal standards of evaluation becomes clear.

When Murray mentions in this interview with Dizzy Gillespie that Wynton Marsalis is one of the two top classical trumpeters in the world, but that Marsalis wondered if he'd make it to the upper reaches of the greatest jazz trumpeters, it implies that jazz performance at the highest levels could be even more challenging than the performance of European concert music. One distinction is the fundamental role of improvisation in the blues idiom, a practice so fundamental to human life that an interdisciplinary academic field (Critical Improvisation Studies) has been established to study it. Another is a difference in rhythmic emphasis and facility. As Murray mentions several times in this volume, the percussive nature of blues idiom music is likely its most definitive feature. Gillespie agreed (while underscoring the harmonic devices of bebop). "Classical musicians don't know anything about an upbeat," said Gillespie. "The conductor, when he brings his hand down, that's 'one' . . . He has no beat for an upbeat. And we live on it. That's why we can play their music, and they can't play ours."

When Murray says, "That particular emotion comes from . . ."

Gillespie interjects: "Yeah, we are the sanctified church, we got that beat." Although in *Stomping the Blues* Murray wrote that "many of the elements of blues music seem to have been derived from the downhome church in the first place," he identified the disposition of black Americans to "turn all movement to a dance beat elegance" as derived from our "captive ancestors." Gillespie, pointing to the holiness or sanctified church as the rhythmic cradle—which fits Murray's thesis but from a sacred angle—quilts a conception of jazz as intimately tied to religio-spiritual sources emphasized by Jon Hendricks, Mary Lou Williams, and Duke Ellington.

Another subtle distinction between Murray and Gillespie surfaced based on their distinct objectives. Murray insisted and demonstrated that jazz, as performed at the upper reaches of aesthetic statement by, say, Louis Armstrong, the Duke Ellington Orchestra, and Charlie Parker, is on a par with the greatest music of any time and in any place. Considering the lowly place of the blues and jazz in the minds of many in the so-called white and black communities in the early days of the music coming to market even on to the bebop era and beyond, such a cultural project was courageous and audacious. Murray also revealed the mythic (the heroic jazz musician engaging existential and bandstand foes/partners through antagonistic cooperation on the break), the ritualistic (purification and fertility rituals), as well as the literary, rhetorical, cultural, and cosmic context of the music's evolution and significance.

As a creative pioneer, both as an instrumentalist and as a stylistic innovator, Gillespie included, yet transcended, the more U.S.-centric vision of Murray's, in a similar manner that Gillespie included the foundations of early jazz and the big-band swing era yet innovated beyond. His transnational vision was that "the music of the Western Hemisphere one day will be unified . . . It's not there quite yet, but they're doing it. The rock and roll guys are doing it. They got jazz and they got blues and they got Latin in their music. I think one of these days the music of Brazil, the West Indies, Cuba and the United States will be unified."

Then Murray pointed out that from W. C. Handy onward, early jazz included Latin American elements owing to infusions of the people and cultures resulting from the Spanish-American War, the building of the Panama Canal, and so on. In "Jazz: Notes Toward a Definition," Murray makes mention of the Latin American influence on jazz as a dance music in the ceremonial context of the juke joint, honky tonk, and ballroom. Yet the vision of *hemispheric unity through music* was Gillespie's, perhaps influenced by his adherence to the Baha'i faith, which during the years of his youth strongly affirmed the concept of "racial amity."

In Murray's conversation with Bob O'Meally for the Smithsonian's Jazz Oral History Project there's a defining moment. Many once wondered why black American literature hasn't risen to a level of accomplishment comparable to the heights reached by black music. Considering the global impact of not just blues and jazz but other forms of music innovated by artists across the black diaspora, this point of view is arguably true, even if only felt intuitively. Professor O'Meally asks Murray to clarify: why the difference? Why would Ralph Ellison say to a young black writer to "check out the Russians" but in reference to a young Louis Armstrong it wouldn't have been necessary to say check out Mozart and Beethoven first?

AM: Well, the difference is that they knew the literature of the trumpet, because they knew about John Philip Sousa and all these people. They knew what that was, but he grew up . . . *where something was actually being created.* You see what I'm saying? Something was being created which he latched on to. And it had all the rest. And besides, they knew it. You would talk to Louis, you know, the guy would say . . . "Well, what did you hear?" [imitating Louis Armstrong]: "We heard it all. We heard all the stuff they playing, we had the radio, we had the phonograph records, we like music!" And the interviewer says, "Yeah, but did you listen to people, you know, like . . . Brahms or Mahler?" He'd say, "Yeah. We're into Brahms. Yeah, all that stuff, and we heard Gustav Mahler! And don't forget Fats Waller!" You see, he was always together with those things [laughs]. It was just music to him. He makes much of when Erskine Tate and those guys were playing classical music. He'd say, "Yeah, they're playing those overtures, man, tell you to turn back five pages. You have to be able to read that stuff. I picked up on reading quite a bit in the pit band."

Jazz, as a North American form, incorporated European, African, and Latin American elements into its synthesis to innovate a *new musical art form*. Armstrong is the stylistic progenitor of the idiom as it developed post-ragtime. For black writers, or writers from any background for that matter, to approach such a level of achievement, they'd have to master and synthesize the literary tradition they're working in and put a contemporary stamp upon it with their individual voice and style. If that voice and style infuse the very language as written in the public domain, then the achievement would be comparable. Perhaps now it's easier to see why Murray so appreciated Hemingway and thought he best translated in American vernacular the style and achievement of the blues idiom.

After the statement in the quote above, Murray essays a remarkable short history of the milieu of music education extant in the early decades of jazz, recalling themes from his conversation with Dizzy Gillespie and an amazing interview about Duke Ellington from 1989. Loren Schoenberg hosted this WKCR radio program at Columbia University in New York, engaging Murray and Stanley Crouch about the sui generis stature of Duke Ellington within jazz and Western music overall. The program has significance far above the attacks of writers such as James Lincoln Collier, Terry Teachout, and Adam Gopnik, who, like thieves in broad daylight, try to blur and mar the iconic status of Ellington, as if his reputation was too uppity. In the context of Murray's body of work and thought, Duke is central as the most comprehensive realization of the vernacular imperative to transmute the raw experience of his life into universal aesthetic statement. Duke also distinguished musical greatness in twentieth-century American terms in contradistinction to the European concert tradition. Even when Ellington rearranged Grieg and Tchaikovsky, he framed it within his own blues idiom aesthetic, values, and style. In fact, if Homo Americanus—according to Constance Rourke: part Negro, part Yankee, part Indian, and part frontiersman—is the cutting edge of Western culture, as Murray often said, then Duke may be the quintessential composer of the century (an idea that wouldn't have been lost on Milhaud, Ravel, and others).

In this swinging discussion, Murray, Crouch, and Schoenberg referenced and played works from Ellington's many decades of musical creativity. Duke's genius becomes translucent through their insights on how Ellington's grasp of blues, ragtime, and stride extended to his capacious gifts as a leader, pianist, arranger, and nonpareil composer. Crouch, for example, astutely relays how Ellington saw the conceptual depths beyond surface technique, and extended basic ideas across time.

Schoenberg emphasized that Ellington represents a new category of composer in Western music. Echoing Crouch's earlier insight regarding the "statement of the harmony with a percussive inflection" in jazz, as well as Murray's emphasis on the definitive incantational and percussive nature of the blues idiom, Schoenberg proclaimed that Duke's particular percussive approach to harmonic structure—which strongly influenced Thelonious Monk—was actually new to Western music. And so some folks don't get the continuum twisted, as Murray said to Wynton in this book: "Nobody called Monk old-fashioned. Monk is Duke. And Duke is ragtime."

Murray expanded the usual perception of the jazz composer as simply writing individual tunes by projecting Duke as a composer for his orchestra (for which he famously composed and arranged with specific musicians in mind) who wrote the equivalent of five or six symphonies a year! The trio of discussants also riffed on the technological limitations of LP length as a formal and structural constraint that Duke used to brilliant pragmatic advantage. Ellington was always steps ahead and above, says Murray:

> Most people somehow or other had the feeling that what he was doing was always totally different from what other people were doing. It was the *apotheosis* of what they were doing. Because *he was a composer.* They could see it, they could feel it—whether they articulated it in that way or not. These other people had arrangers, they did things, you had these other bands that were very popular in hotels and so forth. Their music was popular music derived from more serious aspects of this music. And Ellington was not just providing that type of entertainment. *He was stylizing his own life.* In fact, I remember very well a definition that he gave of jazz. Someone said, "What is your definition of jazz?" And he said, "It is *Negro American feeling expressed in rhythm and tune.*"

By expanding the compositional, technical, and emotional range of
jazz, Ellington became representative of the tones, attitudes, and
textures of twentieth-century America. For Murray, Ellington is
matched only by Louis Armstrong as a prime representative of jazz
as a fine art, exemplary, then, of humanity's potential for mastery and
fulfillment in the face of the blues as such: absurdity, chaos, depression, entropy.

To Murray, that's the ultimate existential value of art. In fact,
art is so fundamental to *Cosmos Murray* that he ventured his own
descriptions, combining denotative clarity and connotative implication. An all-too-brief summation of a braided conceptual base of
Murray's take on art is: Art is *feeling in form* (Susanne K. Langer) as
well as the *processing of form and raw experience into style* (André
Malraux), leading to *style as strategy* and *art as equipment for living*
(Kenneth Burke). Murray's formulations elaborate upon this foundation. He proposed a layered plurality of art: the first via stylization,
another two describing such stylization in idiomatic and universal
registers:

Stylization: "Art is the means by which the raw materials of
human experience are processed into aesthetic statement."
(*From the Briarpatch File: On Context, Procedure, and American Identity*, 29)

Idiomatic: "Art is the extension, elaboration, and refinement
of the local details and idiomatic particulars that impinge
most intimately on one's everyday existence." (Ibid., 3)

Universal: "Art is the ultimate extension, elaboration, and refinement of the rituals that reenact primary survival technology; and hence it conveys basic attitudes toward experience
of a given people, in a given time, place, circumstance, and
predicament." (This definition is synonymous with Murray's
conception of "fine art.") (Robert G. O'Meally, ed., *The Jazz
Cadence of American Culture*, 111)

I'll close with a quote from *The Omni-Americans,* a statement
that considering the content of this book—from Gary Giddins's Fore-

word, Paul Devlin's Introduction, the interviews with and the relatively short pieces by Murray, to my attempt to characterize special
aspects of the volume in this Afterword—should now reverberate
from the idiomatic to the universal:

> The definitive statement of the epistemological assumptions
> that underlie the blues idiom may well be the colloquial title
> and opening declaration of one of Duke Ellington's best-
> known dance tunes from the mid-thirties: "It Don't Mean
> a Thing if It Ain't Got That Swing." In any case, when the
> Negro musician or dancer swings the blues, he is fulfilling the
> same fundamental existential requirement that determines
> the mission of the poet, the priest, and the medicine man. He
> is making an affirmative and hence exemplary and heroic re-
> sponse to that which André Malraux describes as *la condition
> humaine*. Extemporizing in response to the . . . situation in
> which he finds himself, he is confronting, acknowledging, and
> contending with the infernal absurdities and ever-impending
> frustrations inherent in the nature of all existence by *playing
> with the possibilities that are also there.* Thus does man the
> player become man the stylizer and by the same token the hu-
> manizer of chaos; and thus does play become ritual, ceremo-
> ny, and art; and thus also does the dance-beat improvisation
> of experience in the blues idiom become survival technique,
> esthetic equipment for living, and a central element in the
> dynamics of U.S. Negro life style.

Murray detailed why and how the processes of jazz such as improvising on the "break" were a moment of opportunity, not solely a source
of psychoanalytic trauma; how swinging resilience in the midst of
a social and structural briar patch can bring existential fulfillment,
at least for as many measures as we can play in our lifetimes; and
how train metaphors both reflected and expressed elements of black
American life and music within the context of American experimentation and creativity. As with the postmodernists and pragmatists,
he knew that there is no "essential" self. However, a victim model,
a frame of rejection, was antithetical to his temperament, character,
and experience. He embraced a mythic hero mode typified by, among

others in his image house of affirmation through confrontation, the jazz musician and the swinging ensemble. He wanted the "rhapsodized thunder" and "syncopated lightning" of the blues idiom called jazz to speak to the hero in you.

December 2015

ACKNOWLEDGMENTS

First and foremost, I thank Lewis P. Jones III, executor of the Albert Murray Estate, close friend of Albert and Mozelle Murray for forty years, and caretaker of the Murrays in their last years, for entrusting me with the task of assembling this book. Thanks to Michele Murray for encouraging me to carry on the work of her father and extend his legacy. Thanks to Kristen Jones. Thanks to Gary Giddins for his Foreword, as well as his keen editorial eye and expertise. Thanks to Greg Thomas for contributing an important interview with Mr. Murray and for writing the Afterword. Thanks to everyone who generously agreed to allow their unpublished conversations with Mr. Murray (those conversations that the estate did not own) to be included in this book: Wynton Marsalis, Robert G. O'Meally, Janis Herbert, Loren Schoenberg, and Stanley Crouch. Thanks to Lauren Walsh for her translation of the talk on jazz that Mr. Murray wrote in French.

Erik Anderson at the University of Minnesota Press believed in this book and helped guide it through publication. He has outstanding taste and was the ideal editor. Kristian Tvedten did a great job. Doug Armato is very wise and runs one of the best accounts on Twitter. Diedra Harris-Kelley generously allowed me to spend a day in Romare Bearden's archive looking for anything that might be used in this book. (I found nothing for the book, but it was an unforgettable, edifying experience.) Thanks to Edith Bolton. Thanks to Sara Jensen. Thanks to the Houghton Library at Harvard University.

Thanks to my mom and dad, Rosemary Devlin and James Devlin. Thanks to my mom for visiting with Mrs. Murray so often after Mr. Murray passed away. Thanks to my sister, Tara Devlin, and my brother-in-law (and a fellow Ellington buff), Eric Livermore. Thanks to my aunts Maureen Tracy and Patricia Tracy, and to all of my aunts and uncles and cousins. Thanks to Peter and MaryAnn Cooper. Thanks to Naomi Caesar.

Rowan Ricardo Phillips was my dissertation director at Stony Brook University and continues to offer valuable advice and guidance. Henry Louis Gates Jr. has been a helpful and encouraging mentor. Some of Mr. Murray's closest friends generously shared their time and knowledge with me over the years. I'm especially grateful to Charlie Davidson, Dan Morgenstern, Sidney Offit, and George Wein. Mr. Offit is a close friend and mentor. Mr. Wein and Mr. Morgenstern have shared valuable perspectives on jazz, history, and culture with me. Mr. Davidson is a brilliant raconteur and generous friend. Thanks to Matt and Phyllis Clark. Thanks to Edie Shaw Marcus and Meta Shaw Stevens.

Thanks to Ethan Iverson for his perceptive commentary on Mr. Murray's work on his award-winning blog Do the Math and for inviting me to write a guest post on Mr. Murray in 2013. Thanks to master drummer Michael Carvin. Thanks to Phil Schaap. Thanks to Kenny Washington. Thanks to Howard Mandel, Bob Mover, Brandee Younger, Tad Hershorn, Frank Stewart, Genevieve Stewart, Todd Stoll, and Seton Hawkins. Thanks to Jackie Harris of the Louis Armstrong Educational Foundation. Thanks to everyone who interviewed me when *Rifftide: The Life and Opinions of Papa Jo Jones* was published, especially Leonard Lopate, Ken Druker, Josh Jackson, and Bob Waldman. Thanks to Aaron Diehl.

Thanks to all of my colleagues and correspondents. I'd especially like to thank Stephen Sicari of St. John's University, who approved my proposal to bring Mr. Murray to speak on campus in 2003 as a guest of the English department. Thanks to Granville Ganter for allowing his words from that event to be included in this book (and for being a mentor for many years). Thanks to Dohra Ahmad, John Lowney, Raj Chetty, and Steven Mentz. Thanks to the St. John's University students who worked under my supervision during the inventorying of Mr. Murray's books and papers in 2015: Michael Benjamin, Daniel Heffernan, and Tamara Jefferson. Thanks to my colleagues at the U.S. Merchant Marine Academy: LCDR Paul Acquaro, Jane Brickman, Susan Comilang, Georgianna Durant, Laury Magnus, Melanie Ross, Joshua Smith, Jennifer Speelman, Patrick Speelman, Greg Sullivan, Jeffrey Taffet, Kempton Van Hoff, and Rosanne Wasserman. Thanks to the following professors at Stony Brook University: Jeffrey Santa Ana, Eric Haralson, Celia Marshik, Susan Scheckel,

Peter Manning, Michael Rubinstein, Ed Casey, Roger Rosenblatt, and Eugene Hammond. Thanks to Daniel Stein of the University of Siegen. Thanks to Sonia Sanchez and Mungu Sanchez. Thanks to Evan Hughes. Thanks to Matthew Hunte. Thanks to Louis D. Johnston, Cliff Thompson, Jacquelynne Modeste, Roberta Maguire, Walton Muyumba, Herman Beavers, Aryeh Tepper, Joel Dinerstein, Ross Posnock, Greg Clark, and Michael Borshuk. Thanks to Tom Litland. Thanks to John Colgate and Duke Barnett. Thanks to Eric Klinek. Thanks to Phil Clark. Thanks to Christopher Carduff.

Thanks to Mrs. Valena McCants of Mobile, Alabama, an educator and Tuskegee alumna who knew Mr. Murray since the 1930s and generously shared her memories and impressions with me in an interview in 2013. Thanks to Bobbi Ross, close friend of the Murray family for seven decades. Thanks to all of Mr. Murray's friends at cultural institutions in Alabama: Jay Lamar, Don Noble, Jeanie Thompson, William Gantt, Bert Hitchcock, Caroline Gebhard, Al Head, Adam Vines, Kern Jackson, Loretta Burns, and Dana Chandler. Thanks to the Southern Literary Trail. Thanks to the Alabama Writers Hall of Fame at the University of Alabama, Tuscaloosa, and the Alabama Writers Forum.

Thanks to Judy Laffite and Neville Jones, the nurses who took great care of Mr. Murray in his last years. Judy also cared for Mrs. Murray after Mr. Murray passed away. Finally, thanks to all of the new readers who may be discovering Mr. Murray's words for the first time here and thanks to all his readers of many decades.

APPENDIX A
Albert Murray's Canon of Jazz Arrangements

In late 2000 or early 2001 Albert Murray began working on this list of jazz arrangements, which he frequently referred to offhand as a canon. It was intended as a reference point for Jazz at Lincoln Center and was finished by early 2002. I accompanied him on several trips to the enormous Tower Records on Broadway, a few blocks north of Lincoln Center, to buy some of the albums here on compact disc. Murray had many of these works on vinyl but wanted to be able to reference the most recent release.

Murray worked on this list with Sara Jensen, then an information technology employee of Jazz at Lincoln Center (and later a business analyst there), who typed the entries into an Excel spreadsheet. He shared evolving versions of the list with me as Sara completed typing them, and I had a few variants of the lists and fragments of lists on paper. In 2013 I saw Sara (who now works elsewhere) at Murray's memorial service at Jazz at Lincoln Center. She kindly shared the most recent version she had of the list. Both our lists were from fall 2001. The list below, which I found among Mr. Murray's papers, is dated February 2002 and thus is the most recent version. It seems that Murray did not submit or share the list in an official capacity.

"Canon" in its original sense refers to the laws and edicts of the Roman Catholic Church. The word itself has become sort of a hot potato since the so-called culture wars in American higher education in the 1980s and 1990s and debates about the merits of the so-called Western Canon. Lately it has been used to mean continuity within imaginary worlds. A canon traditionally suggests rigidity and permanence. Murray certainly did not have a dogmatic conception of canons of the arts. His understanding was much closer, I believe, to Italo

Calvino's conception of a personal, flexible list of classics, informed by history and developed over a period of long study, which will eventually include many works widely considered to be classics along with idiosyncratic personal favorites. (This is expressed in Calvino's wonderful essay "Why Read the Classics?") I believe Murray intended *for canon in the case of this list to be close to definition 2.c from the* Oxford English Dictionary: *"a standard of judgement or authority; a test, criterion, means of discrimination." Because the list was made for Jazz at Lincoln Center, he probably considered these arrangements to be models for study by arrangers of the future.*

This probably could have been called a list of Murray's "preferred" arrangements. But he put a lot of time and effort into this list and wanted it to be comprehensive. I do not think he intended for it to be exclusive or immutable. This list is the opinion of one expert and scholar, carefully selected after a lifetime of listening. I believe he would have weighed the merits of other equally informed opinions. If someone similarly knowledgeable had said, "What about this, Al?" I believe he would have considered the suggestion. It should also be noted that this list stops around 1960. Murray was a great admirer of the arrangements of Victor Goines (the main arranger for Jazz at Lincoln Center) and said so on many occasions. One omission here that I consider surprising, given how highly Murray spoke of it, is Benny Carter's Kansas City Suite *(performed by the Count Basie Orchestra).*

Each recording included is an outstanding piece of music and new listeners cannot go wrong by starting here. Thanks to the Internet, old and out-of-print music is much easier to find now than in 2002, and therefore Murray's list is even more valuable and useful. There are probably only a very few listeners who couldn't find something new and unexpected here.

The list is in alphabetical order by arranger's last name. Then, each arrangement under each arranger is in alphabetical order. Another benefit of this list is that it is a tribute to the arrangers themselves, some of whom did not share the spotlight with the performers. (Of course, some were also performers.) A few of their names have faded, but they are getting credit here. Unexpected continuities and dimensions in the history of American music in the twentieth century can be discerned from a peek into their lives. Sammy Lowe, for instance, was a prominent big-band arranger and later transitioned away from jazz to become an important rhythm-and-blues and soul arranger, arranging hits for James Brown and others. Another figure who made that transition is Quincy Jones, a surprising omission here. Murray liked a lot of his 1960s work with Basie. Yet Basie's 1950s arranger Neal Hefti is included here, despite Murray's harsh criticism of his work in a letter to Ralph Ellison, included in Trading Twelves. *Then again, Murray really dug the* Breakfast Dance and Barbeque *album. Everyone knows Mary Lou Williams as one of the most important jazz pianists, but this list will draw attention to her arrangements for Andy Kirk.*

The two giant omissions here are Duke Ellington and Billy Strayhorn. Murray planned a separate list for them but never got around to it. Appendix B is an Ellington–Strayhorn list that Murray compiled in the 1990s, most likely for Jazz at Lincoln Center.

Edgar Battle

"Doggin' Around." Performed by Count Basie, from *Complete Original American Decca Recordings.*

"Hard Times." Performed by Cab Calloway, from *Chronological Classics: Cab Calloway and His Orchestra 1940–41.*

"Topsy Turvy." Performed by Earl Hines, from *Chronological Classics: Earl Hines and His Orchestra 1939–40.*

Benny Carter

"Back Bay Boogie." Performed by Benny Carter, from *Chronological Classics: Benny Carter and His Orchestra 1946–48.*

"Cutting Time." Performed by Benny Carter, from *Echoes of Harlem Big Bands.*

"Easy Money." Performed by Count Basie, from *The Best of Count Basie: The Roulette Years.*

"Just You, Just Me." Performed by Benny Carter, from *Echoes of Harlem Big Bands.*

"Lime House Blues." Performed by Fletcher Henderson, from *Tidal Wave.*

"Liza." Performed by Chick Webb, from *Chronological Classics: Chick Webb & His Orchestra 1935–1938.*

"Liza." Performed by Fletcher Henderson, from *Tidal Wave.*

"Lonesome Nights." Performed by Cab Calloway, from *Chronological Classics: Cab Calloway and His Orchestra 1940–41.*

"Prelude to a Kiss." Performed by Benny Carter, from *Echoes of Harlem Big Bands.*

"Re-Bop Boogie." Performed by Benny Carter, from *Chronological Classics: Benny Carter 1946–48.*

"Rhythm of the Tambourine." Performed by Fletcher Henderson, from *Chronological Classics: Fletcher Henderson and His Orchestra 1937–38.*

"Twelve O'clock Jump." Performed by Benny Carter, from *Chronological Classics: Benny Carter and His Orchestra 1946–48.*

Buck Clayton

"Avenue C." Performed by Count Basie, from *Chronological Classics: Count Basie & His Orchestra 1945–1946.*

"Blues in the Dark." Performed by Count Basie, from *Complete Original American Decca Recordings.*

"Blues on the Double." Performed by Duke Ellington, from *Duke's Joint.*

"Hollywood Hangover." Performed by Duke Ellington, from *V Disc Recordings Collector's Choice.*

"It's Sand, Man." Performed by Count Basie.

"Seventh Avenue Express." Performed by Count Basie, from *Complete Original American RCA-Victor Recordings.*

"Taps Miller." Performed by Count Basie, from *Chronological Classics: Count Basie & His Orchestra 1943–1945.*

"Tipping on the Q.T." Performed by Count Basie, from *Chronological Classics: Count Basie and His Orchestra 1945–46.*

Tadd Dameron

"Cool Breeze." Performed by Dizzy Gillespie, from *Chronological Classics: Dizzy Gillespie & His Orchestra 1947–1949.*

"Good Bait." Performed by Dizzy Gillespie, from *Complete RCA Recordings.*

"Our Delight." Performed by Dizzy Gillespie, from *Essential Masters of Jazz.*

"Stay On It." Performed by Count Basie, from *Chronological Classics: Count Basie and His Orchestra 1946–1947.*

"Stay On It." Performed by Dizzy Gillespie, from Complete RCA Recordings.

Eddie Durham

"Baby, Don't Tell on Me." Performed by Count Basie, from *The Essential Count Basie, Vol. 1.*

"Good Morning Blues." Performed by Count Basie, from *Complete Original American Decca Recordings.*

"Lunceford Special." Performed by Jimmie Lunceford, from *Lunceford Special: 1939–1949 Columbia Records.*

"Moten Swing." Performed by Bennie Moten, from *Best of Jazz: Bennie Moten.*

"Sent for You Yesterday." Performed by Count Basie, from *Complete Original American Decca Recordings.*

"Swinging in C." Performed by Jimmie Lunceford, from *Masters of Jazz, Vol. 8, 1940–1941.*

"Swinging the Blues." Performed by Count Basie, from *Complete Original American Decca Recordings.*

"Topsy." Performed by Count Basie, from *Complete Original American Decca Recordings.*

Frank Foster

"Back to the Apple." Performed by Count Basie, from *Breakfast Dance and Barbecue.*

"Blues Backstage." Performed by Count Basie, from *Count Basie Plays the Blues.*

"Blues in Hoss' Flat." Performed by Count Basie, from *Chairman of the Board.*

"Didn't You?" Performed by Count Basie, from *April in Paris.*

"In a Mellow Tone." Performed by Count Basie, from *Breakfast Dance and Barbecue.*

"Manteca." Performed by Dizzy Gillespie, from *Dizzy's Diamonds: Best of the Verve Years, Disc III.*

"Shiny Stockings." Performed by Count Basie, from *April in Paris.*

"The Come Back." Performed by Count Basie.

"Who Me?" Performed by Count Basie, from *Breakfast Dance and Barbecue.*

Gil Fuller

"Angel City." Performed by Dizzy Gillespie, with Gil Fuller conducting Monterey Jazz Festival Orchestra.

"Be's That Way." Performed by Dizzy Gillespie, with Gil Fuller conducting Monterey Jazz Festival Orchestra.

"Big Sur." Performed by Dizzy Gillespie, with Gil Fuller conducting Monterey Jazz Festival Orchestra.

"Born Tired." Performed by Dizzy Gillespie.

"Groovin' High." Performed by Dizzy Gillespie, from *Dizzy Gillespie: The Gold Collection, Classic Performances.*

"Groovin' High." Performed by Dizzy Gillespie, from *Essential Masters of Jazz: Dizzy Gillespie.*

"Manteca." Performed by Dizzy Gillespie, from *Complete RCA Victor Recordings.*

"Manteca." Performed by Dizzy Gillespie, from *Dizzy's Diamonds: Best of the Verve Years.*

"Moon Tide." Performed by Dizzy Gillespie, with Gil Fuller conducting Monterey Jazz Festival Orchestra.

"Swedish Suite." Performed by Dizzy Gillespie, from *1947–49 Dizzy & Orch. Chrono. Classics.*

"Things That Are." Performed by Dizzy Gillespie, with Gil Fuller conducting Monterey Jazz Festival Orchestra.

"Things to Come." Performed by Dizzy Gillespie, from *Dizzy Gillespie: The Gold Collection, Classic Performances.*

"Things to Come." Performed by Dizzy Gillespie, from *Essential Masters of Jazz: Dizzy Gillespie.*

Andy Gibson

"Ebony Silhouette." Performed by Cab Calloway, from *Chronological Classics: Cab Calloway and His Orchestra 1940–41.*

"I Left My Baby." Performed by Count Basie, from *The Essential Count Basie, Vol. 2.*

"Let Me See." Performed by Count Basie, from *The Essential Count Basie, Vol. 2.*

"Shorty George." Performed by Count Basie, from *Complete Original American Decca Recordings.*

"Special Delivery." Performed by Cab Calloway, from *Chronological Classics: Cab Calloway and His Orchestra 1940–41.*

"The Apple Jump." Performed by Count Basie, from *The Essential Count Basie, Vol. 2.*

"The World Is Mad." Performed by Count Basie, from *The Essential Count Basie, Vol. 3.*

"Tickle Toe." Performed by Count Basie, from *The Essential Count Basie, Vol. 2.*

Buster Harding

"9:20 Special." Performed by Count Basie, from *The Essential Count Basie, Vol. 3.*

"Call My Happy." Performed by Earl Hines, from *Chronological Classics: Earl Hines & His Orchestra 1939–1940.*

"Hob Nail Boogie." Performed by Count Basie, from *Blues & Boogie Woogie.*

"Little Jazz." Performed by Artie Shaw.

"Scarecrow." Performed by Benny Goodman, from *Benny Goodman Plays Mel Powell.*

"Smooth One." Performed by Benny Goodman.

"Windy City Jive." Performed by Earl Hines, from *Chronological Classics: Earl Hines & His Orchestra 1941.*

Neal Hefti

"Cherry Point." Performed by Count Basie, from *Breakfast Dance and Barbecue.*

"Cute." Performed by Count Basie, from *Breakfast Dance and Barbecue.*

"Li'l Darling." Performed by Count Basie, from *Live 1958 and 1959.*

"Splanky." Performed by Count Basie, from *Breakfast Dance and Barbecue.*

Fletcher Henderson

"Don't Let the Rhythm Go to Your Head." Performed by Fletcher Henderson, from *Chronological Classics: Fletcher Henderson and His Orchestra 1937–38.*

"If You Should Ever Leave." Performed by Fletcher Henderson, from *Chronological Classics: Fletcher Henderson & His Orchestra 1937–38.*

"King Porter Stomp." Performed by Fletcher Henderson, from *Ken Burns Jazz.*

"Let's Dance." Performed by Benny Goodman, from *B. G. in Hi-Fi.*

"My Melancholy Baby." Performed by Coleman Hawkins, from *Chronological Classics: Coleman Hawkins 1937–39.*

"New King Porter Stomp." Performed by Fletcher Henderson, from *Ken Burns Jazz.*

"Shanghai Shuffle." Performed by Fletcher Henderson, from *Tidal Wave.*

"Sing You Sinners." Performed by Fletcher Henderson, from *Chronological Classics: Fletcher Henderson and His Orchestra 1937–38.*

"Stampede." Performed by Fletcher Henderson, from *Ken Burns Jazz.*

"Stealin' Apples." Performed by Fletcher Henderson, from *Chronological Classics: Fletcher Henderson and His Orchestra 1937–38.*

"Sugarfoot Stomp." Performed by Fletcher Henderson, from *Ken Burns Jazz.*

"The Darktown Strutters Ball." Performed by Coleman Hawkins, from *Chronological Classics: Coleman Hawkins 1937–39.*

"The Stampede." Performed by Fletcher Henderson, from *Chronological Classics: Fletcher Henderson and His Orchestra 1926–27.*

"Wrappin' It Up." Performed by Fletcher Henderson, from *Tidal Wave.*

Horace Henderson

"Christopher Columbus." Performed by Fletcher Henderson, from *Ken Burns Jazz.*

"Big John Special." Performed by Fletcher Henderson, from *Ken Burns Jazz.*

Budd Johnson

"Grand Terrace Shuffle." Performed by Fletcher Henderson, from *Ken Burns Jazz.*

"St. Louis Blues." Performed by Dizzy Gillespie, from *Complete RCA Victor Recordings.*

"Riff Medley." Performed by Earl Hines, from *Chronological Classics: Earl Hines and His Orchestra, 1937–1939.*

"XYZ." Performed by Earl Hines, from *Chronological Classics: Earl Hines and His Orchestra, 1937–1939.*

John Lewis

"Birth of the Cool." Performed by Miles Davis, from *Birth of the Cool.*

"Budo." Performed by Miles Davis, from *Birth of the Cool.*

"Emanon." Performed by Dizzy Gillespie, from *Dizzy Gillespie: The Gold Collection, Classic Performances.*

"Move." Performed by Miles Davis, from *The Complete Birth of the Cool.*

"Move (Live)." Performed by Miles Davis, from *The Complete Birth of the Cool.*

"One Bass Hit." Performed by Dizzy Gillespie, from *Dizzy Gillespie: The Gold Collection, Classic Performances.*

"Stay on It." Performed by Dizzy Gillespie, from *Dizzy Gillespie: Complete RCA Victor Recordings.*

"Two Bass Hit." Performed by Dizzy Gillespie, from *Dizzy Gillespie: Complete RCA Victor Recordings.*

Sammy Lowe

"Bear Mash Blues." Performed by Erskine Hawkins, from *Jazz Archives: Erskine Hawkins and His Orchestra, Vol. 2 Holiday for Swing.*

"Don't Cry Baby." Performed by Erskine Hawkins, from *Chronological Classics: Erskine Hawkins and His Orchestra 1941–1945.*

"Gin Mill Special." Performed by Erskine Hawkins, from *Chronological Classics: Erskine Hawkins and His Orchestra 1938–1939.*

"Nona." Performed by Erskine Hawkins, from *Jazz Archives: Erskine Hawkins and His Orchestra, Vol. 2 Holiday for Swing.*

"Saboo." Performed by Erskine Hawkins, from *Chronological Classics: Erskine Hawkins and His Orchestra 1939–1940.*

"Soft Winds." Performed by Erskine Hawkins, from *Jazz Archives: Erskine Hawkins and His Orchestra 1938–1940.*

"Sweet Georgia Brown." Performed by Erskine Hawkins, from *Jazz Archives: Erskine Hawkins and His Orchestra, Vol. 2 Holiday for Swing.*

Jimmy Mundy

"Airmail Special." Performed by Benny Goodman, from *B. G. in Hi-Fi.*

"Cavernism." Performed by Earl Hines, from *Chronological Classics: Earl Hines and His Orchestra 1934–1937.*

"Feather Merchant." Performed by Count Basie, from *Blues & Boogie Woogie.*

"Fiesta in Blue." Performed by Benny Goodman, from *Benny Goodman Plays Mel Powell.*

"Futile Frustration." Performed by Count Basie, from *Complete Original American RCA Victor Recordings.*

"Miss Thing." Performed by Count Basie, from *The Essential Count Basie, Vol. 1.*

"Queer Street." Performed by Count Basie, from *Chronological Classics: Count Basie and His Orchestra 45–46.*

"Rock-a-Bye Basie." Performed by Count Basie, from *The Essential Count Basie, Vol. 1.*

"Solo Flight." Performed by Benny Goodman, from *Jazz Archive, Vol. 5.*

"Super Chief." Performed by Count Basie, from *The Essential Count Basie, Vol. 2.*

"Swingtime in the Rockies." Performed by Benny Goodman, from *Chronological Classics: Benny Goodman & His Orchestra 1936.*

"Swingtime in the Rockies." Performed by Benny Goodman, from *Live at Carnegie Hall, Disc II.*

"Take Another Guess." Performed by Benny Goodman, from *Ella Fitzgerald, Her Best Recordings 1936–1949.*

"Up Jumped the Devil." Performed by Earl Hines, from *Chronological Classics: Earl Hines and His Orchestra 1941.*

Sy Oliver

"At the Fat Man's." Performed by Tommy Dorsey, from *At the Fat Man's 1946–48.*

"Dream of You." Performed by Jimmie Lunceford, from *Swingstation.*

"For Dancers Only." Performed by Jimmie Lunceford, from *Chronological Classics: Jimmie Lunceford & His Orchestra 1937–1939.*

"For Dancers Only." Performed by Jimmie Lunceford, from *Live at Jefferson Barracks, Missouri.*

"Four or Five Times." Performed by Jimmie Lunceford, from *The Swinging Mr. Lunceford.*

"I Want to Hear Swing Songs." Performed by Jimmie Lunceford.

"Loose Lid Special." Performed by Tommy Dorsey, from *Yes, Indeed!*

"Opus One." Performed by Tommy Dorsey, from *At the Fat Man's 1946–48.*

"Time's a Wastin'." Performed by Jimmie Lunceford, from *Chronological Classics: Jimmie Lunceford & His Orchestra 1937–1939.*

"The Minor Goes Muggin'." Performed by Tommy Dorsey, from *Yes, Indeed!*

"Undecided." Performed by Jimmie Lunceford.

"Yes, Indeed!" Performed by Tommy Dorsey, from *Yes, Indeed!*

Don Redman

"Chant of the Weed." Performed by Fletcher Henderson.

"Copenhagen." Performed by Fletcher Henderson, from *Ken Burns Jazz.*

"Down South Camp Meeting." Performed by Fletcher Henderson, from *Tidal Wave.*

"Henderson Stomp." Performed by Fletcher Henderson, from *The Fletcher Henderson Story, Vol. 1.*

"Hop Off." Performed by Fletcher Henderson, from *Chronological Classics: Fletcher Henderson and his Orchestra 1927.*

"Stampede." Performed by Fletcher Henderson, from *Ken Burns Jazz.*

"Sugarfoot Stomp." Performed by Fletcher Henderson, from *The Fletcher Henderson Story, Vol. 1 & 2.*

"Whiteman Stomp." Performed by Fletcher Henderson, from *The Fletcher Henderson Story, Vol. 1.*

Edgar Sampson

"Blue Lou." Performed by Benny Goodman, from *Chronological Classics: Benny Goodman and His Orchestra 1938–1939.*

"Don't Be That Way." Performed by Benny Goodman, from *Live at Carnegie Hall, Disc I.*

"If Dreams Come True." Performed by Chick Webb, from *Chick Webb and His Orchestra 1937.*

"Stompin' at the Savoy." Performed by Benny Goodman, from *Live at Carnegie Hall, Disc II.*

Gerald Valentine

"Blowing the Blues Away." Performed by Billy Eckstine, from *Dexter Gordon Vol. 2 1944–46.*

"Second Balcony Jump." Performed by Earl Hines, from *Chronological Classics: Earl Hines & His Orchestra 1942–1945.*

Frank Wess

"Midgets." Performed by Count Basie, from *April in Paris.*

"Segue in C." Performed by Count Basie, from *The Roulette Years.*

Ernie Wilkins

"Basie." Performed by Count Basie.

"Birks' Works." Performed by Dizzy Gillespie, from *Dizzy's Diamonds: Best of the Verve Years, Disc I*.

"Dizzy's Business." Performed by Dizzy Gillespie, from *Dizzy's Diamonds: Best of the Verve Years, Disc I*.

"Flute Juice." Performed by Count Basie, from *Live—Complete Roulette 1959–62*.

"Jordu." Performed by Dizzy Gillespie, from *Dizzy's Diamonds: Best of the Verve Years, Disc I*.

"Moten Swing." Performed by Count Basie, from *Breakfast Dance and Barbecue*.

"Moten Swing." Performed by Count Basie, from *The Essential Count Basie, Vol. 3*.

"16 Men Swinging." Performed by Count Basie, from *Live—Complete Roulette 1959–62*.

"Sweetie Cakes." Performed by Count Basie, from *Live—Complete Roulette 1959–62*.

Mary Lou Williams

"Bearcat Shuffle." Performed by Andy Kirk, from *Chronological Classics: Andy Kirk and His Twelve Clouds of Joy 1936–1937*.

"In the Groove." Performed by Andy Kirk, from *Chronological Classics: Andy Kirk and His Twelve Clouds of Joy 1937–1938*.

"Lotta Sax Appeal." Performed by Andy Kirk, from *Chronological Classics: Andy Kirk and His Twelve Clouds of Joy 1936–1937*.

"Mary's Idea." Performed by Andy Kirk, from *Chronological Classics: Andy Kirk and His Twelve Clouds of Joy 1938*.

"Messa Stomp." Performed by Andy Kirk, from *Chronological Classics: Andy Kirk and His Twelve Clouds of Joy 1938*.

"Steppin' Pretty." Performed by Andy Kirk, from *Chronological Classics: Andy Kirk and His Twelve Clouds of Joy 1936–1937*.

"Walkin' and Swingin'." Performed by Andy Kirk, from *Chronological Classics: Andy Kirk and His Twelve Clouds of Joy 1936–1937*.

Gerald Wilson

"Yard Dog Mazurka." Performed by Jimmie Lunceford, from *Chronological Classics: Jimmie Lunceford and His Orchestra 1940–1941*.

APPENDIX B

American Patterns and Variations on Rhythm and Tune: An Ellington–Strayhorn List

Murray created this handwritten list in the early 1990s, in the early days of Jazz at Lincoln Center. The title is Murray's, the subtitle is mine, and the section headings are Murray's. There is nothing on the document that suggests it is supposed to be a definitive list. Each category is on a separate page of loose-leaf paper. This list could be said to be a representative cross section of the Ellington–Strayhorn repertoire (though some pieces are pre-Strayhorn and post-Strayhorn), but by no means definitive. The period covered here is approximately 1930– 72. Murray omits some of his favorite Ellington pieces from the 1920s, such as "Birmingham Breakdown" and "East St. Louis Toodle-oo," as well as major extended works by Ellington such as Black, Brown, and Beige, *and classics such as "In a Mellow Tone," "Jump for Joy," "Creole Love Call," "Reminiscing in Tempo," and many hundreds more.*

Certain aspects of the list are unclear to me. For instance, Murray chooses three pieces from Such Sweet Thunder, *Ellington's tribute to Shakespeare (consisting of twelve compositions), and includes two under* Portraits *("Puck" and "Lady Mac") and one in* Spirit of Place *("Half the Fun"). Why not simply include all of* Such Sweet Thunder, *as Murray expressed his admiration for it as a totality? He lists individual pieces from other suites as well, such as* Deep South Suite, New Orleans Suite, *and one of his personal favorites, the* Uwis Suite *(as in University of Wisconsin). I think that Murray was creating this list not with an eye toward purchasing (in the pre-iTunes era, how could someone buy one movement out of a suite?) or long-term study, but in consideration of concert programming.*

It is an eclectic list, containing well-known, moderately known, and a few incredibly obscure pieces (a judgment based on the number of times the pieces have been recorded, on their current availability, and if they were ever released on compact disc or digitally). This list, representing a sliver of Ellington's and Strayhorn's thousands of compositions and arrangements, would be a fine place for the beginner to start and may suggest a few lesser-known pieces to those who have been studying this body of music for a while.

I. Portraits

Portrait of Louis Armstrong
Night Creature (all three movements)
The Tattooed Bride
The Good Shepherd
Flirty Bird/Happy Anatomy
Sophisticated Lady
Hiawatha
A Very Unbooted Character
Lady Mac
Puck
The Gal from Joe's

II. The Spirit of Place

Sepia Panorama
Mainstem
Uptown Downbeat
Echoes of Harlem
Harlem Airshaft
Delta Serenade
The Second Line (New Orleans Street Parade)
Uwis Suite (1) (College Prom)
Chinoiserie
Half the Fun (Cleopatra's Barge)
Magnolias Dripping with Molasses
Across the Track Blues
The Biggest and Busiest Intersection
Dusk in the Desert

III. Ellington Blue Locomotion

Daybreak Express
Happy Go Lucky Local
Track 360
Loco Madi
The Old Circus Train Turn-Around Blues
Wild Man Moore (arriving in Paris)
Paris Blues (departing Paris)

IV. The Blues as Sonata

C-Jam Blues
Ko-Ko
Diminuendo and Crescendo in Blue
It Don't Mean a Thing if It Ain't Got That Swing
Riding on a Blue Note

V. Ellington's Arrangements

Peanut Vendor
Humoresque
Rose of the Rio Grande
Sidewalks of New York

VI. Ellington the Song Writer

I Got It Bad and That Ain't Good
Rocks in My Bed
I'm Beginning to See the Light
I'm Just a Lucky So-and-So
Just A-Sitting and A-Rocking
Chocolate Shake
Kissing Bug
I Let a Song Go Out of My Heart
Solitude
I'm Checking Out, Goombye

VII. The Strayhorn Book

Take the A Train
Johnny Come Lately

Passion Flower
Chelsea Bridge
Raincheck
My Little Brown Book
Day Dream
Clementine
Midriff
Overture to a Jam Session
Snibor
Rock-Skippin' at the Blue Note
Upper Manhattan Medical Group
Smada
Boodah
Lotus Blossom
After All
All Day Long
The Intimacy of the Blues
Blood Count
Charpoy
Allah-bye
Absinthe
Eighth Veil

INDEX

Aaron, Hank, xliv
Abyssinian Baptist Church
  (Harlem), 165
Adventures of Huckleberry Finn, The,
  131–33
Aeschylus, 19, 90
"Afternoons in Albert Murray's Living Room," xl
"After You've Gone," 220
Agamemnon, The, 19
A Great Day in Harlem, 119
Ailey, Alvin, 114, 178
"Airmail Special," 198
"Alabama Bound," 224
Alain L. Locke Symposium, xxxi
*Albert Murray and the Aesthetic
  Imagination of a Nation,* 114
Alexander, Willard, xlv, 83, 154–55
Alice Tully Hall, 216
Altschul, Arthur, xlv
Altschuler, Bob, 156
Alvin Ailey Company, 114, 116
American, The, 85
American Academy of Arts and Letters, 227
American Composers Orchestra, 142, 149
American Humor, ix–x, 100, 102–3
American Jazz Orchestra (AJO), xli, 200
American Renaissance, 86

America's Coming-of-Age, 85
Anabasis (Perse), 94
Anatomy of a Murder, 212
Anderson, Buddy, 42
Anderson, Ernestine, 216
Anderson, T. J., xlv
Appiah, Kwame Anthony, xxxvi
Apollo Theater, 54, 74, 158–59
Aristophanes, 90
Aristotle, xxxi
Armory (Newark), 159
Armstrong, Louis, xxi, xliv, 8, 15, 18, 22, 24–25, 28–29, 31, 40, 60, 68–69, 87, 150, 165, 172, 181–83, 187, 203, 216, 219, 226, 230, 233–34, 236
Arnold, Matthew, 89
Asbury, Herbert, 144
As I Lay Dying, 176
Asphalt Jungle Suite, The, 207–8
Auburn University, 179
Auchincloss, Louis, xlv
Auden, W. H., xxv, xxxvii
Audubon, John James, 85
Austin, Harold, 155
Austin High School Gang, 121

Bach, Johan Sebastian, xlii, 64
"Back Home in Indiana," 31
"Backwater Blues," 117
Bacon, Francis, 197
"Bag's Groove," 29

Baker, David, xii
Balanchine, George, 178
Baldwin, James, 88, 114
Ballard, Red, 159
'Bama State Collegians, 37
Bambara, Toni Cade, xxix
Bandbox (club), 129
"Band Call," 207
Barefield, Eddie, 79–80
Barker, Danny, 216
Bartók, Béla, 64
Basie, Catherine, 165
Basie, Count, x–xi, xiv, xxvi,
   xliv–xlv, 9–10, 17, 22, 27, 40,
   48–49, 51–55, 61–62, 67–68, 71–76,
   78–81, 87 119, 122–29, 136, 143,
   153–59, 161–65, 168, 201–2, 207,
   222
Basie, Diane, 165
Basie, Harvey Lee, 161
Basie, Lilly Ann Childs, 161
Battle, Edgar, 245
"Beale Street Blues," 14
Bearden, Romare, xx, xlv, xlvi, 98,
   114, 210
"Be-Bop," 43
Bechet, Sidney, 66, 187, 192
Beethoven, Ludwig van, 23, 64, 111,
   233
Bell, Bernard W., xxvii
Bellow, Saul, xxxv, xl
Belton's Society Syncopators, 39
Benedict, Ruth, 86
Bennie Moten Orchestra, 163, 222
Berry, Buster, 80
Bigard, Barney, 50, 204
Billy Berg's (club), 44, 68
Birch, Maceo, 82
Birdland, 122, 128
Birds of America, The, 85
"Birmingham Breakdown," 255
Black, Brown, and Beige, 205, 217,
   255

Blackburn, Julia, xxiv
Blackburn, Thomas, xxv
Black Cat (club), 74
Blake, Eubie, 29–30, 144
Blakey, Art, 48, 61
Blanchard, Terrence, 60
Blanchot, Maurice, xliii
Blanton–Webster Band, The
   (album), 24
Blanton–Webster Band (Ellington
   era), 205
Bloomgarden, Alina, xli
Blowin' Hot and Cool, 119
"Blue and Sentimental," xi
Blue Devils of Nada, The, xviii, xliv,
   149, 229
Blue Devils Orchestra, 71, 75–77, 79,
   83, 162–63
"Blue Juniata, The," 85
Blue Note (club), 67
Blue Room (club), 164
Blues Suite, 114, 116–18
Boas, Franz, 86
"Bonga," 216
"Boogie Bop Blues," 211
"Boogie Woogie on the St. Louis
   Blues," 47
Bostonians, The, 103
Boswell, James, xxxiv
Bourne, Randolph, 85
"Braggin' in Brass," 196
Brahms, Johannes, 111
Braud, Wellman, 204
Breakfast Dance and Barbeque, 245
"Bright Mississippi," 222
Bromwich, David, xxxiv–xxxv
Brooklyn Bridge, 92
Brooks, Jerry, 156
Brooks, Shelton, 30
Brooks, Van Wyck, 85
Brown, Clifford, 60
Brown Decades, The, 84
Brown, James, 245

Brown, Lawrence, 24, 192, 195–96, 213
Brown, Lew, 30
Brown, Ray, 54, 62, 68, 216
Brown, Ruth, 125
Brown, Sterling, 181, 230
Browne, Roscoe Lee, 94
Buchanan, Wes, 42
Burghers of Calais, The, 115
Burke, Edmund, xxxv
Burke, Kenneth, 85, 99, 225, 236
Burleigh, Harry T., 184, 190
Burroughs, Alvin, 61
Butterbeans and Susie, 37–38
Byard, Jaki, xii
Byas, Don, 163, 192

Café Society Uptown (club), 164
Caillois, Roger, ix, 141
"California, Here I Come," 224
Calloway, Cab, 38, 42, 47, 50, 54, 71
Calvino, Italo, xxxvii, 244
Camero, Candido, 180
Campbell, Joseph, 108
Campbell, Mary Schmidt, xxxix
Campbell, Paul, 125
Cantor, Eddie, 121
Capital City Aces, 39
Capitol Lounge, 125
"Caravan," 63
Carnegie Hall, 158, 186–88, 217
Carnegie Hall Jazz Band, xli
Carney, Harry, 211
Carolina Cotton Pickers, 39
Carpenter, Charlie, 47
Carpenter, Richard, 47
Carry, George "Scoops," 51
Carter, Benny, xlii, 46, 57, 105, 216, 224, 244–45
Carver, George Washington, 146–47
Catlett, Sid, 61
CBS Records, 156
Chancellor, John, xlv

"Chant of the Weed," 213
"Chattanooga Choo Choo," 224
Chatterbox (club), xi, 75, 153
"Chatterbox" (composition), 194–95
Cheatham, Doc, 70
Cheney, Sheldon, xxvi
Cherry, Don, 211
Chicago Defender, 193
"Chitlins at the Waldorf," xxix
Cholly, Luzana, 98
Chopin, Frédéric, 27, 201
Christian, Charlie, 159–60, 198
"C-Jam Blues," 23–24
Church, African American:
    Gillespie on, 58, 232; Murray on,
    115–16, 119, 130, 219, 223, 225
Clark, John, 216
Clark, June, 162
Clark Center, 114
Clarke, Kenny "Klook," 61
Classical music: Gillespie on, 57–58;
    Murray on, 34, 59, 177, 181–84,
    198–99, 214
Clayton, Buck, 70, 163–64, 246
Clef Club, 186, 191
Clinko, Arthur, 158
*Clorindy, or the Origin of the
    Cakewalk,* 30
Clotilde (ship), xxvii
Club Harlem, 81
Cobb, Arnett, 198
Cohen, Harold, 154
Cohen, Harvey, xx
Cohn, Sonny, 164
Coker, Henry, 125, 164
Cole, Nat King, 57, 148
Cole, Ralph, 35
Coleman, Gil, 66
Collette, Buddy, 148
Collier, James Lincoln, xxi–xxii, 188, 196, 234
Coltrane, John, 68–69
Columbia University, 234

"Come Sunday," 200, 205

"Comping for Count Basie," xliv

Confessions of Nat Turner, The (Styron), xiii

Confident Years, The, 85

Conjugations and Reiterations, xiv

Constitution of the United States, xiv, 131–32

Conversations with Albert Murray, xix, 105, 114

Cook, Will Marion, 30, 184, 188–90, 193

Copland, Aaron, xlii, 30

"Cops," 207

Cornell University Concert, 100, 102, 204

Costanzo, Jack, 180

Cotton Club (California), 40

Cotton Club (Harlem), 40, 188, 194

"Cotton Tail," 184, 209

Count Basie: A Biodiscography, 165

Count Basie and His Orchestra, 165

Country music: Murray on, 22

Covington, Wes, 36

Cowley, Malcolm, 84

Cox, Ida, 18

Coy, Gene, 76, 78

Creole Jazz Band, 203, 221

"Creole Rhapsody," 204–5

Crippen, Katie, 162

Crouch, Stanley, xxi, xxix, xli, xliii, 3, 15, 186–217, 229–30, 235

Crump, Tom, 46

"Cubana Be, Cubana Bop," 53, 61

Culley, Wendell, 164

Daily Worker, 156

Dallas Institute of Humanities and Culture, 169

Dameron, Tadd, xlii, 53, 55–56, 60, 246

Dance, Stanley, 165

Davidson, Jenny, xxxii

Davis, Bill, 39

Davis, Eddie "Lockjaw," 125, 164

Davis, Gordon, xli

Davis, Miles, 29, 60

Davis, Sammy, Jr., 124, 127

Davis, Stuart, 210

Davis, Walter, Jr., 216

Dawson, William L., 177, 183

"Daybreak Express," xxii, 104, 182, 224

"Day Is Past and Gone, The," 115

"Deep Forest," 47

Deep South Suite, 224, 255

Degas Suite, 211

Derrida, Jacques, xxviii

DeSylva, Buddy, 30

Devlin, Paul, xv, xvii–xlvii, 3, 32, 70–71, 96–98, 102–5, 119–20, 122–23, 130, 134, 138–49, 152–53, 161, 166, 174, 184–86, 218–19, 237, 243–45, 255–56

Diane Rehm Show, The, 166, 172

Dickinson, Vic, 75

"Didn't My Lord Deliver Daniel," 115

"Dig," 29

"Diminuendo and Crescendo in Blue," 216

Dirty Dozen Brass Band, 69

"Disorder at the Border," 43

Divine Days, 92

Dixie Syncopators, 221

Dixon, Eric, 164

"Dizzier and Dizzier," 53

Doc Cook's 14 Doctors of Syncopation, 183

Doctor Faustus, x, xxxii

Doggett, Bill, 49

Donaldson, Walter, 30

Don Giovanni, 177

Dorsey, Jimmy, 45

Dorsey, Thomas A., 38

Dorsey, Tommy, 201

Dostoevsky, Fyodor, 176

Doubleday Books, 70
Douglass, Frederick, ix
Down Beat, 193
Dream on Monkey Mountain, 93
Driggs, Frank, 157
Drummond, Ray, 216
Duke Ellington on Records, xiii
Duke Ellington's America, xx
Duke, Vernon, 30
Dunbar, Paul Laurence, 217
Durham, Eddie, 70, 75, 79–80, 82,
    163, 222, 247
Dvořák, Antonín, 23, 30, 102, 190, 193
Dylan, Bob, 153

Earle Theater, 158
"East St. Louis Toodle-oo," 255
Eblon Movie Theater, 162
Eckstine, Billy, xxi, xxiii, 46, 48,
    51–53, 122–29
Edison, Harry "Sweets," 25, 49, 87,
    155–56
Edwards, David "Honeyboy," xliv,
    130, 133
Elbow, Peter, xxv, xxxiv–xxxv
Eldridge, Jean, 213
Eldridge, Roy, 40, 49, 60, 66, 69, 172,
    220
Eliot, Alexander, xlv
Eliot, T. S., xxiv, xxxvii, 89, 94, 171,
    180, 207
Ellington, Duke, x–xi, xx–xxii, xliii,
    xlvi, 9–11, 13–14, 21–24, 27–28,
    30, 40–41, 50, 54, 63, 67, 72, 76, 87,
    89, 102, 104, 111–12, 123, 129, 135,
    143–44, 165, 168, 172, 181–82, 184,
    186–217, 222–24, 230, 232, 234–37,
    245, 255–56
Ellington, Ruth, 211
Ellington–Strayhorn collaboration,
    87, 245, 255–56
Ellison, Fanny, 175
Ellison, Ralph, ix, xii, xiv, xx, xxiii,
    xvii, xl, xlv, xlvi, 32, 37, 76, 88,
    92–93, 150, 166–67, 174–78, 185,
    227, 229, 233, 245
Elman, Ziggy, 159
Emerson, Ralph Waldo, xxxvi, 86
Emmett, Dan, 121
"Epistrophe," 222
Euripides, 19, 90
Europe, James Reese, 187–89
Evans, Herschel, xi, 26, 156–57, 163
"Evidence," 194
Exiles Return, 85

"Fables of Faubus," 148
Faddis, Jon, 60, 217
Fairfax, Frankie, 44, 49
Famous Door (club), 155–57, 163
Farmer, Art, 216
Farrakhan, Louis, 176
Faulkner, William, xiii, xliv, 176, 219
Felchen, Al, 156
Fine, Ruth, xxxix
Finnegans Wake, 181
*Firearms, Traps, and Tools of the
    Mountain Men,* 140
Fisher, Avery, xlv
Fitzgerald, Barry, 176
Fitzgerald, Ella, 25, 45, 129, 193
Fitzgerald, F. Scott, xliv, 84
"Fix Me Jesus," 115
Flanagan, Tommy, 216
Flowering of New England, The, 85
Flynn, Errol, 146
Forest City Joe, xxii, 96, 104
Forrest, Leon, xxxi, 92
Foster, Frank, 60, 164, 247
"Four in One," 222
Fowlkes, Charles "Poopsie," 125
Frank, Waldo, 85
Franklin, Aretha, 153
Fraser, Al, 32
"Freddie Freeloader," 29
"Frère Monk," 216

From Dvořák to Duke Ellington, 217
From the Briarpatch File, xviii, xix, xl, 229, 236,
Fuller, Walter "Gil," 53, 60, 248
Fuller, Walter "Rosetta," 47
Furtwängler, Wilhelm, 179
"Flying Home," 160

Gable, Clark, 146, 177
Gaines, Ernest J., xxix
Gant, Willie, 162, 207
Ganter, Granville, 102, 104
Gardner, Earl, 216
Gardner, Andrew "Goon," 51
Garvey, Marcus, 94
Gaskin, Leonard, 70
Gates, Henry Louis, Jr., xxviii–xxix, xxxi, 227
Gem of the Prairie, 144
Gene Coy's Black Aces, 78
Gennari, John, 119
George Washington Bridge, 91
Gershwin, George, 30
Gibson, Andy, 248
Giddins, Gary, xxxii, xli, 236
Gifted Ones, The, 54
Gillespie, Dizzy, xiv, xix, xxii, 17, 32–70, 175, 211, 216, 231–32
Gitler, Ira, 70
Globe Theater, 194, 197
Goines, Victor, 244
"Going to Chicago," 118
Goldkette, Jean, 203
Goldmark, Rubin, 30
Golson, Benny, 200
Gonsalves, Paul, 198, 200, 209–10
Goodman, Benny, 75, 153–54, 159–60
Good Morning Blues (Basie/ Murray), x, xviii, xxiii, xxvi, 71, 118, 165
"Good Morning Blues" (song), 117
"Goodnight, My Love," 45
Gopnik, Adam, xx, 234

Gordon, Dexter, 203
Gottlieb, Bill, 211
"Grand Central Getaway," 45
Grand Terrace Ballroom, 40, 48, 72
Grant, Cary, 146
Granz, Norman, 125, 128, 217
Great Paris Concert, The, 202
Green, Bennie, 46
Green, Freddie, xi, 73, 155, 163–64, 207
Greer, Sonny, 144, 161, 192
Grey, Al, 164
Grieg, Edvard, 234
Griffin, Gordon, 159
"Groovin' High," 56, 222
Grosser, Maurice, 142
Gunn, Jimmy, 39
Guy, Joe, 49

Hadnott, Billy, 82
Hairston, Jester, 190
Hall, Shorty, 36
Hallett, Mal, 72
Hamilton, Jimmy, 50
Hamlet, 199
Hammond, John, xi, xxiii, 73, 83, 153–60, 163, 217
Hampton, Lionel, 50, 58, 150, 159–60
Hampton, Slide, 216
Handy, W. C., 13, 63, 221, 232
Hanscom Air Force Base, 169
Hansen, Chadwick, 120
"Happy Go Lucky Local," 181–82, 224
Harding, Buster, 53, 164, 249
Hardwick, Elizabeth, xlv
Hardwicke, Sir Cedric, x
Harlem (A Tone Parallel to Harlem), 199–200
"Harlem Air Shaft," 224
Harlem Club, 49
Harris, Barry, xli, 49, 51, 216
Harrison, Jimmy, 162

Haughton, Chauncey, 50
Hawkins, Coleman, 26–27, 51
Hawkins, Erskine, 37, 147
Hawthorne, Nathaniel, 86
Haydn, Joseph 28
Hayes, Al, 62, 68
Heard, J. C., 61, 67
Heart of Europe, The, 96
Heath, Jimmy, 216
Hefti, Neal, 245, 249
Hemingway, Ernest, ix, xxiv, xxxiii, xliv, 84, 136, 176, 180
Henderson, Fletcher, 26–27, 38, 41, 54, 76, 81, 224, 249
Henderson, Horace, 250
Henderson, Ray, 30
Hendricks, Jon, 232
Herbert, Janis, xliv, 130–33
Herder, Johann Gottfried von, 89, 103
Heredity, xxxii
Hero and the Blues, The, xii–xiii, 20, 25, 100, 108, 178, 209
"Hero to Zero," 212
Heyward, Eddie, 50
Hill, Buck, 216
Hill, Teddy, 40
Hindemith, Paul, 135
Hines, Earl, 46–48, 51–52, 61, 70, 76, 124, 189, 201–2, 210
Hippity Hop (burlesque show), 162
Hitchcock, Alfred, 141
Hite, Les, 40, 194
Hodeir, Andre, 208
Hodes, Art, 120
Hodges, Johnny, x, 184, 192, 195–97, 200, 208–9, 213, 217
Holiday, Billie, xxv, 24, 57, 73–74, 87, 153, 216, 220
Hollander, John, xlv
Holman, Papa, 39
Holmes, Oliver Wendell, Sr., 86
Homo Ludens, 140–41
Honneger, Arthur, 102, 181–82

"Honor, Honor," 115
Horne, Shirley, 216
Horowitz, Vladimir, 27
Horricks, Raymond, 165
Horton, Lester, 115
Hot Fives, 203
House of Seven Gables, The, 86
"House of the Rising Sun," 117
"How High the Moon," 9, 57, 204, 222
"How You Sound," 211
Howard Theater, 27, 38
Howells, William Dean, 85
Hubbard, Freddie, 60
Hughes, Bill, 164
Hughes, Langston, 180–81, 230
Humboldt's Gift, xxxv
Humes, Helen, 156–57, 163
Humoresque, 102
Hurston, Zora Neale, 181, 230
Hutton, Ina Ray, 45

"If You Could See Me Now," 56
Iliad, The, 90
"I'm Bopping Too," 53
"I'm Coming Virginia," 187
"Informal Blues," 217
Inspired Abandon, 196
Interview Magazine, xxiii, 32
"In the Evening," 118
In the Spirit of Swing: Twenty-Five Years of Jazz at Lincoln Center, xlii
Invisible Man, 92, 166, 174, 185
Israels, Chuck, xli
"Is You Is Or Is You Ain't My Baby," 89
"It Don't Mean a Thing If It Ain't Got That Swing," 237
"I've Been Buked," 115
"I've Got Rhythm," 30
"I Want to Be Ready," 115

Jackson, Milt, 68
Jackson, Oliver, 70

Jackson, Rudy, 204
Jacquet, Illinois, 67, 163, 198
James, Daniel "Chappie," Jr., 122–23, 125–28
James, Daniel, III, 127
James, Denise, 127
James, Dorothy Watkins, 122
James, Harry, 159
James, Henry, 85, 214
James, Michael, xxxvi, 84, 139, 142, 230
Jamison, Judith, 114
Jazz at Lincoln Center, xxii–xxiii, xxxiii, xxxviii, xli–xliii, 3, 101, 114, 149, 161, 171–72, 186, 215–16, 219, 225–26, 243–45, 255
Jazz at the Philharmonic, 22, 43, 220
Jazz Cadence of American Culture, The, 236
Jazz Cultural Theater, xli
"Jazz: Notes Toward a Definition," xxxviii, xxxix, 101, 119, 233
"Jelly Jelly," 47
Jensen, Sara, 243
"Jersey Bounce," 47
Jeter-Pillars Orchestra, 82–83
Joachim, Joseph, 190
Johnson, Budd, 47–48, 52–53, 70, 250
Johnson, Gus, 164
Johnson, Isaac, 36
Johnson, James P., 30, 162, 184, 202
Johnson, J. J. (physician), 179
Johnson, J. J. (trombonist), 60
Johnson, Samuel, xxxiv
Jolson, Al, 121, 129
Jones, Eddie, 164
Jones, Elvin, 61
Jones, Etta, 216
Jones, Hank, 216
Jones, Jo, xxiii, xli, xlv, 55, 61, 73, 82–83, 87, 138, 140, 142–44, 146–47, 153, 155, 163–64
Jones, Lewis P., III, xvii, xxxi

Jones, Neville, 138
Jones, Philly Joe, 61
Jones, Quincy, 60, 245
Jones, Reunald, 164
Jones, Sam, 36
Jones, Thad, 59–60, 164
Joplin, Scott, 27, 221
Jordan, Louis, 89
Jordan, Michael, 26
Joyce, James, 176, 180–81
Juilliard School, 30

Kane, Art, 119
Kansas City Suite, 244
Karajan, Herbert von, 179
Kelly's Jazz Hounds, 39
Kennedy, John F., 164
Keppard, Freddie, ix
Keyes, Joe, 74, 78, 154
Kind of Blue, 29
King and the Corpse, The, 178
King Cole Trio, 57
Kirk, Andy, 75, 245
Kirkus Reviews, xxix
"Ko-Ko" (Ellington), 222
Kouwenhoven, John A., ix, 91–92, 111, 214
Krupa, Gene, 158–59

"Lady Be Good," xi
Lafitte, Judy, 138
Lamb, Brian, xxix
Langer, Susanne K., ix, xxxv, 236
Larkin, Milton, 39
Last of the Blue Devils, 78
Latin American music: Gillespie on, 42, 63–64; Murray on, 63–64, 151, 180, 225; Thomas on, 232–34
Laurinburg Institute, 36, 40–41
Lee, George, 72
Leonard, Harlan, 154
Leroy's (club), 162
"Let the Zoomers Drool," 217–18

Leventhal, Nathan, xli
Levy, Stan, 68
Lewis, Cudjo, xxvii
Lewis, Ed, 73, 154
Lewis, Howard, 127
Lewis, John, xlv, 61–62, 203, 250
Liberation Books, xii
Lieberman, William S., xlvi
Life of Johnson, The, xxxiv
Life on the Mississippi, 90
Lim, Harry, 33
"Limehouse Blues," 224
Lincoln, Abby, 216
Lincoln, Abraham, 226
Lincoln Theater, 38, 77, 157, 162
Lloyd Hunter's Serenaders, 76
Lock, Eddie, 70
Locke, Alain, 182
"Loco Madi," 10
Longfellow, Henry Wadsworth, 86
Longo, Mike, 60
Louis, Joe, 123
Louis Armstrong Educational Foundation, 186
"Louis Armstrong in His Own Words," xliv
Lowe, Sammy, 244, 251
Lowe-Porter, H. T., xxiv
Lunceford, Jimmie, 41, 48, 147
Lydon, Christopher, xxxvi
Lynch, Reuben, 78

MacDuffy, Frank, 36
Madame Bovary, 214
Made in America, x, 214
Magic Keys, The, xiv, xxiii, xxxix, 98
Magic Mountain, The, 179
Maguire, Roberta S., xix, 105
Mahler, Gustav, 183, 233
"Main Stem," 11, 224
Malraux, André, ix, xliii, 169, 206, 236–37
Mann, Klaus, 96, 100

Mann, Thomas, ix, x, xix, xxiv, xxxii–xxxiii, 6, 100, 176, 179, 181, 210
Manning, Ted, 76–78
"Manteca," 61
Marlowe, Christopher, 197
Marriage of Figaro, The, 177
Marsalis, Wynton, xvii, xxxviii, xli, 3–31, 34, 60, 172, 214–15, 227, 229, 231, 235
Marxism, 86, 132
Masters of Bebop, The, 70
Mathis, Ayana, xxix
Matthiessen, F. O., 86
Mayview Asylum, 153, 155
McCarthy, Cormac, 176–77
McClean, Jackie, 216
McCoy, Clyde, 73
McGhee, Howard, 43, 220
McLean, Jackie, xlii
McPherson, James Alan, xxix
McShann, Jay, 22, 51
"Mean Ol' Frisco," 117
Melville, Herman, 85, 89
"Memphis Blues," 14
Metronome, 158
Mezzrow, Mezz, 66
Miley, Bubber, 188–89, 191
Milhaud, Darius, 234
Millay, Edna St. Vincent, 19, 142
Millinder, Lucky, 49, 75
Mills, Irving, 194
Mingus, Charles, xxiii, 148–49
Minor, Dan, xxii–xxiii, 71–83, 163
"Minor Goes Muggin', The," 201
Mitchell, Dwike, 134–37
Mitchell and Ruff: An American Profile in Jazz, xliv, 134–37
Mitgang, Herbert, xlv
Mobile Country Training School, xxiv
Moby-Dick, 85, 89, 214
Monk, Thelonious, xlii, 14, 56–57, 69, 194–95, 222, 235
"Mooche, The," 216

"Mood Indigo," 21, 182, 198
Moore, Bobby, 49, 70, 74, 155
Moore, Henry, 115
Morgan, Lee, 60
Morgenstern, Dan, xii, xxvi, xliv
Morocco: Murray in, xxxi, xliv, 32,
　148, 150
Morton, Benny, 163
Morton, Jelly Roll, xlii, 184, 202, 216
Moten, Bennie, 71, 75, 79, 80–83, 163
"Moten Swing," 80, 163
Mozart, Wolfgang Amadeus, 28, 112,
　197, 233
Mumford, Lewis, 84–85
Mundy, Jimmy, 164, 251
Munn, Skip, 75
Munroe, Clark, 62
Murray, David, 65
Murray, Hugh, xxvi–xxvii
Murray, Mattie, xxvi
Murray, Michele, xlv, 114
Murray, Mozelle, xlv, 148
Museum of Modern Art, xlvi
Music Is My Mistress, 142
"Mystery Song, The," 211–12

"Nagasaki," 35
Nance, Ray, 24–25, 183, 198, 213
Nanton, Joe "Tricky Sam," 24, 192
National Book Critics Circle, 95, 227
National Jazz Ensemble, xli
National Jazz Museum in Harlem,
　186
National Records, 126
Navarro, Fats, 60
Neal, Larry, xxix
Neff, Russell, 105–13
"Never No Lament," 196
New England: Indian Summer, 85
Newman, Joe, 125, 164, 192
New Orleans Suite, 255
Newport Jazz Festival, xlvi
New Republic, 219

New School for Social Research,
　215–16
New Yorker, xx
New York Jazz Repertory Company,
　xli
New York Times, 70
New York University, 66, 230
Nicholas Brothers, 53
"Night at the Cotton Club, A," 204
"Night in Tunisia, A," 46
Novel (genre), 92, 213–14
NPR Curious Listener's Guide to Jazz,
　The, 186
Nutcracker Suite, The, 216

Obama, Barack, 139
Oberlin College, 183
Odyssey, The, 90
Oedipus Rex, 19
Offit, Sidney, xxxii, xlv, 139–40
"Old Circus Train Turn-Around
　Blues, The," 10
Olds, Robin, 127
Oliver, King, 38, 60, 204, 216, 221
Oliver, Sy, 201, 252
Olivier, Laurence, 199
O'Meally, Robert G., xxii, xxix, 96,
　149, 172–84, 227, 233, 236
Omeros, 93
Omni-Americans, The, xii–xiii, xxix,
　xxxiii, xliv, 92, 100, 168, 171, 184,
　197, 227, 236
Ordeal of Mark Twain, The, 85
"Ornithology," 9, 222
Orpheus, 98
"Our Delight," 55
"Out the Window," 49

Pacific 231, 102, 104, 182, 223
Page, Oran "Hot Lips," 77–79, 163
Page, Susan, xxiii, xl, 166–73
Page, Walter "Big 'Un," 76–77, 80–81,
　157, 162–63, 183

Paramount Theater (Newark), 158
Paramount Theater (New York City), 158
Parham, Truck, 47
Parker, Charlie, xiv, xliii, 9, 22, 42–44, 46, 48–49, 51, 55–56, 62, 68–69, 87, 172, 220–21, 231
"Parlor Social Stomp," 191
Payne, Sonny, 164
Pearson, Houston, 216
Pemberton, Bill, 70
Percy, Walker, 176
Percussive emphasis in jazz: Crouch on, 187, 191, 194, 202; Gillespie on, 42; Murray on, 12, 16, 42, 45, 195, 222
"Perdido," 148
Peress, Maurice, 187, 200, 217, 219
Perl, Jed, xxxvi, 219
Perrin, Porter G., xxv, 96, 104
Perse, Saint-John, 94
Peter and the Wolf, 224
Peyton, Dave, 183
Phaedrus, xxvii–xxviii
Piazza, Tom, 92
Pilgrimage of Henry James, The, 85
Pinsker, Sanford, xl
Pittsburgh Courier, 38, 193
Plato, xxviii, xxxi, 90
"Please Don't Talk about Me When I'm Gone," 222
Poe, Norman, 35–36
Pope, Alexander, 177
Porter, Cole, 30
"Portrait of Ella Fitzgerald," 205, 217
Pound, Ezra, 92
Powell, Benny, xlii, 125, 164, 202, 216
Powell, Mel, 220
Powell, William, 146
Pozo, Chano, 63, 180
Pratt Institute, 210
Praxiteles, 90
Previn, André, 58

Price, Sally and Richard, xxxii
Problems of Art, x
"Processional," 115
Prokofiev, Sergei, 224
Psychoanalysis, 108
Pudd'nhead Wilson, xxxii

Queen Elizabeth I, 197
Queen Elizabeth II, 164
Queen's Suite, The, 216
Quinichette, Paul, 125, 164

Radio Recorders Studio, xlvi
Raeburn, Boyd, 45
Raft, George, 146
Rainey, Ma, 18, 38
Ramirez, Ram, 66
Randall's Island, 157
Ravel, Maurice, 234
Redman, Don, 66, 191, 253
Rehm, Diane, 166, 172
Reinhardt, Django, 66
Remembrance (Walcott), 94
Remnick, David, 139
Reno Club, 83, 158, 163
Resika, Paul, xlv
Revelations (Ailey), 114–16
Rice, Thomas Dartmouth, 121
Rich, Bernard "Buddy," 201
"Riding on a Bluenote," 197
Rifftide: The Life and Opinions of Papa Jo Jones, xxxiii, xl, xlv, 134, 138, 153
Ritual: Murray on, xiv, xxxvi, 4, 18, 86, 115, 119, 223, 225, 236–37
Roach, Max, xlii
Roberts, Caughey, 154
Roberts, Luckey, 162
Robinson, Sugar Ray, 147
Roché, Betty, 198
"Rockabye River," 217–18
"Rocka My Soul in the Bosom of Abraham," 116

"Rocks in My Bed," 89
Roddy, Ruben, 76–77
Rodin, August, 115
Rogers, Will, 102
Roker, Mickey, 54
Rollins, Sonny, xx
Romare Bearden: The Caribbean
  Dimension, xxxii
Roosevelt, Eleanor, 157
Roots of American Culture, The, 103
Roseland Ballroom, 72, 74, 155
Rosenfeld, Paul, 85
"Rose of the Rio Grande," 202
Roth, Candy, 70
Roulette Records, 125
Rourke, Constance, ix, 21, 85–86,
  89–91, 225, 234
Royal Theater, 38
Royal, Marshal, 125, 164
"Rude Interlude," 212
Ruff, Willie, 134–37
"Rugged Romeo," 184
Rushing, Jimmy, 77–79, 163
Russell, Carl P., 140
Rutherford, Rudy, 68

Saint John's University, 96
Saint Mark's Basilica, 135–36
"Salt Peanuts," 43
Sampson, Edgar, 253
Savoy Ballroom, xii, 40, 157
Sax, Adolphe, 27
Scarlett Letter, The, 86
Schoenberg, Loren, xxi–xxii, 186–218,
  230, 235
Schuller, Gunther, 58
Schwartz, Delmore, xxxv
"Scoops Carry Mary," 46–47
Scooter (character in Murray's fic-
  tion), xiv, xxvii–xxviii, xxxiv, 99,
  184
Scott, Charlie, 36
"Second Balcony Jump," 47

Second Law of Thermodynamics, 98
Second Line and Third Line
  controversy, 119–21
Segregation: Hammond on, 156; Mur-
  ray on, 121, 147
Selections from the Gutter: Portraits
  from the "Jazz Record," 120
"Serenade to Sweden," 198
Seven League Boots, The, 90
Shakespeare Theater, 94
Shakespeare, William, xxxii, 194, 197,
  200
"Sham," 118
"Shanghai Shuffle," 224
Shavers, Charlie, 49
Shaw, Billy, 53, 62, 66
Shaw, George Bernard, 177
Shearing, George, 124
Sheridan, Chris, 165
Shorter, Wayne, 172
"Shorty George," 157
Shuffle Along, 29
Sicari, Stephen, 96
"Sidewalks of New York, The" ("East-
  side-Westside"), 203, 209
Signifying Monkey, The, xxviii
Sims, Sylvia, 216
"Singing the Blues," 203
Sissle, Noble, 29–30
Slavery in the United States: Murray
  on, 23, 88, 101, 117, 145, 222–23
Small, Cliff, 70
Small's Sugar Cane Club, 162
Smith, Ben, 76
Smith, Bessie, 5, 18, 24, 38, 87
Smith, Buster, 76–77, 87
Smith, N. Clark, 183
Smith, Tab, 163
Smith, Trixie, 18
Smith, Willie "The Lion," 30, 145,
  162, 202
Smithsonian Classic Jazz (concert
  program), 101

Smithsonian Institution, xiii, 196
Smithsonian Jazz Oral History Project, 149, 174, 233
Snodgrass, Henry, 82
Socarras, Alberto, 63
Socrates, xxvii–xxviii, xxx–xxxi, 90
"Something Strange," 116
"Something to Live For," 212–13
"Song of Hiawatha, The," 86
Sophocles, 19, 90
Sousa, John Philip, 182, 233
South to a Very Old Place, xii, xxiv, xxvi, xxvii–xxviii, xliv, 176, 209
Soyinka, Wole, 94
Spivey, Victoria, 76, 78
Springsteen, Bruce, 153
Spotlight Club, 62, 211
"Star-Spangled Banner," 31
Steinway pianos, 156
Stevens, Wallace, xxxii
Stewart, Billy "Smiling," 39
Stewart, Bob, 216
Stewart, Dee, 80
Stewart, Frank, xxxix
Stewart, Rex, 184, 191, 195–96, 217
Sticks and Stones, 84
Stitt, Sonny, 62
"St. James Infirmary," 55
"St. Louis Blues," 14, 31, 63, 220
Stomping the Blues, xiv, 33, 52, 70, 86, 107, 119–20, 129, 197, 229
Story of a Novel, The, x
"Straight Up and Fly Right," 147, 222
Strand bookstore, x
"Strange Fruit," 220
Strauss, Richard, 13
Stravinsky, Igor, 182, 199
Strayhorn, Billy, 87, 145, 245, 255–56
Styron, William, xiii
Such Sweet Thunder, 255
Sullivan, Maxine, 46
"Sultry Serenade," 197
Sun Also Rises, The, xxxiii, 214

Sunset Royals, 39
"Swanee River," 218
Swann, Roberta, xli
"Swedish Suite," 66
"Sweet Georgia Brown," 43, 222
"Sweet Is Sweet," 53
"Sweets for My Sweet," 60
"Swing Along," 188
"Swing That Music," 26

"Take the A Train," 198, 207, 209
Tar Baby, 178, 184
Tate, Buddy, 26, 163
Tate, Erskine, 183, 233
Tattooed Bride, The, 205, 215
Tatum, Art, 57, 192
Taylor, David A., xxxvi
Tchaikovsky, Pyotr Ilyich, 234
Teachout, Terry, xx, 234
Technology and music: Murray on, xxii, 10, 24, 59, 102, 104, 117, 144, 182, 215, 223–25
Terry, Clark, 125
Theater: Three Thousand Years of Drama, Acting, and Stagecraft, The, xxvi
"Things to Come," 61, 211
Thomas, Dylan, xxv, 180
Thomas, Greg, xxiii, xl–xli, 84–95, 227–38
Thompson, Carl "Mike," 37
Thompson, Lucky, 68
Thomson, Virgil, 141–42
Thorne, Francis, 149
"Tiger Rag," 104, 224
Times of Melville and Whitman, The, 85
TOBA (Theater Owners Booking Association), 37–38, 162
To Be, or Not . . . to Bop, 32
"Toby," 80
Tone, Franchot, 146
"Topsy Turvy," 47

Toscanini, Arturo, 179
Tough, Dave, 160
"Track 360," 10, 223
Trading Twelves, xlvi, 146, 150, 185, 245
"Tradition and the Individual Talent," xxxvii
"Train Time," xxii, 96, 104
Train Whistle Guitar, xiv, xxvii–xxviii, 98, 171
Trent, Alphonso, 76
Troupers of the Gold Coast (Rourke), x
Trumpets of Jubilee (Rourke), x
Turner, Danny, 55
Tuskegee Army Air Base, 44
Tuskegee Institute, xii, 36–37, 188
Tuskegee Melody Barons, 37
"Tuskegee Song, The," 183, 188
Tuskegee Veterans Administration Medical Center, 180
Twain, Mark, xxiv, xxxii, 85, 89, 131–32

U.S. Air Force, 32, 43, 135, 150, 166, 170–71
Undset, Sigrid, 139
University of Wisconsin, 224
Uwis Suite, 224, 255

Valentine, Gerald, 253
Valentine, Joe, 47, 53
Valéry, Paul, 100
Vanderbilt, Cornelius, 153
Vaughan, Sarah, 25, 46, 48, 148
Vendome Orchestra, 183
Vernacular Eloquence, xxv, xxxiv
Vertigo, 141
View of a Harlem Street, xlvi
Village Vanguard, 33
Village Voice, xxix, 149, 229
Villa-Lobos, Heitor, 64
Vodery, Will, 188–89, 193
Voices of Silence, The, x

"Wading in the Water," 115
Walcott, Derek, 93–94
Walker, Jimmy, 36
Waller, Fats, 30, 162, 183, 192, 233
Walsh, Lauren, xxxix, 114, 150, 152
War and Peace, 214
Warhol, Andy, xxiii, 32
Warren, Earle, 74, 82, 155–56, 163
Warren, Robert Penn, ix
Warwick, Carl " 'Bama," 49
Washington, Booker T., 94, 146
Washington, Charlie, 78
Washington, Jack, 80–81, 163
Washington, Jesse, 80–82
Washington, Kenny, 216
Washington, Mac, 80
Weaver, Raymond, 85
Webb, Chick, 45, 75, 158
Webb, Speed, 37
Webster, Ben, 50, 79–80, 197, 204–5, 209
Wein, George, xli, xlv
Weissman, George, xli
Wells, Dickie, 82, 163
Wesleyan University, 96
Wess, Frank, 60, 164, 253
"West End Blues," 28
Whatley, John T. "Fess," 39
"Whispering," 222
White, Gonzelle, 77, 162
White, Michael, 216
Whiteman, Paul, 203
Whitman, Walt, 86, 89, 139
"Why Read the Classics?," xxxvii, 244
Wieseltier, Leon, 219
Wilcox, Edward, 41
"Wild Car," 207–8
Wilder, Alec, xlv
Wilkins, Ernie, 125, 164, 254
Wilkins, Jimmy, 125
William Penn Hotel, 153–54
Williams, Bert, 121

Williams, Claude "Fiddler," xi, 73, 153, 155
Williams, Cootie, 188, 195, 197–98
Williams, Elmer, 162
Williams, Ernie, 78
Williams, Joe, 164
Williams, Lucy Ariel, 183
Williams, Martin, xii, xli, xlv, 59
Williams, Mary Lou, 27, 70, 159, 232, 245, 254
Wilson, Alice, 35
Wilson, Gerald, 53, 254
Wilson, Shadow, 46, 61, 164
Wilson, Teddy, 159, 184
WKCR, 186, 230, 234
Wood, Booty, 164
"Woody 'n You," 56
WOR, 156
World Don't Owe Me Nothing, The, xliv

World of Count Basie, The, 165
World of Washington Irving, The, 85
Writer's Guide and Index to English, xxv

Yale University, 135
"Yancy Special," 118
"Yankee Doodle Dandy," 31
Yeats, William Butler, 180
"You May Run On," 116
Young, Lester, xi, 26, 43, 51–52, 81, 156–57, 163–64, 172, 203, 220
Young, Snooky, 164
Young, Trummy, 48
"You Oughta," 207
"You're Driving Me Crazy," 222

Ziegfield Follies, 188
Zinnser, William, xliv, 134–37

ALBERT MURRAY (1916–2013) was a renowned essayist, novelist, jazz historian and theorist, literary and social critic, and biographer. Born in Nokomis, Alabama, and raised in Mobile, he held degrees from Tuskegee Institute and New York University. A major in the U.S. Air Force, he attended Air University, Northwestern University, and the Sorbonne and taught at Tuskegee Institute, Colgate University, Emory University, and Barnard College. His books include *The Omni-Americans, South to a Very Old Place, The Hero and the Blues, Train Whistle Guitar, Stomping the Blues,* and *Trading Twelves: The Selected Letters of Ralph Ellison and Albert Murray.* During the 1970s, he began collaborating with Count Basie on Basie's autobiography, which was published as *Good Morning Blues.* His work has been highly influential among cultural critics, creative writers, scholars, and musicians, especially Wynton Marsalis, with whom he cofounded Jazz at Lincoln Center.

PAUL DEVLIN teaches at the U.S. Merchant Marine Academy. He is editor of *Rifftide: The Life and Opinions of Papa Jo Jones* as told to Albert Murray (Minnesota, 2011), which was a finalist for the Jazz Journalists Association's book award in 2012. His writing has been published in *Slate, The Root, The Daily Beast, San Francisco Chronicle, Popular Mechanics, Bomb,* and the *New York Times Book Review.* He has been a consultant for Jazz at Lincoln Center and a curator at the National Jazz Museum in Harlem and is a member of the National Book Critics Circle, Jazz Journalists Association, and PEN American Center. He holds a PhD in English.

GARY GIDDINS is a jazz critic and writer. His books include *Visions of Jazz, Bing Crosby: A Pocketful of Dreams, Weather Bird, Satchmo,* and *Celebrating Bird: The Triumph of Charlie Parker* (Minnesota, 2013). He has received a National Book Critics Circle Award, the Jazz Journalists Association Lifetime Achievement Award, a Grammy, and six ASCAP Deems Taylor Awards for Excellence in Music Criticism. He is executive director of the Leon Levy Center for Biography at the Graduate Center of the City University of New York.

GREG THOMAS is an award-winning cultural journalist, producer, and educator. His writing on American culture has been published in the *Village Voice, Callaloo, The Root, All about Jazz, Salon, The Guardian, American Legacy,* and the *New York Daily News,* for which he was the jazz columnist. He curates and hosts programs for the National Jazz Museum in Harlem and Jazz at Lincoln Center.